By Jack E. Holmes

The University of New Mexico Press · 1967

To WILSON O. CLOUGH and
JOHN D. McGOWAN, Teachers

Contents

Preface

BEGUILING temptations beset the path of those who would assay the political institutions and processes of New Mexico. Colorful individuals crowd a 350-year history, events of a hundred years of partisan struggle invite attention, and nuances of cultural change and conflict offer numerous diversions. Of necessity, these were matters avoided unless they appeared relevant to my central concern—the relationships of political groupings and institutions. But within those limits I found it pleasant, in this day of race riots and militant politics of right and left, to be able to trace the evolution and describe the components of a political system whose members have been urbane enough to accept change, tolerant enough to foster a good measure of cultural diversity, and relaxed enough to enjoy the show.

The three institutions selected for review—party, legislature, and governorship—are those deemed essential to an understanding of the evolution of the state's politics and government since statehood was achieved in 1912. These institutions affect, and they are significantly affected, in turn, by social and economic movements and forces. The three institutions are far from static and a change in one begets change in the others, but each is sometimes examined here as an individual reflection of an underlying political process.

Two other considerations have shaped this inquiry.

If the states were all alike in their politics, one would know them all by studying one. Since they are not, comparative data are in order. Hence, it is a basic and necessary supposition of this and many other recent studies of the politics of the states that common elements of structure and a uniform legal position in the nation permit examination of certain functions and processes that are also common but not invariant among the states. Long-term variations induced in politics and government by various institutions, groups, and individuals then provide elements of comparability which may be screened out from the merely fortuitous or unique. And, although many citizens would doubtless be disposed to dispute it, this study also assumed the validity of the contention that two-party competition provides a useful, if not an essential, ingredient of the good state. So the "two-party model" is used as a principal bench mark and standard for measuring the rate and direction of political change that has occurred in New Mexico in the half century.

Chapters I through IV identify in a broad fashion the sociological, electoral, and regional components of the parties, and measure in some detail the characteristics and results of the inter- and intraparty voting of fifty years. The remaining chapters continue to focus on the parties, but from a radically different perspective. Electoral data are used at intervals, but the emphasis is upon the parties as institutions linking government with electorate. At times the parties are viewed as instrumentalities of electoral groups and forces; in other contexts the parties are seen as forceful entities influencing the activities of governor and legislature.

The organization of statistical and historical material is dictated in some degree by the epochs or periods of different styles of party conflict since the opening of the century. Several periods of intense two-party competition occurred in territorial New Mexico, and the last such interval extended through the quarter century of 1905-1930. That two-party era was complete with all the appurtenances of nominating conventions, long-lived and effective party leadership groups, and a biparty Progressive faction. After 1932 there followed a decade of dominance by a highly integrated Democratic party; and then a twenty-year period characterized by the direct primary, by durable majority party factions, and by a weakened minority party. Each of the three periods of New Mexico's post-statehood politics is therefore described at some length in the effort to find some of the possible attributes or consequences of change, for each developed a characteristic style and a corresponding structure of power. And, only for limited intervals has political leadership resided in the governorship. For a long period the center of power was a Republican party group which used the legislature as its instrument; at other times various Democratic factions have fought for supremacy while the legislature became a center of governmental authority. It is to account for these sequences and shifts of power and activity that this inquiry has been cast in terms of legislature and governorship as well as the political party.

II

Readers familiar with such investigations will readily discern that this excursion into New Mexico's politics keeps another model quite consistently in view, for the researches of V. O. Key, Jr., particularly *Southern Politics* (Alfred A. Knopf, 1949) and *American State Politics* (Alfred A. Knopf, 1956), were the lodestones fixing the directions taken here.

Other debts are also due. The Social Science Research Council, through its Committee on Political Behavior, generously provided a grant-in-aid in support of the research leading to this book. Charles M. Hardin, then of the University of Chicago, reviewed the study as a set of proposals, Morton Grodzins, University of Chicago, lent his counsel, and Professor Duncan MacRae, Jr., also of Chicago, saw it through several drafts. Professors Charles B. Judah, Dorothy I. Cline, and Allan R. Richards of the University of New Mexico, and Brother August Raymond Ogden, College of Santa Fe, Santa Fe, also patiently read drafts and provided helpful criticism. Lee S. Greene, University of Tennessee, and William Buchanan, Washington and Lee University, reviewed the portion dealing with Los Alamos and Oak Ridge. And I am also indebted to Lynn Dexter Bates for drawing the charts. Unfortunately, the many public officials and politicians of New Mexico who so willingly and courteously provided information must remain in the anonymity they were assured would be theirs. To them all, named and unnamed, grateful acknowledgment is made.

JACK E. HOLMES
University of Tennessee

Politics
in New
Mexico

ONE

People, Places, and Party Balance

A̲N assessment of the electoral history and fortunes in New Mexico of the two major parties requires a few preliminaries, for the state is no exception to the rule that economic and social demography have an important bearing upon politics. Areas marked by particular kinds and times of settlement became and, to a large degree, remain distinguishable by consistent patterns of political behavior that condition the course of change and the strategy of successive campaigns. Habits of nomination and volatility of candidate preference, coupled with a high degree of party attachment, can be traced back to the old days.

This chapter first provides a brief tracing of the state's bipartisan politics in the voting for president, governor, and legislature over a period of sixty years. The two-party classification of the state is described in terms of criteria employed in several recent formulas. The locations of New Mexico's counties and cultural subareas are then outlined in relation to groups and events that have been, or promise to become, significant in the state's politics. A map, a brief description of the physical environment, and some rudimentary population statistics are set out, and the chapter concludes with a review of sectional groupings and electoral habits brought into prominence by the third-party era and the New Deal.

GOVERNOR, PRESIDENT, AND LEGISLATURE
IN THE FRAMEWORK OF STATEWIDE VOTING

During the territorial era the only statewide election was that for territorial delegate to Congress. Democratic candidates won six of the thirteen elections of 1884-1908, and the Democratic percentage of the two-party vote ranged from 37 to 56 per cent. The mean of the Democratic percentages in the period was 48 per cent.

The narrow limits set in the territorial period have not been expanded in the gubernatorial and presidential elections of fifty years
of statehood. Table 1 indicates that in the fourteen nonpresidential
elections in which the governorship has been contested, the Demo-

TABLE 1. RELATION OF DEMOCRATIC VOTE FOR GOVERNOR TO
          VOTE FOR PRESIDENT

(The state constitution originally provided for four-year terms, but set a
five-year term for the first set of officers and provided that the first election be held in 1911).

Year of Election	President	Party	Democratic percentage of two-party vote	Governor	Party	Democratic percentage of two-party vote
1911-12	Wilson	D	53.5	W. C. McDonald	D	51.0
1916	Wilson	D	51.8	E. C. de Baca	D	50.9
1918				O. A. Larrazolo	R	48.6
1920	Harding	R	44.7	M. C. Mechem	R	48.3
1922				J. F. Hinkle	D	55.5
1924	Coolidge	R	47.0	A. T. Hannett	D	50.1
1926				R. C. Dillon	R	48.1
1928	Hoover	R	40.9	R. C. Dillon	R	44.3
1930				Arthur Seligman	D	53.3
1932	F. D. Roosevelt	D	63.7	Arthur Seligman	D	55.4
1934				Clyde Tingley	D	52.2
1936	F. D. Roosevelt	D	63.2	Clyde Tingley	D	57.5
1938				John Miles	D	52.3
1940	F. D. Roosevelt	D	56.7	John Miles	D	55.6
1942				J. J. Dempsey	D	54.5
1944	F. D. Roosevelt	D	53.5	J. J. Dempsey	D	51.8
1946				T. J. Mabry	D	52.8
1948	Truman	D	56.8	T. J. Mabry	D	54.7
1950				E. L. Mechem	R	46.3
1952	Eisenhower	R	44.5	E. L. Mechem	R	46.2
1954				J. F. Simms, Jr.	D	57.0
1956	Eisenhower	R	42.0	E. L. Mechem	R	47.8
1958				John Burroughs	D	50.5
1960	Kennedy	D	50.4	E. L. Mechem	R	49.7
1962				Jack Campbell	D	53.0
1964	Johnson	D	59.5	Jack Campbell	D	60.2
1966				David F. Cargo	R	48.3

cratic candidates have won ten, but the average winning majority is only 53 per cent in the group which ranged from 51 to 57 per cent. In the four such elections lost, the average Democratic share of the vote was 48 per cent, and the range of electoral margins of the strongest and weakest candidates of the party reached a total of only 11 percentage points in the thirteen elections.

The story is essentially the same in the gubernatorial contests associated with thirteen presidential elections. In only two did the presidential candidate (Franklin Delano Roosevelt in 1932 and 1936) win by margins exceeding 60 per cent of the total, and in none did the Democratic presidential candidate drop below 40 per cent. The corresponding gubernatorial races have been even tighter, although the vote for governor has usually been within two or three percentage points of the vote for the presidential running mate.

In every election since statehood, New Mexico's voters have given a majority to the nation's choice for president; and only in 1924 and 1960, in the course of the presidential elections, did the voters fail to return a governor of the president's party. In each such instance, the national and state candidates whose votes diverged won or lost office by narrow margins. Hence, New Mexico has long been among that large and representative group of states which contributes to the shifts and tides of national politics even while they respond to national issues.[1] At eight of the off-year elections, however, the voters chose governors not of the incumbent president's party—a result likely to occur when margins of victory are small, and state issues most readily dominate popular attention.[2]

A longer sequence of elections is graphed in Figure 1 to show the relationship of the vote for each Democratic candidate for governor to the percentage of legislative seats won by his party. In general, since 1930, it confirms the experience of other states in showing the percentage of seats held by the victorious dominant party to be considerably higher than the percentage of the vote for its gubernatorial candidate. Several of the elections beginning with that of 1950 also suggest that New Mexico's voters may have duplicated the feat of those of Ohio and several other states in deliberately choosing a governor of one party and a legislature of the other.[3]

The percentage of the two-party vote for the Democratic candidates for governor has varied through a range of only 16 percentage points since statehood, and, as is shown by Figures 1 and 2, the Democratic

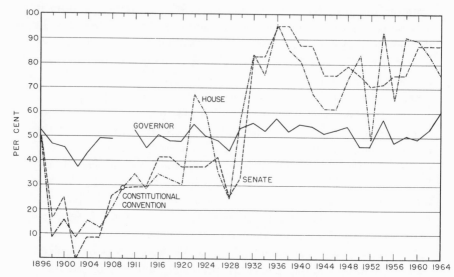

FIGURE 1. Relation of percentage of Democratic legislators and constitutional convention delegates to the two-party vote for territorial delegate and governor, 1896-1964. (Congressional vote in 1914.)

trend line gain in the fifty years is only two percentage points in going from 50.7 to 53.0 per cent. By this measure, New Mexico's politics is one of a close and stable two-party balance.

At this point, if the reader will bear with it, a brief explanation of the ideas and data represented by Figure 2 may aid him mightily in reading it and some of the other charts and tables to come.

One should note first that the jagged graph line (statisticians call it the "curve") represents the percentage of the state's two-party vote for the Democratic candidates for governor at successive elections. In the first election of 1911 the Democratic candidate received 52.6 per cent, in 1916 the Democrat won with 50.9 per cent, and not until 1964 did a candidate reach 60 per cent. If one asks whether Democratic candidates have done better, on the whole, than Republicans, or if the trend for the Democrats has been up or down, and by how much, Figure 2 answers those questions also.

The straight line, drawn from 50.7 on the left of the chart to the point 53.0 per cent on the right, represents a moving average which statisticians call a "line of regression." It is simply a method of averaging which takes account of all the highs and lows as well as the direction and degree of change. Thus, Figure 2 indicates that Democratic candidates for governor have only very slowly improved their statewide voting records in gaining 2.3 percentage points, but Figures 10 and 11 in Chapter 4 indicate large and consistent gains or losses in two major areas.

The dashed lines parallel to the regression line are also useful, for these give a relatively undistorted measure of the tendency of an electoral unit to shift its party majorities in successive elections, and so give the unit a "variability rating." More technically, however, the use of high or low party percentages to compare elections separated by several years can be very misleading if the political unit concerned has been making a large long-term shift in its political sympathies. The variability rating used here is derived from calculating "S_y"— the standard error of estimate from the line of regression—and is expressed in Figures 2, 10, 11 as the dotted lines parallel to the regression line at a distance of 2 S_y. The mathematical relationship of the

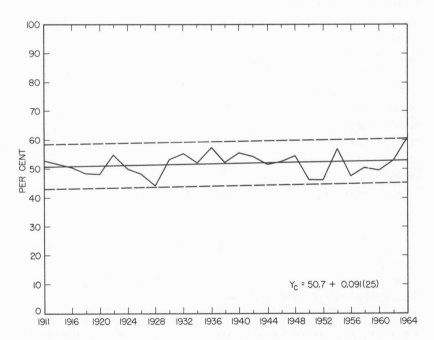

$$Y_c = 50.7 + 0.091(25)$$

FIGURE 2. Democratic candidates for governor register a slight gain over the course of 26 elections.

two dashed lines to the line of regression is that of a 95 per-cent confidence limit (that is, nineteen of twenty election results could be expected to fall within the dashed lines); but their use here is merely that of a handy device for removing the effect of secular trend in measuring "fluctuations about that trend."[4]

Not unexpectedly, the evenness and limited range of the two-party, statewide vote for governor results in another characteristic customarily associated with a high order of competition. Thus, an interval of the nine elections of 1932-1948 comprises the only extended period since statehood in which one party formally controlled all the top agencies of government. In this respect, the state shares the characteristics of twenty-five others of a close two-party balance wherein from 40 to 70 per cent of the time the governor confronted a legislature of which one or both houses were under the control of the opposition.[5] If one excludes the nine sessions of the New Deal and Fair Deal eras, 53 per cent of the time legislative and gubernatorial party control has been divided; for on ten of the nineteen remaining occasions in New Mexico, one or both houses have been in the control of the governor's opposition. Five of the nine elections of 1950-1966 produced the same result.

A similar classification involving the votes of 1914-1952 for president, governor, and U.S. senator places New Mexico near the lower margin of a group of twenty-six two-party states by virtue of its 33 per cent of second-party wins.[6] Another approach, based on the percentage of legislative seats held in both houses and control of the governorship at three points in time—1937, 1941, and 1951—finds only nineteen two-party states, and places New Mexico among the thirteen weak minority-party states."[7]

The data and classifications so far used to describe the party balance of New Mexico's politics serve principally to indicate that, on the statewide level, a rigorous and close interparty competition has existed for the offices of president and governor, and that elections have frequently served to deprive the party holding the governorship of control of the legislature. Such measures do not reveal the profound shift in the party balance marked by the New Deal.

In the series of elections spanning 1911-1928, the two parties contested on the statewide level for 106 executive, judicial, and congressional positions. Republicans won 58 per cent of the contests on the state tickets and 60 per cent of the legislative seats. Electoral margins were typically close for all of the state-ticket candidates, so the first eighteen years were Republican by virtue of a rather narrow legislative control rather than by dominance at the polls. It was a two-party system in every sense.

Party balance in the elections from 1930 was tipped heavily to the Democratic side. Although the fifty-year Democratic score in the gubernatorial voting percentages rose only two points to 53 per cent on a 1911-1964 trend line, candidates of that party won 97 per cent (223 of 229) of all the state-level and congressional elections of 1930-1964. Of legislative seats in the period, Democratic members held 77 per cent. As Chapters Seven and Eight may make clear, however, Republicans have remained strong enough to put a damper upon Democratic factionalism and to impel that party to impose restraints upon the primary system of nominations.

THE PHYSICAL ENVIRONMENT

New Mexico shares the topographic features, climatic extremes, and the various degrees of aridity common to the states of the Rocky Mountain West. The north-central counties of Rio Arriba, San Miguel, Taos, Colfax, Mora, and Santa Fe are situated on a great broken plateau, ranging from six to thirteen thousand feet in elevation, that slopes down into the state from Colorado (Figure 3). The other principal mountainous areas are in Lincoln and Otero counties in the south-central area of the state, and in Catron and Grant counties on the Arizona border to the west. It is these Alpine and sub-Alpine areas which furnish the perennial streams and much of the ground water used in the irrigation sustaining the relatively wealthy agriculture of the counties of the southern and eastern areas of the state, as well as the majority of the static Spanish-American settlements.

Only those counties of the northeastern area on the Texas border—Union, Harding, Quay, Curry, and Roosevelt—can boast of much in common with the short-grass plains of the western Mississippi valley. Their rainfall of fifteen to twenty inches and their elevation of four to five thousand feet are sufficient for good range-forage production, although the rainfall is short of the amount needed for the nonirrigated or dry-land farming tried there with disastrous results from 1910 to 1930. Otherwise, except in the mountainous areas, most regions of the state can anticipate an annual rainfall of six to twelve inches—an amount ordinarily sufficient only for range livestock production, so in most areas the rural population is extremely sparse.

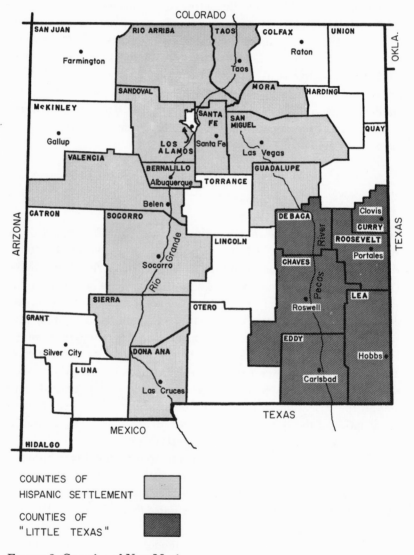

Figure 3. Counties of New Mexico.

GROWTH, CHARACTERISTICS, AND SHIFTS OF POPULATION

New Mexico was late in following the course of growth taken by the other western states.[8] In the 1900-1910 decade its rate of population growth was significantly above that of the nation and the other western states, but only in the last three decades has its rate of growth consistently been from two to four times that of the nation and on a par with that of the West as a whole. That the rate of increase has been heavily dependent upon interstate migration is made obvious by the right-hand column of Table 2, showing the percentages born in other states.

TABLE 2. RATE OF CHANGE AND GROWTH OF NEW MEXICO'S POPULATION 1870-1960.

Year	Population	Increase in percentage		Percentage born in other states
		U.S.	N.M.	
1870	91,874	...	...	...
1880	119,565	26.0	30.1	...
1890	160,282	25.5	25.4	...
1900	195,310	20.7	21.9	20
1910	327,301	21.0	67.6	39
1920	360,350	14.9	10.1	36
1930	423,317	16.1	17.5	36
1940	531,818	7.2	25.6	37
1950	681,187	14.5	28.1	43
1960	951,023	18.4	39.6	46

The state's percentage of foreign-born has consistently been low—a trait shared generally only by the states of the South. During the decade of 1910-1920, the ratio of foreign-born rose to 8 per cent—a brief influx caused chiefly by the rapid growth of the mining industry of three counties in which the European foreign-born clustered. This barely perceptible peak of nonnative population (somewhat more than half being persons born in Mexico) occurred from thirty to fifty years later than the much higher ratios reached in most other states in the West.

The foreign-born Mexican population of the state as a percentage of the total has ranged between 3.5 to 5.5 per cent during the fifty years of statehood, and it has tended to reside in the agricultural and mining communities of the southern tier of counties adjacent to the Texas-Mexican border. The Negro population has increased during the last two decades, but remains at less than 2 per cent. Less than 6 per cent of the 1960 population was composed of Indians—a long-prevailing ratio.

It is apparent that New Mexico's has been a "native-white" population to an unusual degree, but its composition and location have changed drastically nonetheless. The percentage of persons of Hispanic surname dropped below 50 during the 1940's; the rate of immigration has been increasing; and the location and urban-rural ratios of the population have changed profoundly.

In 1900, the 195,000 residents of the territory were still concentrated in the traditional area of settlement along the Rio Grande. In the nine Hispanic counties of Bernalillo, Doña Ana, Mora, Rio Arriba, San Miguel, Santa Fe, Socorro, Taos, and Valencia resided 132,000 persons—67 per cent of the population of the territory. This population, and that of most of the adjacent areas, was largely of native-born citizens of Hispanic surname. As late as 1915, Spanish Americans numbered 57 per cent of the state's total population and constituted 75 per cent or more of the population of eleven counties—between 50 and 75 per cent in three, and from 25 to 50 per cent in four others of the state's twenty-six counties.[9] By 1950, the proportion of residents of Hispanic surname had dropped to 37 per cent in the state, and only ten of the thirty-two counties mustered an Hispanic population of 50 per cent or more.

The 1900's—the decade preceding statehood—produced a rapid rate and redirection of growth. The population of the nine principal Hispanic counties increased by 9 per cent. In the whole territory, however, population increased by 68 per cent to reach 327,000 at the end of the decade, and those counties away from the Rio Grande and northern mountains trebled their population by going from 54,000 to 177,000.

But perhaps of the greatest significance for New Mexico's politics are the rapidly shifting, intercounty population ratios and the types of immigration occurring. The diversity and numbers of the new citizens have not been without impact, but New Mexico has not shared the experience of Florida, in which they apparently contributed, for a

time, "towards a politics without form and without issue."[10] New
Mexico's new groups and political areas are examined in subsequent
chapters in several contexts which indicate that the political system
has shown considerable capacity to limit or contain the changes imposed by population growth and shift.

By 1960, nine counties provided 71 per cent of the state's total
employment, accounted for nearly 100 per cent of the total gain of employment during the preceding decade, and accounted for nearly all
of the state's population gain of 270,000. Six counties experienced a
gain less than their natural increase would provide them, and the
remaining half of the counties suffered population losses. In consequence, the population of the larger urban areas increased more than
80 per cent, while that of places of 2,500 to 10,000 and those of 1,000
to 2,500 decreased by 14 and 32 per cent, respectively. The urban
proportion of the population, ranging from 18 to 33 per cent from
1920 to 1940, reached 50 per cent in 1950 and 66 per cent in 1960.

But urbanization has so proceeded that New Mexico's larger municipalities have more in common with Nashville, Louisville, or Charles-
ton than with the towns and cities of the northeastern and north-
central states. With the exception of mining areas in Colfax, Eddy,
McKinley, and Grant counties, urban areas have not developed the
types of labor force that contribute to unionization. They have tended,
rather, to a social and economic structure compatible with middle-
class conservatism if not Republicanism.

The impression is that artisans and semiskilled persons coming
lately into the state are largely from neighboring states and the Middle West. But New Mexico's urban areas are white-collar rather than
blue-collar, and some have begun to take on an academic tinge. Its
communities of technically and professionally trained people associated with military and research organizations represent a cross
section of the recent output of the nation's major private and state
universities. The matter is of great significance for the conduct of the
state's politics.

EARLY SECTIONAL COMPONENTS IN THE MEASURE OF POLITICAL
        CHANGE AND THIRD-PARTY POLITICS

For a generation after statehood, the party division in New Mexico
was based upon a sectional and cultural division. Those forces associated with urbanism or stemming from the unionization of mining

labor were yet to make themselves strongly felt, and the statewide
party balance was one of the closest in the nation. Underlying the
narrow statewide electoral margins, however, the peculiarities of the
sectional components of party strength fell into patterns significant
in the marked party shift of the 1930's.

The ten counties which in 1950 were still 50 per cent or more of
Hispanic population were the 1911-1928 basis of Republican strength,
and not until 1950 were they to begin casting less than 40 per cent
of the state's total vote.[11] Immersed in the highly competitive two-
party politics of faction and coalition through which the Republican
party for a time dominated the state, these counties had no ear, for
various cultural and economic reasons, for the siren songs of Populism.
As a group the Hispanic counties cast about 60 per cent of their
vote for Republicans and, except for a mild flirtation in 1912, refused
to trifle with Progressive or other third-party candidates during the
twelve-year period spanning the Theodore Roosevelt and LaFollette
candidacies. Yet, it was through these Hispanic counties—the counties
most impervious to Progressivism and most clearly characterized by
rigorous two-party competition—that the liberal, Progressive-Republican faction of U.S. Senator Bronson Cutting came to dominate the
party by 1930. The sharp differences in the reactions of the Hispanic
counties from those of other areas of the state show clearly in Figure 4.

Of the counties shown in Figure 4, those that responded most
readily to the various Socialist, Progressive, and Farmer-Labor candidacies of 1911-1924 were the eight of the east side, situated in the
plains areas adjacent to or near Oklahoma and Texas. These were
Union and Quay and the six counties which have come to be called
Little Texas—Chaves, Curry, De Baca, Eddy, Lea, and Roosevelt.
Four other scattered counties in which third-party politics had a
marked influence were Luna and Otero on the Mexican and Texas
border to the southwest, San Juan in the northwest corner, and Torrance in the central area. Their common characteristics were few, but
important. They typically contained large areas of land open to mining or homestead entry; their settlement occurred chiefly between
1890 and 1910, they contained no land grants, and they contained a
small percentage of population of native Hispanic origin. Two principal elements, however, which lead to their classification here as
"Progressive" counties are their early (and sometimes long-con-

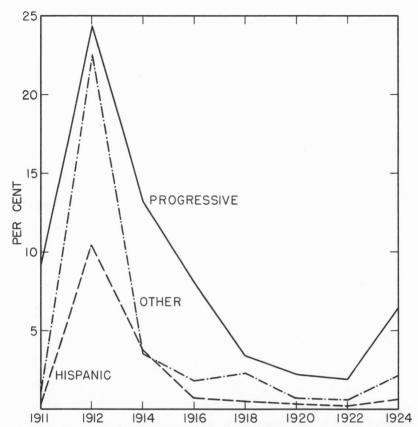

FIGURE 4. Minor and third-party votes as a per cent of total vote for governor in three groups of counties, 1911-1924. (Congressional vote in 1912 and 1914.)

tinued) preference for the Democratic party, and their early responsiveness to grass-roots movements and third-party enthusiasms. Ten of the twelve have made a long-term shift to the Republican party.

Some part of the measure of the political tendencies of the Progressive and Spanish-American counties is provided simply by their contrast with each other. But a bench mark from which the movement of both groups may be measured is provided by a polyglot residue composed of the remaining counties of the state.

The most important of the bench-mark counties is Bernalillo, the site of Albuquerque and, from the time of statehood, a center of factional strength. It tended for long to be marginally Democratic and

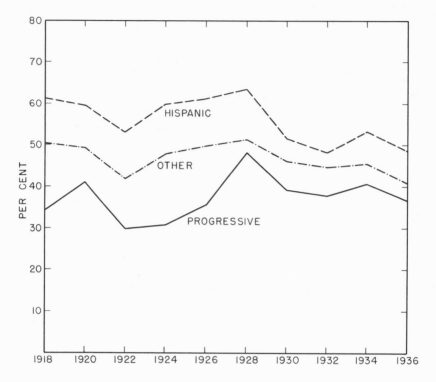

FIGURE 5. Shifting of the marginal balance: Percentage of total vote to Republican candidates for governor in three groups of counties.

by 1912 was beginning to exert a considerable economic as well as electoral influence. Although Bernalillo County returned 30 per cent of its 1912 vote to third-party congressional candidates, it was then more Hispanic than not, and it did not otherwise fit the pattern of ruralism and late development found in Little Texas and the other Progressive counties. The bench-mark group of counties contains, also, a subgroup of three which early came to have considerable electoral weight. These—Grant, Colfax, and McKinley—were different in many respects and far removed from each other geographically. In the beginning, they were reasonably evenly divided politically. Early during the period, the three were each rapidly developing as mining centers—coal in Colfax and McKinley; copper, lead, and zinc in Grant. These counties, plus the new potash and uranium areas of Eddy and Valencia counties, are now the state's most important centers of trade-union influence and harbor the firmest blocs of Democratic voters.

Figure 5 indicates the measure of the change which broke the marginal Republican dominance of the early years. The Republican vote dropped in 1922 under the impact of agricultural depression. In 1928, it went up most sharply in the Progressive counties—in part as a protest against the Catholicism of presidential candidate Alfred E. Smith, but the shift was also probably an endorsement of the economic policies of the time. In 1928 and after, the regional differences in the vote declined sharply. They were still quite perceptible, but thereafter each region and county tended to a closer approximation of the common pattern.

The shift to center, 1911-1936, of the state's voting areas is the approximate measure of Republican losses, which cut away a marginal control to convert the state to an area of Democratic dominance. Figure 6 measures the trends by which the Hispanic and the Progres-

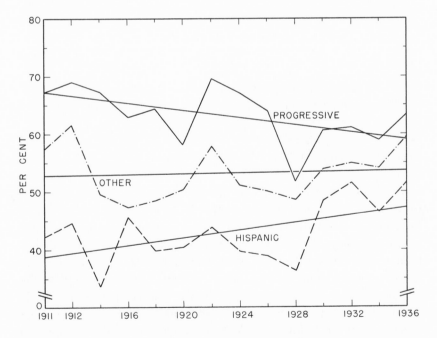

FIGURE 6. Erosion of regional differences: Democratic percentage, two-party vote for governor.

sive county groups each moved toward the center by about nine percentage points. The Hispanic counties then cast over 40 per cent of the state's vote, so the shift of the Hispanic counties toward a more even party balance was sufficient to permit heavy Democratic majorities of other areas to prevail.

TWO

The Political Acculturation of
Hispanic New Mexico

O N one of the occasions when Senator Dennis Chavez expressed an easily provoked ire at a fellow Democrat, he remarked:

> "If they go to war they're Americans; if they run for office, they're Spanish-Americans; but if they're looking for a job, they're damned Mexicans."[1]

Senator Chavez was stating a conviction held by many among those of Hispanic descent. That he was able to make the remark as a ranking member of the United States Senate is conclusive evidence that the Spanish-American citizenry of New Mexico has long possessed a political power that cannot be ignored.

Some cultural and institutional roots of that power are the subjects of this essay. They are roots so fundamental that the state's politics simply cannot be explained without them. Impressive evidence suggests, however, that New Mexico's Hispanic politics is unique primarily because of the degree of success it has enjoyed. The political order may, in fact, be primary and what we examine in New Mexico may be yet another example of an acculturating group successfully maintaining a valued identity. If so, this example fits as another, albeit somewhat special, case into the file on the ethnic in American politics.

POLITICAL CULTURE OR ETHNIC POLITICS?

New Mexico's political experience is at variance in one important respect from that of most of the United States. With the exception of Spanish-Mexican settlements on the West Coast, New Orleans and its French inhabitants, and a few Dutch settlements, few areas can boast of having a going polity based upon a European political tradition, ready to welcome or resist the imposition and development of a political system based upon the Anglo-American tradition.

In the case of New Mexico, political institutions of Spanish origin had been functioning for over two hundred years when the United States assumed control of the area in 1846. The formal institutions of government were neither elaborate nor busy, for there was little to do but maintain trade routes, preserve the area from Indian incursions, and provide a rudimentary system of administration and justice through the appointive prefects and alcaldes.[2]

Scattered north and south along the Rio Grande and its tributaries were numerous small settlements which achieved a functioning status best described as traditional village. More imposing communities such as Las Cruces, Socorro, Albuquerque, Santa Fe, and Taos were strung along the Rio Grande at sixty- or seventy-mile intervals. These carried on some of the limited functions of governance, and the more important ones of commerce and organized religion. For many generations, however, a common pattern was that of a village within or adjacent to a land grant. The earlier grants in the central and southern portions of the state were customarily to individuals. The grantees, their sons who succeeded them, and the Franciscan clergy who were associated with the larger villages and grants provided those continuing functions of governance, leadership, and education which molded the community. As likely as not the grantee or his successor would be the alcalde or prefect; if not, it made little difference, for he and the priest allocated the land, dispensed charity and justice, arranged and performed the more important marriages, and did most of the other things needed to adjust the workings of their communities.

It is of this area—the lower valley or Rio Abajo—that Harvey Fergusson has written:

> This lower valley of the early eighteenth century, although surrounded by unmapped wilderness, was itself a well-settled and well-cultivated place where men had lived for generations. From Bernalillo to Socorro the great houses were only a few miles apart.[3]

Over the course of the decades of Hispanic settlement, the sharp valley regions of the mountains to the north came to sustain the bulk of the population, for it was here that the numerous small streams most readily lent themselves to the irrigation technology of the time. Elsewhere, the Indians and terrain permitting, the grants of the central and southern areas were utilized as sheep or cattle ranches, and the village economy often became the adjunct of a pastoral one. And everywhere, the tempo of change had been so slow that a century ago the political and social life of large parts of the territory was much as Brayer described it—quiescent, based upon subsistence farming, or dominated by a relatively small group of relatively wealthy merchants and ranchers—but the leavening of the future was already at work, for the first generation of a little band of German-Jewish merchants and peddlers was already deployed at every crossroads serving, in Parish's words, as a "significant catalytic agent in the reasonably peaceful convergence of New Mexico's three cultures and other ethnic groups."[4] From such beginnings the Spanish Americans of New Mexico have achieved an excellent social and economic result in comparison to that obtained in Texas, Colorado, Arizona, and California.

Bolstered by the state's constitution, expressed in the statutes, sustained by organization and a high level of voting, maintained out of a conviction of its necessity, Hispanic political power has led to an endless debate over its nature and purpose. A lengthy series of studies of New Mexico's politics and cultures has done little to resolve the debate.[5] Of those contributing to the discussion, only the practicing politicians have bothered to count the votes with which the Hispanic community maintains its place in New Mexico's politics; and the nature of the institutional linkage between the Hispanic and the larger community is but seldom taken into account.

But it must be granted that the search for explanatory principles or factors decisive in determining the nature of the state's Hispanic politics is a baffling endeavor. Nor does the experience of Hispanic communities elsewhere in the Southwest offer many obvious clues.

A low level of Hispanic voting has long persisted in the Rio Grande valley in Texas; the level has been consistently high for sixty years in the same valley in New Mexico.[6] Where the vote in the heavily Hispanic and rural Texas counties of Duval, Starr, and Webb has been highly manipulable, the rural Hispanic vote of New Mexico has frequently changed in slow, incremental steps and coalesced into durable intraparty factions. The rural and city vote in New Mexico's counties of predominantly Hispanic populations has consistently inclined toward a two-party division at the precinct as well as the county level. When the Hispanic voter moves to larger towns dominated by "Anglo" (any non-Hispanic) citizens, he is apt to register soon in the Democratic party, where he contributes heavily to its primary and general election vote. In New Mexico areas most similar to West Texas, several county organizations of the Democratic party rely heavily upon Hispanic precincts; but in mining communities, the Hispanic voters are apt to accept the trade union as a prime object of loyalty and to be less prone to stay with the ticket. Instructive analogies might also be found in the precinct and city-wide politics of Albuquerque, New Mexico, and El Paso, Texas. Hispanic voting and ethnicity are important in each, and there are cultural parallels to be discovered at this big-town level as surely as they are to be found in rural areas. But Albuquerque's politics is probably much more sensitive than El Paso's to Hispanic educational and economic interests, and Nogales, Arizona, presents still another case—one which departs materially from the pattern in other areas in Arizona—for that border city has achived a community based upon a blending of Hispanic and Anglo elements throughout the power and economic structures.[7]

The counties of the Rio Grande in south-central Colorado contain the northern extension of the early movement of the Hispanic population. A few durable pockets of Republicanism persist in the Spanish-American counties of Colorado, but that state's Hispanic residents enlisted as Democrats long before such a movement became obvious in New Mexico.[8] Political habits and levels of activity in the two areas are plainly different. In New Mexico, in short, Spanish Americans usually run their towns when they are numerous enough to do so; in Colorado, Texas, and Arizona, they do not.

Explanations of the politics of Hispanic New Mexico often reflect findings of a number of sociological and anthropological studies. Indeed, a broad range of evidence in this state and elsewhere points to the existence of "political cultures," but it is questionable whether the cultural and institutional elements upon which sociological studies of the area have focused are of much utility in explanations of political systems as highly structured as those of New Mexico. It is contended in the following pages that the voting record of Hispanic New Mexico reflects communities whose voters long ago developed a highly organized, stable, and competitive two-party politics at village as well as precinct and county levels. It is also contended that these results could not have been predicted from the several studies relying heavily upon analysis of cultural or institutional influences of family, church, or *patrón*.

The Prevailing View of the Political Role and Style of the Spanish-American Voter as an Aspect of Culture

Much attention has been paid of late to the frequently conjoined concepts of culture and values—useful constructions which lend themselves readily to a high degree of compression and abstraction, if not to precise and universal definition. The concepts are used variously as assumptions in complex research and as reasonably well-agreed-upon methods of delineating essential elements found within social groups. They have been frequently employed in New Mexico, particularly in studies of relatively small and easily identifiable localized groups and communities. From these studies, in turn, explicit and implicit generalizations have been applied with varying degrees of caution to broader groups and more complex situations. The leap from the institutions and life styles of small villages to the complexities of a state's politics is sometimes taken with startling aplomb.

Of the several studies of the Spanish Americans of New Mexico, the most influential in recent years is Florence R. Kluckhohn's dissertation on the village of Atarque in western Valencia County.[9] The field work for the Atarque study was done in 1936 and 1937—in a decade in which examinations were under way of several other rural Hispanic settlements of the state.[10] There followed then a series of studies through the late 1940's and the 1950's of Atarque and several small but non-Hispanic communities or areas of the same region on the western plateau of Valencia County.[11]

The various field studies agree on the profound importance of family, and generally regard it both as the nuclear, multigeneration unit upon which the Hispanic villages are based and as an essential instrument in the control of the individual's relations with other institutions. The roles of church and *patrón* are also heavily stressed, although, in some, the *patrón* (sometimes "good" or at least kindly) is distinguished from the *jefe político*, the political leader or boss (usually "bad"). All stress the infrequency of other types of social or interest groups and organizations such as those found in most American communities. Opinions among the various authors concerning the extent of knowledge, interest, and effectiveness in politics of the Hispanic villagers differ a great deal,[12] and in several reports there is a strong trace of the pejorative in discussions of the state's system of politics. Writings based upon firsthand knowledge are not numerous, but from them there has been derived a somewhat Procrustean synthesis exemplified in works of Margaret Mead and Lyle Saunders.

According to this synthesis, among the central facts was cultural isolation which perpetuated many of the customs and mores of Spain, even though there was a significant imitation of Indian ways.

Villages were not only isolated from centers of civilization in Spain and Mexico, but also from each other. Those villages which survived quickly incorporated the elements of skill which lent themselves to economic self-sufficiency, and, although barter was always useful, commercial enterprise was rudimentary or nonexistent. The village economy was semicommunal. Land was cultivated by large family groups incorporating several generations; tools and equipment were freely shared and borrowed as were labor and products. "And thus, although the village community was highly self-sufficient, the individuals in it were not. The economic unit was the community, not the individual."[13] Within the semicommunal village, family and church were the dominant institutions. Family and village often tended to be almost synonymous, while religion—"a devout Catholicism"—was the center, "the core of all institutional activity."[14] The third institution was the *patrón* system. "A large landowner, a person of wealth, an influential politician—anyone with prestige, power, resources, and a sense of obligation toward a given community might become a *patrón*." He was a person "with whom the villagers assumed a reciprocal relationship of mutual assistance and dependency."[15]

Mead sees the *patrón* as the link between the village and the larger community, and in this aspect the *patrón* even supersedes the father or oldest family male, important though he be in the family scheme of things.

Leadership is provided through the *patrón* system, whereby the leading man in the community, whether because of his financial status, his knowledge of the outside world or his personal power, assumes a position of responsibility for the villagers. The *patrón* system reproduces the family picture for the community, and the *patrón* holds the position ascribed to the father in Spanish American culture. To be Spanish American is to be a father or to be dependent, or both, in different contexts. For most fathers, it is to be dependent upon a *patrón*. The older, in general, are in authority over the younger, men over women, and, to some extent, the rich over the poor.[16]

After noting differences between the land use and land holding patterns of the communities of the western part of the state and those northeast of the Rio Grande valley, and such developments as the self-governed acequia or irrigation system, Mead continues:

Throughout the structure, authority and responsibility for leadership, power and obligation for dependents, tend to focus on one person. *There are no voluntary associations here, with elected leaders.* (Italics added.) Society is characterized by already present units: the paternalistic kinship group, the village with which it may prove to be coextensive. Within this, in the appropriate position, the *patrón* rises in authority.[17]

The conventional analysis implies a prevailing tendency to preservation of a condition of internal social equilibrium centered upon traditional concerns and the person of the *patrón*. A picture emerges of tightly knit villages in which there is a normal inclination to a political unanimity reflecting an underlying social unanimity—a condition leading, in stable times, to a local one-party dominance maintained by the *patrón* in his role of father figure and conservator of village solidarity. A one-party stance results from the normal equilibrium of the village, and a two-party balance of around 50 per cent is divisive of the community.[18] Consequently, a response to external forces of change, or a shift in the party allegiance of the *patrón* implies a major change so that, for example, the village once 80 per cent Republican changes, if it does, to an equally one-sided Democratic vote. Similar changes may come as a result of the activities of a *jefe político*, but this actor is indifferent to the preservation of the core values of the community. The *jefe* merely seeks, and frequently finds, a vote he can easily control and move from party to party.

The results which might be anticipated from the foregoing systems of analysis appear in New Mexico only in areas in which Hispanic

voters are a local minority; but, in those cases, more conventional
explanations appear to suffice.

Community and Party: Some Potsherds from the
Electoral Middens

A curious alignment of circumstance, and of questions and answers,
is apparent in various studies of Hispanic communities of the state.
Most of the villages studied were quite naturally targets of opportunity
chosen for their availability to the researcher, or for their appropriate-
ness to concerns in which matters political were more or less inci-
dental. In the selection of the places studied there was, of necessity,
no grand design by which to fit a cross section of villages into the slots
of a carefully wrought sample. But, as a fortuitously random sample,
the villages studied comprise by quite improbable chance a statistical
oddity producing a skewed result. So, too, do inferences drawn from
the *patrón* conception. That *patrones* and local political bosses have
long existed in New Mexico is beyond dispute, but neither their supposed frequency nor their power accounts for the electoral or organizational pattern the political record discloses.

Valencia County, during the territorial period, became a source of
legend and the apogee of the type of political and social organization
which had developed along the Rio Grande south of Santa Fe. One
of its *jefes grandes* was the redoubtable Col. J. Francisco Chavez, said
to have been a parliamentarian of extraordinary ability.[19] Chavez was
succeeded by Solomon Luna, a wealthy and soft-spoken sheepman
whose ability and political following made him one of the most influential men of the 1910 constitutional convention. A few years later
Luna died, at age fifty-three, by drowning in a vat of sheep-dipping
fluid. He was succeeded by Eduardo Otero—a man of somewhat less
but still formidable skill and influence.

Of Colonel Chavez and his successors to the leadership of Valencia
County, it has often been said that when an election was in doubt they
could always win it by voting their sheep. The statement is both pun
and canard—their constituents always did well enough so that there
was no reason in well over a generation to vote the sheep, for in that
period no election was in doubt. The county voted 1,465 to 229 to
adopt the 1910 constitution, and it voted by a similar majority to reject an amendment designed to make the constitution easier of amendment. Earlier votes on the election of territorial delegates to congress

were usually by equally impressive margins, and in the first state election only 15 percent of the county's vote went to the Democratic candidate for governor. (A history of similar but Democratic majorities in the counties of Little Texas has never been held to be evidence of controlled voting. There, of course, the historical reasons for one-sided majorities are much clearer.)

There is no competent political or social history of Valencia County which can inform us of the details in the development of the ascendancy there of Colonel Chavez, Solomon Luna, and the Republican party. One might suspect that wealth, external positions of power and influence, and a great deal of accumulated political experience had much to do with it. No doubt Chavez and Luna attained their wealth, in part, through their family connections which in turn relied upon the productivity of family-controlled pastoral empires. But they were intelligent and forceful men who were no strangers to the larger arenas of politics. There is also little doubt that they relied upon subleaders in the various communities. And these, by the standards of the times, were useful, comfortable communities in which for many years there was little impetus for change. To vote solidly for the men and party who were part of the fabric of community and who maintained that stability was not unnatural.

But in other predominantly Hispanic counties, the vote for Republican candidates was usually a precarious 60 per cent, and in several the party was often only breaking even. No monopoly of political power existed in the typical Hispanic county. There were, of course, small areas such as precincts or villages in which a man or a family might for a time maintain a hegemony of authority, but even in these, if one accepts the evidence of the voting records of fifty years, there must often have been alternative sets of leadership in active competition.

Table 3 sets out for a span of thirty-six years some percentages of the total vote for Republican candidates for governor in several villages treated by the authors who wrote or made their investigations during the period 1936-1942. The villages listed are those identifiable from the precinct designations of the election returns. Atarque was the dominant village of the Jaraloso precinct of Valencia County.

Electoral margins enjoyed in 1916 and 1924 by the Republican candidates in the eight precincts were frequently somewhat higher than the average of the vote in other Hispanic precincts across the

state. For some years prior to 1932 there were few great economic or
social issues which might have served to lead the Hispanic villager to
question his political allegiance. In 1932 and after, the voters of the
eight precincts usually responded about as other voters did to the
issues and personalities involved in state and, particularly, national

TABLE 3. PERCENTAGE OF VOTE FOR REPUBLICAN CANDIDATES FOR
GOVERNOR IN PRECINCTS TREATED IN RESEARCH OF 1936-1942

County and precinct	*Percentage of vote for Republican candidate*				
	1916	*1924*	*1932*	*1940*	*1952*
DOÑA ANA					
2 Doña Ana	71	75	40	47	63
10 Berino	59	68	58	53	79
11 Chamberino	70	68	54	56	47
23 Picacho	..	43	44	35	68
SANDOVAL					
2 Sandoval	56	80	47	52	45
SAN MIGUEL					
37 El Cerrito	78	98	37	63	39
TAOS					
19 Talpa	46	56	35	46	41
VALENCIA					
24 Jaraloso (Atarque)	73	95	71	78	89

politics. If local and county political organizations were as described
or assumed in some of the works relating to these areas, then one
would expect shifts of considerably greater magnitude than those
which occurred.[20] If one makes the more justifiable assumption that
competent politicians will usually exercise their talents in the expectation that they can exert a measure of effective influence upon 10 to
20 per cent of the electorate, then that expectation is borne out in
Table 3.

If there were, in fact, *patrones* in residence in these precincts prior to 1932, then one might conjecture that *patrón* and *gente* alike were generally quite content to be Republicans. If all the *patrones* were merely *jefes políticos* after 1932, it appears that only in Jaraloso-Atarque were they able to keep the opposition reduced to a negligible faction. Far from being the typical or modal Hispanic precinct, Jaraloso-Atarque is nearly unique, for there are only a score or so like it in the state.

A series of inflexibly one-sided party majorities is an unreliable clue to a vote controlled by a local boss or organization; for to be found across the land are unbossed clusters of voters who maintain an astonishing party loyalty. The more frequently rewarding indicator of electoral faction, boss, or machine is a highly flexible series of votes. Behavior of the embattled precincts of Mora, Rio Arriba, San Miguel, Santa Fe, and Taos counties in the state's northern Hispanic heartland provides evidence permitting a tentative judgment of the incidence of controlled voting.

The paired elections of 1928 and 1936, and those of 1920 and 1936, are both good measures of a marked shift in party strength in the Hispanic counties, but the longer interval may provide the best comparison: First, it avoids perturbations induced in party orbits by the bipartisan "Progressive" faction headed by U.S. Senator Bronson Cutting. In numerous precincts of northern New Mexico, Cutting was able to place his factional group at the support of either party or to withdraw it—maneuvers he could accomplish with finesse and celerity. As a result, the electoral margins of the regular parties varied consistently (if not greatly) in the directions taken by Cutting in the elections of 1922-1934. (As senatorial candidate in 1928, Cutting was stoutly Republican; in 1932, he supported Roosevelt and the Democratic gubernatorial candidate; in 1934, Cutting ran as the Republican senatorial nominee and strongly supported his own Progressive Republican statewide and local party tickets.) Second, the course of secular political change for many groups and areas of the state appears to have been a linear accumulation of somewhat irregular increases or decreases in party strength (see Figures 2, 10 and 11). The presence of the Cutting faction, and the absorption by the Democratic party of most of its members after Cutting's death in 1935, served to expedite and steepen the rates of change in many precincts. As a result, 1936, rather than 1932, was the critical election in New Mexico for the formation and confirmation of new political faiths.

To Republicans, 1920 was a sound and satisfying year; 1936 brought a bonanza to Democratic candidates and a lasting realignment of voter loyalties. One hundred of 148 rural and small-town precincts yielded Democratic gains ranging from 1 to 30 percentage points—changes of an order which should raise no eyebrows. More likely as domain of *jefe* or *patrón* are precincts which moved in sharp opposition to the trend, or those which gave the trend an extraordinary support. Twelve precincts flouted the Democratic trend and reduced the party's vote by 10 to 34 percentage points; a score produced Democratic gains of 30 to 65 points. Some were precincts in which politics was strongly influenced by the Penitentes—religious

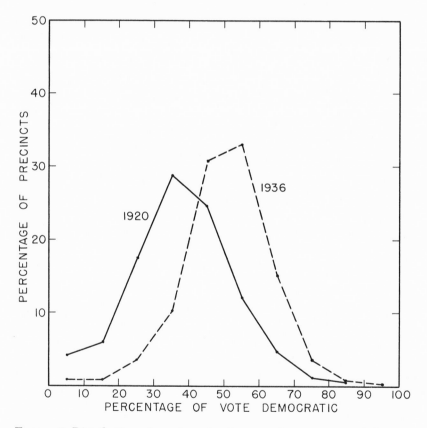

FIGURE 7. Distribution of precincts by Democratic percentage of the two-party vote for governor in five Hispanic counties of north-central New Mexico, 1920 and 1936.

groups verging on apostacy, and serving the sociological functions of a sodality. Others were merely indulging a passion for politics. A few at either extreme of party change were doubtless producing their notable votes at the behest of some local family or leader.[21]

Figure 7 compares the frequency of party vote percentages in the two elections of 1920 and 1936.[22] Whatever the nature of the psychological and sociological variables involved, the voters and political institutions of the five counties produced a classic example of a smooth and fluid partisan shift.

The most frequent Democratic percentage in 1920 was in the 30-40 range; in 1936 it moved 20 points to the 50-60 range. Profound as it was, this shift was duplicated in numerous counties and precincts across the nation. More germane to the argument here is the demonstration in Figure 7 that the number of precincts with an extremely lopsided party preference was small in each election. Seventy per cent of the precincts fell within the range of 30 to 70 per cent Democratic in 1920; in 1936 that range accounted for 89 per cent of the precincts.

THE INSTITUTIONAL ROOTS OF POLITICAL SKILLS

A shrewd knowledge of the mechanics and nuances of politics is not inborn. Nor is that knowledge necessarily an ingredient of a social heritage, although it may be fostered by relevant institutions and perfected by a succession of generations. In New Mexico's case, scarcely two generations separate the Kearny Code of the military occupation and the 1910 constitution, but sixty-four years were enough; for the pupils were apt, the tutors proficient, and institutions already at hand had long fostered political skills. At the beginning, the anecdote goes, the young men of Taos asked their famed, and unfrocked, politician-priest what kind of government the United States was. Padre Martinez replied that it was a republic, and added that a republic was a "burro on which lawyers jog along better than priests."[23] At the close of the territorial era, Col. Venceslao Jaramillo, Republican state chairman, had occasion to address his party's convention. Colonel Jaramillo stressed protection, particularly of the sheep industry, called President Taft a statesman, and went into the "race issue" with a suave reminder to his colleagues of the party's dependence upon Hispanic votes.[24] The period of tutelage had ended.

The key factors and institutions underlying this prompt and efficient accommodation to a new political system are not those usually accorded sociological primacy. Elemental agencies such as church and family dominate an intricate and diffuse range of activities and relationships, but in New Mexico's case provide only the broadest of contexts for political analysis. If radically different cultures come into conflict, then the more basic institutions lying at the center of the struggle may be greatly altered. If the cultures are substantially alike, then conflict and accommodation may proceed at quite different levels and involve other less basic elements. In this case no great clan or tribal organizations intervened; nor was there a clash of significantly different beliefs. Both groups were European, both Christian, and they shared more basic conceptions than they disputed. This new confrontation of the Protestant and Catholic ethics involved no severe strain, for the modes of resolving that issue had already been worked out elsewhere in Europe and the United States.

Conflict was present, of course, but it was not so serious that it prevented the evolution of a political system incorporating and merging factors important to both groups. There evolved, rather, a notable emphasis upon political institutions and processes—an emphasis probably not at all incompatible with central elements of the Hispanic subculture. As Herskovits states the matter:

> Not all aspects of a culture (as in a vocabulary) are given equal emphasis. . . . The things that outstandingly mark the culture of a people . . . also tend to dominate their lives. Because such matters are important to them, people will think and talk a great deal about personalities, events, and possibilities lying in this aspect of their culture.[25]

The emerging system made crucial adjustments with a minimum of strain. In the critical territorial years, the lawmaking process was American and Anglo-Saxon; the majority of legislators was Hispanic; and the leadership of both parties was representative of both cultural groups. Statutes governing descent and distribution of property, marital and family matters, and the control of land and water promptly became a blend of the continental and the common law.

So, the institutions at issue here are those of a lesser scope—those called into existence to cope with matters of a specific focus. The assignment of herd or guard duty, determination of the type and priority of repairs to an irrigation system, the assignment of water rights, and the organization of a joint venture of several families or villages are all of an order of activity likely to result in specific institutional arrangements. Merely to list them is to make obvious their political nature. Several formal organizations of a broad membership arose in many areas to perform the needed or desired activities, and these provided a training of considerable utility for those who grappled with the problems and requirements of the new polity.

In what follows, comments about the nature of Hispanic political organizations and the high levels of political participation may convey a misleading impression of the level of educational attainment. Few of the villagers were literate, although many were informed. The essential point is that indigenous groups provided the means for checking or controlling those to whom they delegated their personal or group powers of agency. Riggs has examined a similar phenomenon in other cultures. In those, associations he likens to sodalities are engaged in remolding or creating secondary social institutions. He describes their functions as follows:

> How about goals? We contrast the functional diffuseness of primary groups with the functional specificity of associations. . . . The goals [of the sodality or "clect"] are more diffuse than those of a traditional family. . . . They may cover a combination of political, religious, and economic activities.[26]

The Government of Land Grants and Irrigation Systems

A review of the mechanisms of social control and cooperation of an Hispanic village must include an elective system for the governance of the economic essentials of land and water.

Brenan has described several facets of Spain's political economy which have a parallel with those of New Mexico's northern areas. He notes, for example, a village- and land-tenure system once general in Leon, and in parts of Extremadura and Old Castile in which land was divided into allotments. And among "the valleys of the Pyrenees are to be found communities of shepherds who own all the pasture lands and run their affairs on similar lines."[27] In these and other instances, the land, except for houses and gardens, belonged to the village. Brenan holds that the peculiar agrarian conditions of the area, the isolation of many villages, and the delay in the growth of capitalistic institutions all may have played a part in developing popular but complex irrigation enterprises. Guilds of confraternities also "till recently owned land and worked it in common to provide old age and sickness insurance."[28] Brenan also shows that the creation of agricultural and pastoral communities based upon land grants dates back to the ninth and eleventh centuries.

The land-grant technique was brought along to Mexico and New Mexico, where, in the latter, according to sources cited by Sanchez, there were twelve grants of less than 1,000 acres; thirty-five of 50,000 to 100,000 acres; and nineteen grants of more than 100,000 acres.[29] Sanchez notes that many of the grants, including some made to individuals, became the property of the community, while others were made initially to the community, in which:

> Only the homesteads and farming lands were owned privately. The rest of the land was owned in common and was managed by a community board of directors. Grazing and water rights were assigned by community boards or councils. A mayordomo de la acequia, or ditch boss, apportioned the water and supervised the ditches. The rivers were diverted, reservoirs were built, and canals were dug cooperatively. Each land owner was required to do his pro-rata share of the work on the basis of acreage farmed.
>
> . . . .
>
> This system of land use and management became the dominant factor in the economic and civic life of the settlers.[30]

The Mora grant (what is now essentially the county of Mora) was made by Mexico in 1835 to "José Tapia, and seventy-five others. . . ."

> It appears that each of the seventy-five grantees received in severalty a small piece of land suitable for cultivation, and that the remainder of the grant was given to them in common; in the words of the act, "for the benefit of the grantees and for common pasturage."
>
> . . . .
>
> After the acquisition of New Mexico by the United States, the Mora grantees applied under the laws of Congress for a patent of their

lands. . . . Subsequently a survey of the grant was made by the United States, and a patent issued thereon in 1876.[31]

A review of the statutes governing land grants and acequias indicates that the political and administrative training received in the typical land-grant community or irrigation enterprise must have been considerable. According to the 1897 codification of acequia statutes, all rivers and streams were declared public, and acequias were "bodies corporate, with power to sue or to be sued as such."[32] Officers of acequias were three commissioners and one mayordomo, each of whom had to be the owner of an interest in the ditch. Officers were elected annually, and the commissioners were vested with authority to assess fatigue work. The mayordomo was the "executive officer of said ditch and [had] the superintendence of all work thereon and the distribution of the waters thereof."

Statutes establishing self-government of the land grants were similar. Owners or proprietors of any grant "to any colony, community or town or to any person or persons . . . shall become a body corporate and politic." Any ten or more owners in common could file a petition to be vested with corporate powers. Each person owning any interest in the grant could vote at the biennial elections. Corporate powers of the grant were exercised by a board of nine trustees elected by the owners and proprietors of the grant. The trustees could sue in the corporate name, and make rules and regulations "as necessary to the protection and improvement of such common lands. . . ." They could impose taxes or improvement assessments and determine the number of animals to be permitted to graze. Where the acequias selected or elected a ditch boss, the land grants often provided for one or more graziers or herders who were selected by the inhabitants.

The Brotherhood of Penitentes: Religious and Political Third Force

There has also long existed in New Mexico a lay religious and fraternal organization called the Penitent Brothers of Jesus of Nazareth, or Los Hermanos Penitentes. The chapels of the Brothers early became schools for politics, and a formidable counterweight to other institutions both sacred and secular.

It appears that the origin of the organization was similar or related to that of the secular Tertiaries of Saint Francis in Europe, and it is probable that such elements of New Mexico's Penitentes as chapel self-government and flagellation were also importations drawn from Europe. Archbishop Edwin V. Byrne of Santa Fe wrote that the origins of the brotherhood are obscure but that:

> It seems that it began somewhere in the beginnings of the last century when the Franciscan padres left New Mexico by order of the new government of Mexico. No other priests were sent to take their place. Groups among the faithful tried to keep up Catholic practices, without priestly guidance, and, though certain excesses crept in, it is to these groups of Penitential Brethren that we owe, in a manner, the preservation of the faith in those hard and trying times.
>
> But why do we make this declaration now? Precisely because many, even Catholics, harbor an erroneous idea concerning this association. It cannot be denied that the association itself is at fault because of certain excesses and abuses in the past. There are still scattered instances of individual bad lives, as in other societies, and this or that group still makes of itself a political football, thus giving a bad name to the Brethren.[33]

The recall of the Franciscan missionaries in 1834 and 1835 coincided with a period of social ferment in the area. Settlements were being extended into the mountainous areas of the northern upper river, or Rio Arriba country, and there was beginning to be considerable traffic by traders and trappers in the north. By 1846, when General Kearny occupied the territory, almost the whole of the area tillable by the irrigation methods of the time was occupied. Fergusson's history relates that: "It was in the rugged upper valley that the fraternity of the Penitent Brothers, wholly a plebeian organization, had its headquarters and its greatest strength."[34] A few moradas, or chapels, existed to the south in the Manzano and Sandia mountains near Albuquerque. There were and are several moradas in eastern and north central Valencia county. Their eastern limit was apparently in Guadalupe and Colfax counties.

Most writers who have described some facet or other of Penitente practices or villages have stressed that the organization has generally drawn its members from "the poorer men of the community—probably those whose interests are least well represented by the *patrón*, and whose influence is otherwise negligible."[35]

Fray Angélico indicates that the rituals of the Hermanos were public in the early days and that the men of the moradas provided the priestless villages with religious ceremonies for "which they greatly hungered," but that not all, by any means, of the villagers were members. Nor was membership restricted by the poor to the poor.

The *ricos* and more sophisticated men, if they joined at all, tended to be only "brothers of light" who, as in the quip by the author of *Fray Gerundio,* were content to light the way for their more simple and sincere brethren and their scourging, and, after the American occupation, to peddle them as vote-blocks at the polls. Some were also ready to become Protestants when the Archbishop invaded their sphere of influence.[36]

The morada or chapel would often be, and still is, within a few hundred yards of, or sometimes adjacent to, a church. The building was usually small and of one or two rooms. If the village was fairly populous, there might be two or more moradas, as in the village of Talpa in Taos County, where four could once be seen from one spot.

Each morada was, and some still are, a highly organized social entity. During the long period when they operated outside the mantle of the church, a fully staffed morada elected ten officers at the annual elections. The ritual attendant upon the religious observances, the practice of self-flagellation, and the judicial responsibilities of the morada each required the presence of specialized officers. Lummis lists four officers, whose capacities were directed to the rituals of flagellation or worship. There was also an *enfermero* or nurse who attended the ill, a *celador* or warden who attended to the morada and executed sentences imposed for a misdeed, a teacher of novices, a *mandatario* or collector, and a secretary.[37]

The chief officer of each morada, the *hermano mayor* or older brother, might be young, but he was a man of considerable authority. He had the duty of general overseeing of the other officers, served as a court in disputes between members, and represented the morada before official agencies or outside parties. He, too, was elected.

Some moradas may still elect this full complement of officers, but the practice now tends to the election of those with religious functions and to the *concilios,* or councilmen. Three of the latter are now elected in each morada to assist the *hermano mayor* in his official functions, particularly in those involving adjudication of disputes or in those involving representation of the morada in official Penitente or church affairs.

The organization existed for a hundred years without the sanction of the church. When Kearny's entry enabled the restoration of the rights of the church, the returning clergy found much in the organization they disapproved of. In 1886, Archbishop Salpointe of Santa Fe directed in a circular letter that the Penitentes cease their flagellation and return to the laws of the Third Order of St. Francis. When two years lapsed with no results, he dispatched another letter:

> With regard to the society called Los Penitentes we firmly believe, that it fully deserves all blame. Consequently it is not to be fostered. This society, though perhaps legitimate and religious in its beginning, has so greatly degenerated many years ago that it has no longer fixed rules but is governed in everything according to the pleasure of the director of every locality, and in many cases it is nothing else but a political society.[38]

The circular directed that Mass would not be celebrated in the chapels, "where the Penitentes observe their rites and abuses," and added that they were to be deprived of the Sacrament.

Religious and lay writers alike have placed considerable stress on the political activities of the Penitentes and almost always they have strongly indicated their disapproval.

The historian Twitchell thought it probable that half to two-thirds of the Hispanic population of the northern area "at some time has been identified with the order" but that its popularity had declined because of the ascendancy gained over the organization by "political demagogues" who used the brothers "as tools for the consummation of designs of a questionable nature."[39] A later writer states that:

> Today, as earlier, any man who can cultivate and secure the allegiance of the Hermano Mayor . . . can command many votes. The entire group will vote as he instructs it. Padre Martinez was not the last man to use the order for political purposes.[40]

Russell also states, and more correctly, that the Republican political organization of the state had "long counted on the Penitente vote."[41]

A novel by Fergusson may come closer to the mark, however, than the typical work of interpretation or analysis. Therein, in dealing with the period 1850-1880, he quotes the alcalde of a mountain village who sought to persuade a Scot—hence an Anglo in Hispanic parlance—to become a member.

"You know the Penitentes are many. Here in the upper river country we outnumber all others. Moreover, we act and think as one. In the town of Mora on the other side of the mountain we have our headquarters and there lives the great brother who rules us all.

. . . . .

"We are poor and ignorant," the Alcalde said. "Under the Mexican government all we could do was to care for our own, and also some times we could take care of our enemies. Those who are wise have always respected our power. But under the American government we might do much more. I am an ignorant man myself but I know that votes are power now and we have many votes. What we need is someone to speak for us in Santa Fe—someone who knows the written word and also the ways of the Americans."[42]

Fergusson's reference to "the great brother who rules us all" is intriguing, but it is probably a bit of poetic license, for a church historian recorded early in this century that "the society has no general organization or supreme authority. Each fraternity is local and independent with its own officers."[43] The office of *hermano supremo* was established in 1936 when, with the assent of Archbishop Gerken, several members seeking to bring the organization under the sanction of the church designated Don Miguel Archibeque of Santa Fe to assume such a post. Most moradas had long declined to acknowledge the authority of the archbishop, but some members felt that an organization was needed to foster, over a period of time, a group of moradas which adhered to the church and which might bring others along. The last group of twenty-two moradas of San Miguel County's thirty-eight did not affiliate with the church-sanctioned organization until 1955.

According to Don Miguel, the moradas of several counties sometimes maintained, prior to 1936, a county *concilio* or council organized on a formal basis of representation by moradas, but such county groups did not form a formal union. Districts were first created in

1937 in southern San Miguel and in Rio Arriba counties, and by 1955 the Brotherhood was organized in nine districts or *concilios*. The more isolated chapels are directly under the supervision of the *hermano supremo*, the others comprise three districts in San Miguel, one in Mora, three in Taos, and two in Rio Arriba counties. By 1960 there remained perhaps 135 chapter houses in New Mexico and southern Colorado. Estimates of the size of the membership are far from precise, but the 1960 rosters probably included some two to three thousand members.[44] Moradas consisted then of ten or more members, and were divided when they reached a membership of ninety or so. Don Miguel estimated the average size of the active chapels to be fifty members—an estimate that seems too high, for many of the villages scarcely numbered fifty male adults in 1960. A general meeting, which each *hermano mayor* is urged to attend with his *concilio* members, is now held in Santa Fe each June. As many as three hundred have attended, but the conclave has sometimes assembled with only a hundred or so members present to hear formal addresses by the archbishop and other officials of church and Brotherhood.

Penitente Political Activity: The Case of San Miguel County

It is difficult to separate fact from legend in an accounting of the politics of the Brotherhood. According to some sources, the Penitente vote was "deliverable" and highly subject to manipulation. According to others, it was a vote inflexibly controlled by the Republican party. Probably it was neither. A manipulable vote is most useful to a party machine when it is seeking to control its own primaries, but New Mexico did not adopt a primary law until 1939. And a dominant party normally seeks to make its general election vote as high and stable as possible. Strenuous efforts were frequently made to influence precinct organizations to select county convention delegations acceptable to this or that faction, but blatant attempts to dominate were apt to provoke party schisms or rump movements. And if the general election vote of the Penitente precincts had been inflexibly dominated by the Republican party, it is improbable that officers of both parties would have felt impelled to expend in them as much time and effort as they did. Much more likely is the proposition that the Penitente precincts comprised a vote large enough, and variable enough, to make them a marginal factor critical in the election strategies of both parties.

The leaders of the Republican organization of San Miguel County from 1905 to 1935 enjoyed a substantial amount of power, but never anything approaching a monopoly. Dissident factions among the Republicans strove for leadership; and the Democrats, through those years, were frequently above 40 per cent in elections. So were they in Guadalupe, Mora, Rio Arriba, and Taos, the other counties of the state's Hispanic heartland.

Within those counties, political leaders, whether of the Brotherhood or not, were unquestionably "powerful," but they were so in the limited sense in which authority must have due regard for supportive factions. Almost invariably, political leaders had to "politic" for dominance over their own party. Since there was no common and automatic unanimity, agreements had to be reached in the bargaining and negotiations that are the stuff of politics. Usually a common party front could be achieved within a county (it had to be, or the opposition would win), but even within the county party there tended to be strong and obdurate pockets of opposition. Factions were always incipient. In a county like San Miguel, the scattered groups of Penitentes were too pervasive; and, probably, too much a functioning part of the Republican party to permit them consistently to behave, as politicians would view it, with a feckless opportunism. But, since the Penitentes were a minority in the localized Hispanic group which, in turn, was a part of the structure of a statewide party, they apparently sometimes did as the polity permits such groups to do: that is, use their weight as a balance of power within the Republican party and between the parties and other groups as well.

In the view of some observers, the Penitente groups would have used their power more effectively and more rationally by accepting clear-cut goals in the manner of a pressure group. They tended instead to indulge in another customary attribute of political groups, for most persisted in maintaining a consistent political identity with one party and loyalty to it. Hence, to induce a switch of 10 or 20 per cent in the precinct usually required a considerable expenditure of time and effort. But the men of the moradas played the game *con gusto* and in the expectation that their vote or convention support would be courted.

A politician who spent a lot of time plying his trade in the northern counties estimated that in the 1920's there were probably 25,000 to 30,000 people involved in Penitente politics of the state. The estimate seems high, for the same individual observed: "We always figured the Penitente vote in San Miguel was good for three thousand. This figure was good late into the 1930's." But if by "involved" there was meant to be included the bulk of those voters who were living in Penitente precincts, as distinguished from members, the figure is reasonable enough, and so is that of three thousand for San Miguel County. For a generation the Penitente precincts of San Miguel County cast three thousand votes, but by no means were all of those votes cast by members of the Brotherhood. However, if, as claimed, Penitentes were of the more plebian element, then they were probably representative of the majority of their fellows whether or not all were members.

Working politicians insist that the Penitente vote could not be "delivered." In the words of one, "that vote wasn't for sale as a group. It had to be worked and solicited." An Anglo political leader and lawyer who practiced both arts in the northern counties maintains:

> The leading personalities in northern county politics did not attempt to tell the people of Penitente villages or members of the *moradas* what to do. The technique was low pressure. It involved a lot of talk and, in general, the talk was designed to reach an agreement on each candidate. In the *moradas* and other political meetings, various candidates would be discussed at length, and those who were trusted and who knew the candidates would carry the ball or act as spokesmen for the men of their preference.
>
> When this was determined [i.e., who was favored for each office] there was little question of how a convention would go in the county.[45]

A gruff old Republican cacique (or "big wheel" as the Taos Democratic chieftain who applied the term translated it) observed that the Penitentes:

> were the balance of power then [1920's] and are probably still influential, but their strength is being dissipated. Most are now Democrats.
>
> Most of them were illiterate and poor, but they were often good speakers, and they were often—those who got into the conventions —capable and good politicians and still are.

The lawyer-politician earlier quoted describes the homegrown juris-
prudence of the Penitente areas and throws an inferential light upon
the pervasive quality of the group's influence: (The phenomenon described is a frequent one in acculturating groups striving to maintain
an identity and a degree of cohesion among their members. A more recent example in New Mexico is provided by Navajo and other tribal
courts, but in this case there is a legalized division of jurisdiction.)

> The moradas would mete out punishment and everyone in the
> community would be thoroughly aware of the misdeed, its back-
> ground, and its punishment. Then, if such cases came officially into
> court, as likely as not members of the organization would be found
> on the jury; and, if not, the juries were certainly willing to act on be-
> half of first principals. The cases were normally dismissed by acquit-
> tals as not guilty. They were actually usually guilty as hell, but they
> had been punished and there was normally no desire to punish a
> second time.

Although it is doubtful that the Hermanos were once ruled by a
"Grand Klagle," as one observer expressed it, there was considerable
emphasis by others that Mora County was for a long while a center of
particularly pervasive Penitente activity, but that by the time statehood was granted, that center had shifted southward to neighboring
San Miguel County. And San Miguel was then one of the most salient,
but embattled, of the Republican strongholds.

Two Republican leaders of the time and place were long widely ac-
claimed in San Miguel County as having been "very powerful" among
the Penitentes. At any rate, Lorenzo Delgado and Secundino Romero
were able and influential politicians. Romero, a large and mustachioed
man, looked the *patrón* or *jefe político*. Head of a prominent family,
"Sec" Romero was court clerk, sheriff (on those several occasions
when his brother Cleofas or his foster-brother Lorenzo Delgado were
not), and speaker of the house of representatives. Delgado, a wiry
(when young) and smooth-shaven man of lesser size, never looked the
patrón. Clerk of the house, sheriff, and the man who bested Romero
in a head-on political fight, Delgado's style was more the affable one
expected in a service club president; and, although he never married,
his personal charm was such that the lady he chose as his partner to

lead the grand march to open a ball or dance felt herself to be queen for the evening. Few men in New Mexico politics have displayed much of *charisma,* but by all accounts, Delgado had that quality.

A few items from the political careers of Delgado and Romero of San Miguel County are used in the following pages as indicators of electoral habits of the Penitente areas. The other principals involved are Holm O. Bursum, I, a major Republican figure; Ezequiel C de Baca of San Miguel County, successful Democratic gubernatorial candidate in 1916; and Bronson M. Cutting, Republican liberal maverick and U.S. senator, 1927-1935.

The votes evoked by the series of hard-fought contests used in Table 4 to test the results of Penitente voting were clearly influenced by the presence of candidates identifiable as compatriots or fellow members of the Hispanic community. Other things being equal a candidate bearing a name like Baca or Lucero could poll a heavier vote than a candidate named Smith or Bursum. And if a candidate of any name were judged "simpático" by members of the Penitente fraternity that, too, could be traced in the election returns. The point demonstrated here is that voting in the Penitente precincts shared the characteristics of the voting in other Hispanic but non-Penitente precincts. In the Penitente precincts those characteristics were etched a little more sharply; they were a little more discernible. But the reminder may be in order that in neither case do the characteristics measured describe an extreme reaction to the presence of particularly favored candidates. Other groups in the United States have frequently shown their responses to ethnic considerations much more sharply. In the New Mexico case the bonds of party have acted as a powerful restraint. The cases are legion in which a "Bursum" did defeat a "Baca" in the Hispanic counties, but in many the "Bursum" or the "Smith" may have trailed his ticket by a few points.

In the 1916 elections, the second after statehood, the five north-central counties turned in a typical vote.

Each party had carefully constructed tickets designed to yield optimum results. Democrats, favored by war, Wilson, and a realistic appraisal of the results of population shifts and growth, won in the state by taking seven of eleven places of the statewide ticket. Their gubernatorial nomination of Ezequiel C de Baca of San Miguel County was a good move, although Republicans did reasonably well with most of their ticket in the northern counties. B. C. Hernandez, Republican candidate for Congress, was an able politician from Rio Arriba County who had long been one of the leaders of the state party. Holm O. Bursum was one of the major figures in the Republican party and an astute political manager, but his county of Socorro lay far to the south. Lindsey, for lieutenant governor, had been placed on the ticket to lend it more appeal to the eastern part of the state. Lindsey's opponent, Democrat W. C. McDonald, was just finishing a four-year term as governor. The five-county vote for Lindsey and McDonald was about par for each party for most of the state ticket. Table 4 indicates the diver-

TABLE 4. VOTE FOR HISPANIC VERSUS ANGLO POLITICAL LEADERS IN FIVE
HISPANIC REPUBLICAN COUNTIES, 1916

County	*Congress* Hernandez (R) Walton (D)		*Governor* Bursum (R) C de Baca (D)		*Lt. Governor* Lindsey (R) McDonald (D)	
Guadalupe	1,098	1,132	1,023	1,205	1,098	1,124
Mora	1,651	1,436	1,463	1,610	1,606	1,476
Rio Arriba	2,310	1,173	1,962	1,622	2,090	1,390
San Miguel	3,119	2,024	2,606	2,521	3,005	2,131
Taos	1,433	785	1,116	1,107	1,351	868
Total	9,611	6,550	8,170	7,965	9,150	6,989
Percentage Republican	59.4		50.6		56.7	

gencies from their vote of the vote for Bursum and C de Baca; and for Hernandez and Walton—Anglo and Republican Bursum against an effective and popular Spanish American from a big county, and Hispanic and Republican Hernandez against an Anglo who did not live in the region.

The question of the possible membership of Hernandez and C de Baca in the Penitente organizations of their counties is moot. Certainly, however, neither was a stranger to them and each was as capable of working politics with Penitente groups as they were with others.

Using the vote for lieutenant governor as the gauge, we infer from Table 4 that Hispanic Republican Hernandez got about three percentage points more of the total vote than his party would have gotten for him; and that Hispanic Democrat C de Baca got about six percentage points more of the vote than his party would have gotten for him.

It is a reasonable deduction that about 450 of Hernandez' vote of 9,611, and 970 to 1,000 of C de Baca's vote of 7,965 came from sources of strength outside regular party channels or party votes. Some part of their additional margins would have been available simply from friends and neighbors in their own and adjoining counties; some accrued because of their Spanish names; some additional part must be attributed to their skill and resourcefulness; but a residue is probably due to the Penitente vote in the five counties. San Miguel County provides a measure of its marginal but sometimes decisive weight in periods of tight elections.

In the 1916 elections, twenty-six country precincts of San Miguel County's then fifty-six contained (so far as it could be ascertained) one or more moradas. Those precincts cast 39 per cent of the vote of the county—1,988 of 5,140. (The reminder may be in order that vote totals jumped by 60 to 70 per cent after passage of the woman's suffrage amendment.)

Republican Hernandez of Rio Arriba County won in twenty-two of the twenty-six precincts and tied in one. Republican Lindsey of Roosevelt County made the same precinct score with a lower percentage of the vote, but party *jefe* Bursum won in only fifteen, while losing the non-Penitente precincts to C de Baca, San Miguel's favorite son. Table 5 shows the alignment of the vote, and the highest and lowest Republican percentage of the vote in the county's Penitente and non-Penitente precincts.

Table 5 indicates that C de Baca received 390 more votes than fellow Democrat McDonald, who received a vote quite typical of that received by other members of his ticket. Of C de Baca's margin over his ticket, 179, a little less than half, came from twenty-six Penitente precincts, and 211 came from the remaining thirty. C de Baca ran about nine percentage points ahead of his ticket in Penitente precincts and about seven in the others. By this measure, the difference in the reactions of the precincts is not significant. The Penitente vote was more Republican than that of the remainder of the county, but it otherwise reacted just about as did the bulk of the vote.

Differences in the range or limits of the Republican percentages in-

TABLE 5. VARIABILITY AND RANGE OF THE VOTE IN PENITENTE AND NON-PENITENTE PRECINCTS, SAN MIGUEL COUNTY, 1916

Voting area	*Congress*		*Governor*		*Lt. Governor*	
	(R) Hernandez	(D) Walton	(R) Bursum	(D) C de Baca	(R) Lindsey	(D) McDonald
In all						
precincts	3,119	2,024	2,606	2,521	3,005	2,131
Total	5,143		5,127		5,136	
Percentage Republican	60.6		50.8		58.5	
In 26 Penitente						
precincts	1,346	642	1,086	893	1,272	714
Total	1,988		1,979		1,986	
Percentage Republican	67.7		54.9		64.0	
Range of vote for Republican	28-94		24-87		28-92	
In 30 remaining						
precincts	1,773	1,382	1,520	1,628	1,733	1,417
Total	3,155		3,148		3,150	
Percentage Republican	56.2		48.3		55.0	
Range of vote for Republican	44-79		29-72		42-77	

dicate, however, that the Penitente precincts were apt to produce a more one-sided vote. The question then remains, whether, within those broader ranges, the vote of the individual Penitente precincts was more variable than that of the non-Penitente areas. Table 6 groups the precincts by the number of percentage points by which each separated the highest and lowest of the three Republican candidates of the previous table. The Penitente precincts were more likely to keep the vote for all three candidates within a 10-point spread. At the other ex-

TABLE 6. INCIDENCE OF VOTE-SPLITTING IN PENITENTE AND OTHER
    PRECINCTS
(Republican candidates for congressman, governor and lt. governor, San
Miguel County, 1916)

Classes and	*Percentage points separating highest and*			
number of precincts	*lowest of three Republican candidates*			
	1-10	*11-20*	*21-30*	*31-plus*
Penitente (26)	57.7	23.1	11.5	7.7
Non-Penitente (30)	43.3	46.7	3.3	6.7

treme, they had a higher tendency to cast a vote in which the difference
between candidates was over 20 points, but the differences there are
not great.

One-fourth of San Miguel County's Penitente precincts produced
majorities in 1916 for one or the other of the parties of 70 per cent or
more. Among them precinct 37—El Cerrito—was indeed Republican,
as found by its chronicler, but it was almost singularly so.[46] Since few
gave such one-sided majorities, it appears that the typical precinct
was probably one in which the precinct chairman of each party worked
hard at his business. Each may have been a small-scale boss or *jefe
político*, but it is unlikely that many of those precincts could have contained two *patrones*. There is small doubt, either, that the typical Republican precinct chairman might have been a member of the local
Penitente morada, but several of the twenty-six precincts turned a ma-
ority to C de Baca and they, plus a few others, were to do so for other
Democratic candidates in a long series of elections.

While most moradas were Republican, it is probable that they and
their communities were subject to the stresses of an intense factionalism
that led many to a division into opposing party camps.[47] The contrary
would require the assumption that, since the great majority of Penitentes were Republicans, nearly all others in each precinct were necessarily Democrats—a dubious proposition, for the larger ranchers, store-
keepers, etc., of the time were prone to be Republicans although they,
as a class, were not supposed to be of Los Hermanos Penitentes.

A comparison of the voting in the Penitente precincts with that in
the others in four San Miguel County elections of 1922-1928 may provide an additional clue to the characteristics of the two sectors of the

electorate. The period covered by Table 7 spans the brief era in which Delgado left his party and twice ran as a Democrat—for sheriff in 1924 against his old ally and mentor, Secundino Romero, and for lieutenant governor in 1926 when his new ally, Bronson M. Cutting, deserted him.[48] Delgado then ran again for sheriff in 1928 as a Republican.

When Delgado locked horns in 1924 with his old ally, Romero, the total vote in the Penitente precincts dropped off by about 250 and stayed low in the next two elections. Of the remaining 2,700 votes in the Penitente areas, approximately 350 to 400 probably represented a switch, for the Republican majority dropped from 1,016 to 296. An

TABLE 7. PENITENTE VOTING? FOUR ELECTIONS INVOLVING DEMOCRATIC
AND REPUBLICAN CANDIDACIES OF LORENZO DELGADO

	Election and Party of Candidacy			
	1922	1924	1926	1928
	(Sheriff)	*(Sheriff)*	*(Lt. Gov.)*	*(Sheriff)*
	DELGADO	Romero	Sargent	DELGADO
	(R)	(R)	(R)	(R)
	Lucero	DELGADO	DELGADO	Sena
Area and Vote	(D)	(D)	(D)	(D)
Vote cast in:				
Penitente precincts	2,944	2,696	2,783	2,643
Remaining precincts	6,093	5,978	5,791	6,014
Total county vote	9,037	8,674	8,574	8,657
Republican majority in:				
Penitente precincts	1,016	296	–91	647
Remaining precincts	1,071	–302	–573	222
County	2,087	–6	–664	869
Percentage Republican in:				
Penitente precincts	67.3	55.5	48.4	62.2
Remaining precincts	59.6	47.5	45.1	51.8
County	62.1	50.0	46.1	55.0

additional 200, or a few less, changed in the 1926 election to follow Delgado, so that the approximate total involved in the switch in the Penitente precincts was 600 votes—about 22 per cent of the vote. Most of this vote taken by Delgado into the Democratic fusion must have switched over also in the races for governor, congressman, and several others on the state and local tickets, for the proportion of voters who switched in the other races was about 20 per cent in the Penitente areas and about half that in the remaining areas. Consequently, for several on the state Democratic ticket, some 1,100 to 1,200 votes, or 12 to 14 per cent of the county's total, switched in the course of the two elections.

Few of the Penitente precincts were resistant to the stresses and strains of the four campaigns of 1922-1928, but Table 8 (derived from

TABLE 8. INCIDENCE AND EXTENT OF SHIFT IN PARTY PERCENTAGE IN
PENITENTE PRECINCTS OF SAN MIGUEL COUNTY
(Four elections of 1922-1928 involving Democratic and Republican candidacies of Lorenzo Delgado)

	Precincts shifting	
Percentage-point shift	Number	Percentage
0-10	3	10
11-20	4	14
21-30	9	31
31-40	8	28
41-50	3	10
51-60	0	..
61-80	2	7
	—	—
	29	100

Appendix, Table A-2) shows that only five of the twenty-nine precincts made shifts of heroic proportions. The record is more indicative of intense political activity and local bargaining than it is of domination by *patrón* or *jefe político*.

In the elections of 1916, 1924-1928, 1934, and 1942, six Penitente precincts never gave a Democratic gubernatorial candidate a majority.

Eight once gave one such candidate a majority, six permitted their vote to go twice to the Democrat, three precincts gave majorities to four Democratic gubernatorial candidates, and one did so five times. Eight precincts went through the four elections of 1922-1928 without a change, and in 1942, after twelve years of Democratic administration in the state and a full decade of depression, a majority of the precincts turned in Republican majorities in four key races.

So, in brief, if the Penitente vote of San Miguel County is a fair sample of other such votes in the state, it was Republican as has been claimed, and only recently has it come to a Democratic attachment. But if that vote was ever a vendible commodity, in the sense that it could be made to break significantly away from tradition, and friends and neighbors, then it was an angular and difficult thing to package, wrap, and consign.

But when elections are close, then a few hundred votes bulk as large on the horizons of politicians as the Rockies to the westward traveler, and the presence of a man or a cadre who can move such votes is apt to be the source of legends as glittering as those spun by travelers returned from El Dorado.

The Constitution, and Other Measures of Political Skills

Sixty-four years of practice in the ways of gringo politics ended in 1910 with the writing of a constitution containing some extraordinary guarantees of Spanish-American civic and political rights. To assess these features of the constitution as measure and result simply of Hispanic political power would not, of course, be altogether accurate, for the legal position accorded this "minority" was an institutional product fashioned by a partisan grouping in which the Hispanic members were merely one of several essential elements. One half of the seventy Republican delegates to the one-hundred-member convention were Spanish American. The other half included a dozen or so Republicans of the rank and file, but most were key figures in the Republican Old Guard, or "Santa Fe Ring" as it was sometimes called.[49] Party leaders who never before, and never again, held elective office made sure they would be on hand to shape the framework of the new state. It was not merely coincidental that the dominant economic interests of the state were represented in that close-knit group. Nor was it an accident that the indispensable member of the Old Guard leadership of the constitutional convention was Solomon Luna—spokesman and leader of the Hispanic members who "formed a comparatively solid block welded by a common interest . . . the preservation of their traditional way of life and the language of their fathers."[50]

The camaraderie of political fellowship and many lasting personal attachments are not to be discounted, but the relationship binding Anglo representatives of mining, railroad, and commercial interests to Hispanic members of party and convention had earlier become less one of mutual than of complementary needs. In seeking its goals, each side was profoundly aware that it needed the support of the other. For their part of the bargain, Hispanic members achieved a constitution which should remove any doubt that the nexus between politics, economics, and group power had long been quite clear to a decisive, if not large, number of Hispanic citizens.

Except for a proviso or two like that requiring judges to be "learned in the law," the constitution contains few of the restrictions of a type found in the laws of many of the states, for certain qualifications frequently required for holding office or exercising the right of franchise are expressly barred in New Mexico. Every resident citizen of the United States is qualified to vote and "to hold any public office in the state."[51] Furthermore:

> The right of any citizen of the state to vote, hold office or sit upon juries, shall never be restricted, abridged or impaired on account of religion, race, language or color, *or inability to speak, read or write the English or Spanish languages except as may be otherwise provided in this constitution* and the provisions of this section and of section one of this article shall never be amended except upon a vote of the people of this state in an election at which at least three-fourths of the electors voting in the whole state, and at least two-thirds of those voting in each county of the state shall vote for such amendment.[52]

Broadly though the right is stated above, it does not stand isolated in the constitution and the statutes of the state.[53] It is deeply embedded, and the strictness of the standard for any reduction of it at the polls makes as absolute as legal institutions can the capacity of the Hispanic citizen to bar other groups or those in control of the formal agencies of government from undertakings which would denigrate his political capacity. To see so explicit a statement of a group veto (particularly in the light of its implications for other states) could well disquiet many Southern defenders of the status quo; but New Mexico can perhaps take credit for being the first to have given Calhoun's doctrine of the concurrent majority a formal expression that governs a major aspect of politics *within* a state.

Certain other provisions like those of Article XII are notable: Section 8 provides that the legislature shall provide for the training of teachers in the normal schools "so that they may become proficient in both the English and Spanish languages, to qualify them to teach Spanish-speaking pupils." Section 10 provides that children of Spanish descent shall never be denied "the right and privilege of admission and attendance in the public schools . . . and they shall never be classed in separate schools." Section 11 confirms as a state institution "the Spanish-American School at El Rito."

These provisions did not occur spontaneously or unheralded in the brief span of the constitutional convention of 1910. They had precedent, and one found its way into the constitution in the face of a congressional stricture to the contrary. It may be true "that there was no particular opposition" to them, but it may be vouchsafed that they are there because Hispanic leaders knew their interests well enough to insist on their inclusion.[54]

The Kearny Code—the articles of government of the military occupation of 1846-1850—simply declared that "all political power is vested in and belongs to the people," but the Treaty of Guadalupe Hidalgo (1848) required that Mexicans not electing to remain citizens of Mexico were to be admitted "at the proper time . . . to the enjoyment of all the rights of citizens of the United States." The Organic Act establishing the territory (1850) gave formal acknowledgment to the treaty commitment but gave the territorial legislature an option, that was never exercised, of restricting the suffrage:

Every free white male inhabitant, above the age of twenty-one years, who shall have been a resident of said territory at the time of the passage of this act, shall be entitled to vote at the first election, and shall be eligible to any office within the said territory, but the qualifications of voters and of holding office at all subsequent elections, shall be such as prescribed by the legislative assembly: Provided, That the right of suffrage, and of holding office, shall be exercised only by citizens of the United States, including those recognized as citizens by the treaty with the Republic of Mexico.[55]

But despite the fact that New Mexico's territorial legislature had never elected in sixty years to prescribe a generalized literacy or language qualification for the suffrage or officeholding, Congress stipulated in the Enabling Act of 1910:

> That said state shall never enact any law restricting or abridging the right of suffrage on account of race, color, or previous condition of servitude, *and that ability to read, write, speak, and understand the English language sufficiently well to conduct the duties of the office without the aid of an interpreter shall be a necessary qualification for all state officers and members of the legislature.*[56] (Italics added.)

So the 1910 constitution that was submitted to the people contained related provisions in Articles VII and XXI which plainly posed a dilemma for Hispanic leaders and a problem in construction for lawyers. It was not then known whether the provision in Article XXI as required by Congress in the Enabling Act would prevail in the pending judicial test, but the wording of Article VII was deliberate, and a gamble on the possibility of removing or negating the offensive requirement of Article XXI while relying on the guarantee expressed in Article VII to assist in securing acceptance of the constitution.

To have obtained an enabling act for statehood was a victory for many of the social and economic interests associated with the Republican party; to neglect to limit or remove the requirement imposed by Congress was to risk the defeat of the proposed constitution.

One measure taken was to write into the constitution the requirements in Articles II, IV, VII, XII, and XX which granted or confirmed rights previously or potentially useful to Hispanic citizens. Then, when it became necessary to refer directly to the requirement of the Enabling Act, the majority and the committee on revision clearly signified their disapproval of it by reciting in Article XXI (relating to the compact with the United States) the required guarantee of the suffrage and then stating: *"and in compliance with the requirements of the said act of congress,* it is hereby provided that ability to read, write . . . shall be a necessary qualification. . . ." (Italics added.)

Meanwhile the constitutional convention adopted a resolution commending the committee on revision for the great care used "necessitating almost continuous sessions . . . for some days and nights past." Charles Spiess, an able legislative draftsman and political strategist, was later called upon to respond to a eulogy commending his work as convention president. The response stressed two results of the convention. One was the correspondence between the proposed constitution and what Spiess conceived to be the Republican position; the comment on the other was no doubt in recognition of a political requirement that could not be ignored. Said Spiess:

The politics of today is represented by a long line, which commences with the socialist on one end and terminates with the reactionary on the other, who does not tolerate a suggestion that the old order of things should be changed; but you have . . . safely steered . . . among the different ideas. . . . You have by its provisions guaranteed the equal protection of the law to every citizen of New Mexico; you have preserved the religious, political, social, and civic rights to every one of our citizens, and placed them beyond the power of assault from any source whatsoever.[57]

The constitution was adopted and Congress was then easily induced, after the 1911 Supreme Court decision in *Coyle v. Smith*, to remove

TABLE 9. RELATION OF VOTE ON TWO CONSTITUTIONAL AMENDMENTS TO "ANGLO-HISPANIC" POPULATION PROPORTIONS

Percentage population Hispanic[a]	Number of counties	Percentage of voters for Gov. and Pres. voting on measures		Percentage voting Yes[b]	
		1911	1912	1911 "Blue Ballot"	1912 Removal of literacy qualification
0-24.9	9	95	81	83	31
25-74.9	10[c]	92	80	57	67
75-100	7	96	94	45	88

a *New Mexico Blue Book, 1915*, p. 142.
b Derived from *New Mexico Blue Book, 1917*, pp. 221 and 227.
c Union County 1911 vote not available on "Blue Ballot."

the restriction of the Enabling Act so that the legislature might propose
a constitutional amendment for removal of the disputed requirement.[58]

The objection might be raised that the convention action on the
constitutional provisions merely demonstrates that a limited group of
political leaders required those provisions. There is strong evidence,
however, that Anglo and Spanish-American voters alike were either
aware or readily induced to become aware of the underlying issues.

The vote on the 1912 amendment to remove the congressionally
imposed qualifications for officeholding, and the vote on the 1911
"Flood" or "Blue Ballot" amendment to make the constitution easier
of amendment are contrasted in Table 9. The sharply negative correlation of the two elections is clearly dependent upon the proportions of
Hispanic and Anglo voters of the various counties.

HISPANIC MINORITIES AND DEMOCRATIC PARTISANSHIP

In communities and counties in which Hispanic voters are a stable and
self-assured majority, the natural, nearly inevitable division is one of
Republican versus Democrat. In this case partisanship reflects community, not ethnic, divisions; and, although the majority party may
enjoy long periods of dominance, the minority party remains as a
formidable force with a strong attraction for factional groups seeking
alterations in the balance of community interests. But the partisan
alignment is quite different in communities or situations in which
Hispanic voters occupy a minority position. In this case, the not unexpected result is an increasing identification with one party—the
Democratic. This relationship subsuming minority groupings of Spanish-American voters into customary components of the Democratic
party can be taken as axiomatic, but, as the following illustrations indicate, the forms and expressions of that relationship may change
from town to town and from time to time.

A Democratic, Spanish-American voter in Albuquerque is in a situation quite different from that of one in Roswell, and neither would
quickly understand the politics of Silver City and its fringe of Grant
County mining towns.

Grant County's Hispanic citizens came to political self-consciousness
in an environment dominated by mining companies and by the "Big

Hats," as miners call the ranchers; but a change, curiously long delayed, has recently occurred in the politics of the county. Although Spanish-American candidates there were seldom seen and even less frequently successful before 1958, a half-dozen mining town precincts encircling Silver City and three voting divisions within Silver City called "Chihuahua Hill" can now return overwhelming margins for Hispanic candidates in the Democratic primaries and safe majorities for Anglo candidates favored by the Mine, Mill, and Smelter Workers' Union. Consequently, Hispanic candidates are now frequently successful, and the union can even make its weight apparent in the general elections when it lends its endorsement to a Republican.

A few results in the 1962 elections illustrate the ethnic cohesiveness and trade union influence lately apparent in Grant County. The Democratic nominee for one of the two congressional posts was incumbent Joseph M. Montoya—a candidate entirely *simpático* with Hispanic voters of the area. Montoya's opponent, Jack Redman, led the losing Republican ticket in the statewide voting. On the county ticket several Democratic Hispanic candidates won easy majorities, but one (Carrillo) who had the hard luck to confront a Republican Spanish American endorsed by the union received a much smaller majority. Table 10 groups the county's thirty precincts by their accessibility to Spanish-American and trade union influences.[59]

By 1960, Spanish Americans made up slightly over a quarter of the population of Bernalillo County, residing, usually, in the areas in which history first placed them. A majority live in the "Valley" precincts of Albuquerque and on or near the floodplains of a twenty-five-mile, north-south reach of the Rio Grande. Some live in villages of the small valleys of the Sandia and Manzano mountains lying parallel to the Rio Grande at a distance of eight miles or so, and perhaps 20 per cent of the county's Hispanic voters live scattered throughout the newer precincts. From 1910 to 1940, Hispanic voters numbered about half of the county's total, but after World War II the county's population doubled in a few years, and then doubled again. Most of this new, and largely middle-class, Anglo population lives in Albuquerque's "Heights"—a loosely filled, inverted triangle of about forty square miles. The base of the Heights triangle lies nearly against the mountains, its apex is near the University of New Mexico and the 1940 limits of the city. The county's Hispanic precincts were once major factors

TABLE 10. Ranch, Main Street, and Mine Union in the Ethnic and
Party Voting of Grant County General Elections, 1962

	Percentage of vote for Democrat		
	Congress (1) Montoya (D)[a] vs.	Commissioner (2) Carrillo (D) vs.	Percentage difference
Type of area	Redman	Norero[b]	(1) - (2)
Seven heavily Hispanic mine town precincts[c]	86	57	29
Three Silver City "Chi- huahua Hill" precincts[d]	81	65	16
Thirteen small and scat- tered rural precincts	56	54	2
Seven "most Anglo" city and mine town precincts[e]	49	49	0

[a] Endorsed by Mine, Mill, and Smelter Workers' Union.
[b] Endorsed by Union.
[c] Central, 1-A; Hanover, 11; Hurley, 12-B; Santa Rita, 13-B; Fierro, 20; Bayard, 21-A, and 21-B.
[d] Silver City, 3-A, 3-D, and 3-F.
[e] Silver City, 3-B, 3-C, 3-E, 3-G, 3-H; Hurley, 12-A; and Santa Rita, 13-A.

in the organizations and strategies of each party and possessed a decisive strength in the general elections; they are now most influential
in the Democratic primary.

Data are not economically available for ranking the 220 or so voting divisions of Bernalillo County's forty-seven precincts by their
percentages of Hispanic voters, but an array of ten divisions and their
voting results in 1962 provides a reasonably accurate profile of a few
characteristics of the elections of 1958-1964. These are voting divisions or precincts frequently mentioned or described to me by activists
of both parties. They range from heavily Hispanic and most Democratic
to least Democratic and most Anglo. The "sample" provides no best
representative of the highest-income neighborhoods and it jumps a
group of divisions lying at the middle of the ranges of ethnic and
economic characteristics. Tables 11 and 12 arrange the ten divisions
in an order determined by their average Democratic percentage in the

general election vote for seventeen state and county candidates in contests which did not pit Anglo against Hispano. From this base, Table 11 shows the apparent frequency of ethnic favoritism in the old His-

TABLE 11. PARTY AND ETHNIC VOTE IN RELATION TO PARTY STRENGTH IN BERNALILLO COUNTY GENERAL ELECTIONS, 1962

Precinct or voting division	*Average Democratic percentage in*		*Difference in "Anglo-Hispano" vote (2)-(1)*	*Range of vote from highest to lowest Democrat*
	17 non-ethnic contests	*Contests of 8 Hispanic Democrats vs. "Anglos"*		
	(1)	*(2)*	*(3)*	*(4)*
24C East San Jose	89	90	1	8
27D Barelas	79	84	5	19
2B Atrisco	71	72	1	12
5A Commodity Warehouse	71	75	4	18
18A Five Points	64	64	0	13
25A Eugene Field School	55	51	–4	19
46F Acoma School	50	44	–6	23
37C Highland High	43	34	–9	25
36C Jefferson Jr. High	39	30	–9	31
40D Fairgrounds Building	37	25	–12	37

panic precincts to be eclipsed by that in the newer and more Anglo divisions. A diminishing Democratic (and Hispanic) percentage is also strongly associated with an increasing range of cross-party voting or ticket-splitting (column 4).

Measures relating ethnicity to comparative levels of political activity and group voting in the same ten Bernalillo County divisions are provided by Table 12. The Democratic primary vote for Rodriguez, contesting three Anglos for a legislative nomination, is a not unduly distorted reflection of the proportions of Anglo and Hispanic voters in the ten divisions.

The slight enthusiasm of Hispanic residents for cross-party voting

TABLE 12. Ethnic Ratios Reflected in Voter Turnout in Primary
and General Elections in Bernalillo County, 1962

Precinct or voting division	Democratic general election percentage, in 17 non-ethnic races	Percentage of Democratic primary vote to Rodriguez	Democratic primary vote as percentage of total general election vote	Total primary vote as percentage of total vote in general election
	(1)	(2)	(3)	(4)
24C	89	86	80	83
27D	79	79	56	68
2B	71	79	54	67
5A	71	64	55	69
18A	64	46	51	61
25A	55	40	34	45
46F	50	35	26	44
37C	43	18	33	52
36C	39	19	32	51
40D	37	9	32	49

indicated by column 4 of Table 11 is consonant with a high order of
party identification. So also is the relatively high level of participation
in the primaries, although, in this case, ancient habits must be taken
into account (columns 3 and 4, Table 12). The greater capacity of the
more Anglo neighborhoods of Bernalillo County to produce split ballots is related (among other things) to higher levels of income, newspaper readership, and similar scales. But the smaller inclination of
residents of the Anglo divisions to vote in the primaries is the mark of
a new urban group of voters whose levels of partisan involvement and
political activity are lower and much less consistent than those customary in the Hispanic neighborhoods.

The high voting level of the Hispanic precincts is not unexpected
on other grounds, for it is in accord with the experience of many self-
aware ethnic groups elsewhere in the United States. The lower primary
turnout of the Heights Anglo precincts is more perplexing, for voting

levels are conventionally related to income and educational scales. (Chapter 4 explores these matters further in connection with the theory that urbanization produces a group of voters largely disengaged from local politics but with a high level of attention in national elections.)

Spanish-American voters in Roswell's "Little Chihuahua" divisions have long been exposed to the cultural abrasions inherent in their group subordination to the somewhat insensitive ethos of the Little Texas counties of New Mexico. And, good Democrats though they are, Roswell's Hispanic voters are also handicapped because there is no strong party organization into which they can fit their voting divisions as an essential part. There is a courthouse crowd (largely Anglo) of proven aptitude for primary-election politics, but it is not a power, for it exists within the limits of a rather narrow community sufferance. Municipal politics and elections in Roswell and other towns of the area are quite a-partisan. Few people are involved as participants, and in most there appears to be a rather small group of people in charge of things—a situation leading to few occasions in which Roswell's community leadership is impelled to solicit support from relatively small ethnic groups. The formal county party organization is also narrowly based, for it includes only two precincts in the city, and these, in turn, are divided into thirty-two polling places or divisions. And, although the county organization must frequently gird of late for hard combat with Republican candidates, local tradition is Southern enough to require that the formal organization preserve a reputation for a measure of neutrality in the primaries. In short, county and municipal political arrangements provide few points of leverage for the voters of the Hispanic divisions. In this politics of faction, the Hispanic vote is sometimes divided or manipulated by leaders more or less for sale in the primaries. Normally, however, these Hispanic voters respond in classic ethnic fashion to favored and identifiable candidates in the primaries while retaining a strong party loyalty in the general elections.

The contests used in Table 13 to mark broad differences in voting habits of the two segments of the population of Chaves County are those of Joseph M. Montoya seeking re-election as congressman, and Jack M. Campbell versus incumbent Republican Governor Edwin L. Mechem. Campbell, a resident of the county, had served several terms in the state legislature and was the popular speaker of the house.[60]

TABLE 13. ETHNIC SUPPORT LEVELS TO TWO DEMOCRATIC, STATE-LEVEL
CANDIDATES, CHAVES COUNTY, 1962

Candidate and county area	Percentage of vote to two state-level Democratic candidates	
	Primary	General election
Montoya		
4 most Hispanic divisions	77	68
Remainder of county	65	33
Campbell		
4 most Hispanic divisions	64	65
Remainder of county	55	38

Montoya and Campbell, both Catholic, shared their Chaves County defeat with several other state-level candidates and the legislative delegation, so the religious factor in the 1962 election there may be substantially discounted. The surge of adverse conservative votes that buried them came from the middle-income and the blue-stocking divisions, and from the rich farmlands. Primary turnout in the more Hispanic divisions was 75 per cent of the general election vote. It was only 63 per cent in the rest of the county.

The bits and pieces dug up in the foregoing exercises in political archeology are not complete, but all fit these conclusions: The politics of most of Hispanic New Mexico came long ago to parallel the politics of other two-party areas in the United States; where the Hispanic citizenry is a localized minority, it maintains a devotion to political activity but it becomes identified with one party. In either case, if the ethnic flavor differs somewhat from that in most states, it is mainly in the spicing, much as chili differs from clam chowder. And Hispanic political strength is so firmly embedded in the institutions of the state that only continued losses in relative numbers will readily alter it. Whether or not that political power has been used to gain an optimum social advantage is a question reserved to the last chapter. New Mexico's experience is not without relevance to the current politics of civil rights.

THREE

Little Texas and Los Alamos, Urbanites and Indians

THOSE who lament the American predilection for drawing political borders in utter disregard of geographic or economic logic could find ample cause for tears in New Mexico. A planner's nightmare, the state is a social scientist's dream, for history, political forces, and the contrariness of humanity have contrived to juxtapose some quite unlikely combinations of people. Within the most arbitrary but analytically convenient of boundaries live Spanish Americans (the old settlers), transplanted Texans, indigenous Indians, urban residents representative of a broad cross section of the United States, and scientists—the latter being an entirely new societal breed. A factor making comparison easy and useful is a set of legal and political institutions common to the lot.

Politics has an air of a wondrous alchemy when election bulletins reveal that John F. Kennedy received 48 per cent of the presidential vote in Albuquerque and in the Navajo polling place of Hospah, and that the Kennedy majority of 51 per cent in Los Alamos was nearly a match for his vote of 52 per cent in the Spanish-American mountain county of Mora and in the Little Texas county of Eddy. These data are not without significance, but a search for the meaning of such odd pairings is more bemusing than instructive unless it is understood that New Mexico's several cultural areas move in discrete orbits and in different directions in their response to forces common to them all. The mundane objective pursued in this chapter is to add to the preceding one by assessing political and voting characteristics of the several groups following Spanish Americans upon the scene. Discussion of their frequently opposing contributions to the state's partisan balance is reserved, in the main, for the following chapter.

ROOTS OF A FLEXIBLE ONE-PARTY POLITICS IN THE EAST SIDE'S
LITTLE TEXAS

Of twelve counties which once shared a common enthusiasm for Progressive and third-party politics, only those of the eastern edge of the
state, in close proximity to Oklahoma and Texas, have continued to
maintain a relatively durable one-party politics.

The availability of the counties to the various streams of settlement
no doubt determined a good many of their subsequent political characteristics.[1] It was in the decade 1900-1910 that the six counties of the
southeast corner earned their title of "Little Texas." By 1900, some
37,000 of New Mexico's residents had been born in other states. Of
these about two-thirds came from the states of the Middle West and
the East Coast to scatter throughout the areas open to entry. The remainder came from Texas and Missouri; and the Texans were prone
to settle in counties nearest the Texas border. This increasing immigration from Texas deposited 35,000 Texans in New Mexico by 1920.[2]

Certain other items of relevance in a description of the political
culture of Little Texas are somewhat harder to impart. There is, as
residents of the area are apt to claim, a high level of local civic pride.
Stemming in part, no doubt, from the nature of the state's tax structure, but in considerable part from civic virtue, the county courthouses
are not the "sunbaked, tobacco-stained" edifices of the rural South.[3]
Local school boards have apparently responded to every demand of
their administrators. Expensive and well-maintained schools and public
buildings dot the landscape.

Four out of five registered voters of Little Texas have long been
labeled Democratic, but that fact provides only the most general of
clues to much of their voting. They are diligent voters at the primary
elections they have insisted on having, but their presidential-year,
general-election turnout would be phenomenal in the South. It appears,
in short, that the voters of the East Side's Little Texas have become
more acculturated as New Mexicans than they might suspect or admit.
Yet, in large degree, they are still undoubtedly a breed apart in New
Mexico's politics, just as they were in their voting for radical and
third-party candidates from 1912 to 1924.

Little Texas: Political Laboratory Unit

Curiously, but perhaps by coincidence, the areas in which third-party or reform politics was strongest in New Mexico are the areas in which there had long been the smallest degree of two-party competition. And (a matter explored more fully in Chapter IV), these are the areas in which politics is still usually the most volatile and its results most variable. It is notable also, that, in spite of the long-standing and heavily Democratic preference of several of these counties, they have recently become essential among the voting components which occasionally give important aid in maintaining the Republican as a lively second party.

Two aspects of politics in Little Texas qualify the area as a laboratory unit. Situated in a two-party state, her politics locally is largely free from the restraints involved in the state's areas of an even two-party balance. New Mexico's politics seems to impose limits on the variability of electoral margins and turnout in the more competitive areas. Hence, electoral margins in Little Texas voting in the gubernatorial and presidential elections are likely to shift more drastically than those elsewhere in the state. New Mexico's Little Texas is largely free, as well, from the different set of restraints imposed in the parental homeland by the remaining influences of the race issue.[4] Fortunately, for purposes at hand, the area has also proven itself to be one sensitive to economic and social issues—to radicalism and to ultraconservatism —just as it has shown itself to be far from insulated from the impact of national politics.[5]

Although the Progressive candidacies had a strong appeal everywhere in the state except in the strongly Hispanic counties where competitive and highly organized, two-party politics was strongest, their efforts were most effective in the counties of the eastern border. Even those eight counties divided into two subregions in their reactions to the Theodore Roosevelt and LaFollette candidacies.

The agrarian-homestead society of Union, Quay, Curry, and Roosevelt counties of the northeast, bordering on Colorado, Oklahoma, and the Texas Panhandle, had been agitated by the Populism of the 1890's. Over 40 per cent of Colorado's 1892 vote and over 20 per cent of that of Texas had been Populist; and two years later a belated Progressive candidacy for New Mexico territorial delegate to Congress received 5 per cent of the territory's vote. A third of the four-county presidential vote of 1912 went to minor parties with 19 per cent of their total to Roosevelt, while 14 per cent went to the Socialist candidate. Recently settled Oklahoma led the nation in 1912 in casting 17 per cent of its

vote for the Socialist candidate—a ratio all but matched in this neighboring area of New Mexico.[6]

The four counties of the southeast—Chaves, DeBaca, Eddy, and
Lea—were then predominantly ranching areas and marginal to the
short-grass plains. Their dominant economic group consisted of boot-
wearing cattlemen rather than the homesteaders of the four counties
of the northeast. The two minor parties mustered 30 per cent of the
area's vote in 1912, but in the subsequent presidential elections of
1916-1924, the Democratic percentage of the total vote ranged from
60 to 70 per cent of the total to stay relatively close to the long-term
average for the area; for the minor parties never again exceeded more
than 6 per cent of the total. In the four homestead counties of the
northeast, however, electoral variations were much more marked. The
1916 Socialist candidate drew 10 per cent of the vote of the northeastern counties, and in 1924 the LaFollette candidacy attracted there
one-sixth of the total vote, equal to his share of the national vote.

Over the course of the presidential elections since statehood, the
pull of Republicanism in Little Texas appears to have been reasonably
strong, if not entirely consistent. The Progressive counties generally,
and the counties of Little Texas particularly, have manifested a rate
of secular change that ranges from moderate to steep in their increasing percentage of the two-party vote to the Republican candidates. The
long-term influence of national two-party politics has no doubt led this
erosion of the area's Democratic attachment, but the stream of national
influence was concealed or diverted for some time by the strong third-
party crosscurrents in the traditional politics of Little Texas.

If all of the minor-party and protest votes of the early years are
applied to the Republican percentages, the downward curve of the
Democratic majorities for the period 1912-1936 becomes somewhat
flatter by virtue of starting from a less lofty point, and Republican
gains are less impressive. The relatively two-party profile resulting,
however, is more intriguing than informative; for although those
voters who sought alterations in public policy were doubtless greatly
agitated by the events of the day, the one-party form of their politics
may have served to deny them the capacity to influence policy in the
manner possible elsewhere in the West.

Electoral turbulence, as described by the variability in the percentage of the vote going to a party in an area, is found in the following chapter to be associated with the degree of one-party dominance.[7]

New Mexico's one-party areas change their party majorities more drastically than those in which party competition is close.

Intense party competition may lead the parties to become more flexible, and more sensitive, so that they become more prone to absorb ideas or shift policy positions.[8] That is, competition forces the parties to make such adjustments as are needed to preserve relative strength. To the degree that parties tend to make marginal rather than major adjustments in their policy, adjustments may result in correspondingly marginal realignment of the electorate with the result that the vote to either party varies within a narrow range.[9] Conversely, where the vote is less useful in producing marginal or other adjustments, more drastic or radical alterations in the vote may be necessary in order to influence policy makers.

Thus, Key suggests that the LaFollette candidacy was costly to Democratic votes in several industrial and urban areas in the East, and particularly so in the West where LaFollette ran ahead of Davis in ten states.[10] Key judges that the vote was a warning to western Democrats and Republicans alike, and suggests that the Progressive influence served to sharpen "the alternatives" between the parties as well as to prepare the way for a realignment of the electorate.[11] These tendencies may have been operative in New Mexico's Little Texas counties as well, but their effects are obscure. It appears, however, that a conservative group, rather than representatives of the more liberal wing of the party, came to control in most of the Little Texas counties. If the conservative position was in fact pre-empted locally by the individuals dominating the Democratic party in the eastern counties, as it was nationally and at the state level by Republicans, an open shift to the Republican party after the 1912 failure of Theodore Roosevelt's Progressivism would probably have gained little (if it had been palatable) for those of the more liberal persuasion.[12] In this respect, the Progressives of Little Texas may have suffered from party alignments traceable to the ancient dilemma of the South even though the race issue per se has never been of much consequence in New Mexico. The system in Little Texas did not provide for ready entry into the power structure. Third-party movements elsewhere in the Mountain West were usually absorbed with little strain into the two-party politics prevailing there. In Wisconsin, the Progressive movement apparently served to delay the creation of a strong Democratic opposition, but even there the Progressive party eventually provided a way station for some liberal Republicans who became Democratic.[13] In New Mexico, the Democratic liberals of Little Texas had no secure home in their own party until the New Deal era. But now, to the extent that the relatively liberal elements of the national party have come into possession, it is their conservative fellows in the New Mexico hustings who are prone to give aid, comfort, and a good many votes to the ancient Republican enemy.[14]

Presidential Republicans or Conservative Democrats:
The Truman Victory of 1948

The votes deposited by currents and eddies at work in the election of 1960 have led a team of analysts to dub the contest "a reinstating election."[15] That is, when the narrowness of Kennedy's margin is accounted for, the results of the election indicate that there had been no basic shift in the electorate during the preceding eight years. A majority of "party identifiers" was returned to power.[16] Truman's more decisive 1948 victory produced in New Mexico a result so closely related to ratios of party strength, so integrative of party factions, that it might with equal justice be described as a "politician's election."

The Truman election was marked in Texas by a continuance of the turbulence accompanying the appearance of the "Texas Regulars" in 1944. It had no such result in New Mexico, and produced instead a significant, but temporary, decline in the vote for Republican presidential and gubernatorial candidates.

Of a political breed identified by Key and Heard, the Presidential Republican is characterized as a "strange political schizophrenic" who votes in Democratic primaries to influence state and local matters, "but when the presidential election rolls around he casts a ballot for the Republican nominee."[17] Never a numerous group, the Presidential Republicans of Little Texas may also be evolving into a different strain.

Although the attraction of presidential politics is strong in Little Texas, political activity there in the off years is considerably below that of the remainder of the state—characteristics the area shares with several southern states when they are compared with most other areas of the nation.[18] The mean of the decreases in the vote from presidential to off years in Little Texas for the general elections of 1940-1958 was 30 per cent, or nearly double the average off-year decrease of 16 per cent in the rest of the state.

Other attributes of the major- and minor-party voting for president, and the tie to it of the voting for governor, are suggested in Table 14 for two contrasting periods.[19]

TABLE 14. LITTLE TEXAS HARBORS FEW "PRESIDENTIAL REPUBLICANS"

Year of election	Republican vote[a]				Republican presidential votes in excess of those for governor	
	Governor		President			
	Number	Percentage	Number	Percentage	Number	Percentage
1916[b]	2,922	34.3	2,649	30.7	−273	−9.3
1920[c]	4,553	33.4	5,180	38.2	627	13.8
1924[d]	4,018	30.4	5,165	39.8	1,147	28.5
1928	6,856	45.0	8,875	58.9	2,019	29.4
			. . .			
1944	9,691	34.6	11,085	38.3	1,394	14.4
1948	9,097	24.2	10,270	27.8	1,191	13.1
1952	25,755	51.2	26,639	53.7	884	3.4
1956	23,252	44.3	28,203	53.5	4,951	21.3
1960	28,944	45.8	35,549	55.5	6,605	22.8
1964	26,393	40.1	30,610	44.9	4,218	16.0

[a]For the period 1916-1924, all votes for Socialist, Progressive, or Farmer-Labor candidates are credited to the Republican candidates; the two-party vote is used for the remaining elections.

[b]Third-party vote for president was 9.0% of total vote, with 757 for the Socialist candidate and 24 for the Progressive. The Democratic gubernatorial candidate was E. C de Baca. His "short" vote is probably attributable to his Hispanic name.

[c]Farmer-Labor candidate received 2.2% of total vote for governor; 2.5% of total vote for president.

[d]Progressive candidate for governor received 6.5% of total vote cast; LaFollette received 11.9% of total vote for president.

The drop in the off-year vote is frequently associated with a drop in the percentage of the general election vote to the Republican candidate for governor—indicative, probably, of an underdog reluctance of "regular" Republicans to go to the polls. But presidential Republicans could also contribute to the off-year drop: As voters of Democratic registration, their significant choice in off years would be limited to the state and local primary. To persons relatively immune to majority party influences, a vote in the off-year fall elections would be an unrewarding act unless some particular objective were sought by supporting the gubernatorial nominee.

The slight excess shown by Table 14 of Republican presidential over gubernatorial votes indicates a scant number of Presidential Republicans in Little Texas. These, Heard found, were most prevalent for the years 1920-1948 in Texas, Arkansas, and Florida.[20] In those states the median excess of Republican presidential votes over those for governor ranged from Florida's 52 per cent to 71 in Texas. Southern states in which Presidential Republicans were apt to be few, in probable consequence of a relatively even and strenuous two-party competition, were North Carolina, Tennessee, and Virginia.[21] Hence, the experience of Little Texas, in two-party New Mexico, ranks its limited proclivity to presidential Republicanism with the latter states rather than with neighboring Texas.

A somewhat different measure of voting differentials may serve to identify a local variant of the Presidential Republican. Table 15 ex-

TABLE 15. Percentage of Vote of Little Texas for Republican Candidates

Series of Elections	Percentage of vote for Republican statewide candidates		
	President	Governor	Five others
1940-1948	31.9	29.4	29.2
1950-1960	54.2	44.1	34.5
Republican gain	22.3	14.7	5.3

tends its measure across the votes to five Republican candidates for state-level offices as well as the votes for the party's candidates for president and governor. Some of the voters who produced the results of the elections of 1950-1960 would perhaps be better called "top-of-the-ticket" Republicans. In this series Republican candidates for United States senator and representative also did well on occasion, while votes for legislative candidates were more apt to trail in the manner of those of the lesser state-level candidates.

The Little Texas situation may be analogous to that of the last decade's elections in Texas when the increasing difficulty of Democratic conservatives there in controlling their party was matched by an increasing willingness to vote for Republican candidates for governor and the federal offices.[22]

It is suggestive that the returns of 1940-1948 set a common plateau for president, and for governor and other state-level officials. The Republican level of voter support of the decade, at about 30 per cent, is similar to the long-term level Heard found in the more two-party states of the South. Rather than Presidential Republicans, the returns indicate a likelihood of a persistent and reasonably cohesive local minority party whose strength was suddenly augmented in the 1950's by Democratic votes released by a complex of economic and social issues.

Truman's election brought a sharp, but temporary, reversal of his party's ebbing presidential vote in Little Texas. The Roosevelt vote there of nearly 80 per cent in 1932 and 1936 had diminished to 71 per cent in 1940, and to 62 per cent in the following election. Consequently, the sudden resurgence to 72 per cent in 1948 presents some riddles, for it reversed the pattern set by Texas.[23] Throughout the South, the Truman economic program excited apprehension in some circles, and the civil rights program of 1947 and 1948 engendered a vigorous and varied opposition. In Texas, as in the other southern states, the episode possibly contributed to a slow sorting of the electorate into liberal and conservative components.[24] But Truman's vote in Little Texas exceeded by a few points his vote in Texas, where the economic and social issues of the day were being vigorously debated. Economic and social matters were less divisive that year in the areas west of the Texas-New Mexico border.

The county-by-county results throughout New Mexico in the presidential and gubernatorial elections of 1948 are an unusual reflection of party strength as measured by party registrations. The rank-order coefficient of correlation of the counties' vote for Truman with the percentage of Democratic registration is .897. Figure 8 indicates that few counties depart significantly from the sharply sloping regression line set by the group. The graph strongly suggests that saliency of issues and the attractions of the candidates had relatively little to do with the outcome of the election, and that 1948 was a year in which party identification prevailed.[25]

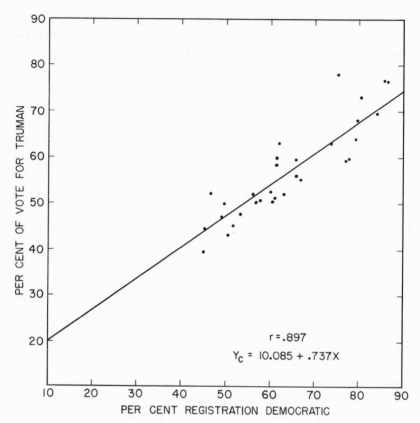

FIGURE 8. The year of the party vote: Relation of the vote for Truman to Democratic registration in New Mexico's counties.

The inference that partisanship prevailed can perhaps be supported by the proposition that personalities of the candidates, local alignments, and economic issues came in 1948 to a rare congruence in Little Texas.

It has been noted that the racial issue in Little Texas is even less salient than it is in Texas—in this respect the least southern of southern states. The last segregated schools in Little Texas were quietly going out of business, and little agitation marked their closing. Civil rights distressed but few of the local citizenry. Other, but less concrete, distinctions must be sought between Truman and the later candidates, for no great differences separate the apparent economic philosophies of Truman, Stevenson, Kennedy, and Johnson. Economic views with which the four candidates are identified have been consistently both highly visible and anathema to numerous influential Texans of the cities from Dallas to El Paso, but in 1948 they did not cut deep in New Mexico's portion of the Pecos valley.

Truman's position as a border-state politician brought him close to home in Little Texas, where he was nearly a southerner and nearly a westerner. Ambiguities inherent in his position as a man of the border states may also have served to give him a variable image in the eyes of those not disposed to make sharp ideological distinctions.[26] Those probably numerous, but seldom heard, liberal voters of Little Texas could take heart in the Truman economic and social program; those disposed to protect the status quo could doubtless look with some equanimity upon the conservative aspects of the Truman career; all could rejoice in his indubitably Democratic pedigree. Probably, too, the personalities of the candidates had an appreciable effect. Few New Mexicans would dispute the proposition that the citizens of Little Texas possess a rather distinctive ethos. It is a culture rendering most unlikely the possibility that the increasing urbanity of its voters had so far progressed that personal attributes of Dewey would induce those voters to desert Truman, whose very speech and dress made him congenial.[27] In Eddy, Lea, and Roosevelt counties—the heartland of Little Texas—the Truman vote reached nearly 80 per cent.

Conversely, the candidacies of Stevenson and Kennedy were more clearly of a sort to appeal to the newer elements of the Democratic coalition—to the ethnic and labor groups of the northern cities, perhaps regarded with a trace of xenophobia by certain of the residents of Little Texas.[28] Economic issues became more salient. Elements of the economic doctrines identified with Stevenson, Kennedy, and Johnson, implying a high degree of federal intervention in the economy, were little conducive, it appears, to a high degree of confidence in the now prosperous children of the old agrarian rebels of Little Texas. Whether or not a will to express the old impulses was among the motives inspiring the liberal part of the electorate to contribute to the spectacular vote for Truman is probably a matter impossible of demonstration. There is more assurance, however, that subsequent candidacies have found a widespread and adverse sensitivity among the well-to-do and conservative adherents of the established order. The progressive-conservative cleavage Key noted in Texas appears to have reopened in Little Texas. To anticipate some of the statistical evidence of the following chapter, it appears that the nexus of political change is again primarily economic, and that the current conservative-liberal conflict involving government is largely the struggle of the haves and the have-nots. Most of the Hispanic counties are marching steadily to a firm union with the Democratic party; the relatively wealthy counties of Little Texas find an increasing appeal in the conservative camp of the Republicans.

Scientists and Bureaucrats at Home on the Range

A new yeast has been added to the politics of New Mexico. Scientists, engineers, technicians, and administrators manning the local outposts of the science establishment, together with wives and children, make up a complete community in Los Alamos. Other contingents comprise a string of similar, but much less self-contained, colonies extending southward to the Mexican border. Scarcely more numerous than the state's sixty thousand Indians, these now well-settled residents are a factor of significantly greater weight on the political scales; yet, New Mexico's scientists have been much less studied in their home places than have its Texans, Spanish Americans, and Indians.

Outlined here are some of the more obvious aspects of the politics of Los Alamos, where, "on the Hill," the percentage of people engaged in research and its applications is much higher than in Albuquerque, Alamogordo, Las Cruces, and Socorro. Some attention is also paid, for comparison, to Oak Ridge, Tennessee, which was also developed during wartime by the Manhattan District of the Army Engineers and later administered by the Atomic Energy Commission in support of research and developmental laboratories. Curiously enough, insofar as I know, no town like Los Alamos or Oak Ridge has ever figured in the novels of a domestic C. P. Snow or a Mary McCarthy, and the lives and loves of their inhabitants have gone nearly as unremarked as their civic politics. Cultural anthropologist Margaret Mead has acquired a file of information about the lives and education of young people in Oak Ridge, and Ruth McQuown and Gladys Kammerer of the University of Florida have studied factors leading to the creation of political communities among settlements called into existence by the space activities at Cape Kennedy, but the types, extent, and effects of involvement of scientists in state or community politics are largely unassayed. The influence of aggregations of scientists upon state politics, and the reactions of scientists or their communities to state politics, are similarly obscure.

Greenberg discerns a "disinclination of scientists to take part in the public process," claiming it rare for scientists to be members of school boards or candidates for office, for they wish to practice science without interference and without much regard for its consequences.[29] Leiserson proposes that the professional objectivity of scientists is associated with their "low political (electoral) involvement," and Fischer holds that few scientists have a firm or sophisticated understanding of the political system which sustains them.[30] Applied, as they are, to national politics and to sojourners of Washington's Cosmos Club, such claims are hard to dispute, but they are not usefully descriptive of these science towns, where the record indicates that a large percentage of scientists (or their wives) are active, but flexible, partisans who are intensely involved in elections and community affairs, and highly aware of local and state issues. Although the presidential elections of 1948-1964 reveal a curious lode of conservatism in these towns, their voters can display a civic zeal as readily as an enlightened self-interest—qualities which may be a fortunate characteristic of communities so composed.[31] These voters have shown a diminishing tendency to register as Democratic party members, yet they are more likely than most to vote, to endorse a new tax, to favor activity in the public sector, or to change reactions to a candidate.

In most respects, in short, the civic attributes of Los Alamos or Oak Ridge should surprise few observers who have tried to establish the correlates of political activity. Much more interesting are the propositions that the women of science town provide an unusually high proportion of the civic shock troops and partisan activists, while their scientist husbands apply to civic policy-making a method closely related to the problem-solving ethos of their laboratories. Sometimes, however, these scientist voters appear to be unaware of the limits imposed by their conventions and perceptions, and, when lively local issues arise, they are apt to find the rank and file of voters marching off under other banners.

It is unlikely, of course, that Los Alamos or Oak Ridge are more than loosely equivalent to other towns, suburbs, or university areas heavily committed to research and development. There is warrant, however, for the presumption that large proportions of the 15,000 inhabitants of Los Alamos and the 27,000 of Oak Ridge are a citizenry reasonably representative of the million and a half or so scientists, engineers, and administrators who are aggregated with their dependents into a variety of towns and neighborhoods—Huntsville, Alabama; Richland, Washington; Ann Arbor, Michigan; and certain suburbs of Los Angeles, San Francisco, Houston, and Boston.

Some intriguing contrasts are apparent when these "new towns" are compared with those older or more typical. Oak Ridge and Los Alamos share a common culture. Fourteen hundred miles apart, they are far more like each other as dwelling places and as communities than either is akin to its more immediate neighbors. When confronted with questions of governmental organization, each of these AEC towns has sent its delegations of inquiry to the other rather than to its immediate neighbors, for the seven miles separating Oak Ridge and Clinton, Tennessee, poorly symbolize a civic and cultural distance that is just as real, if less apparent, than that which separates Los Alamos from Española or Tucumcari, New Mexico. Nor are these new towns like bedroom suburbs, for they quickly acquired or came endowed with a full and complex range of governmental services, and the place of work is but a few minutes from home. Many older communities have a politics incorporating traditional power groupings and influential families. Not so in Los Alamos or Oak Ridge. Although these little polities came into being almost overnight, and although, by some conventional measures, their citizens might seem to be a homogenized lot, their power structures are not starkly pyramidal and they involve a relatively large number of people. Developed in isolation from their state political environments and those of neighboring communities, these towns, while mindful and protective of their own identities, are now highly sensitive to state as well as to national politics. If, in their civic capacity, their scientist residents take a little too self-consciously the Platonic injunction that only the good should rule, they also help regulate the civic enterprise with an irreverence for old forms that befits a notable inclination to tinker with institutions and processes.

These attributes of science town and similar subcommunities are of more than trivial consequence for the politics of New Mexico, if not of Tennessee. Small though they be, these sensitive aggregations of voters sometimes have the capacity to be the critical marginal weight in electoral and legislative contests—matters which have not escaped the attention of candidates, party leaders, and, in all likelihood, of impressive numbers of the voters themselves.

Party Roots in Shop and Laboratory

Only after some twenty years has Los Alamos come to resemble somewhat a prosperous suburban community. Main street does not yet exist, nor has Los Alamos ever been at all like a company town. The atmosphere is more like that of a well-funded college community, for its existence is centered about the Los Alamos Scientific Laboratory— a contract agency of the University of California. The division sometimes separating town and gown does not obtain, but there is a parallel distinction (which in Oak Ridge is much more highly marked) between that segment of the population and bureaucracy most directly associated with the laboratory and what may loosely be termed the supportive community.

Some 1,500 of the 4,000 Los Alamos employees of the University of California are ranked as staff members and research assistants of the technical divisions of the laboratory; the remainder serve in a broad array of clerical, technical, and administrative positions. Engineers number about 35 per cent of the laboratory staff roster. The remaining 900 or so staff members include a sprinkling of persons trained in the arts, medicine, social sciences, and law, but over half of the non-engineers are chemists, mathematicians, and physicists. Half of these latter scientists and about 7 per cent of the engineers hold the Ph.D. Some 500 persons are employed on the Hill by the Atomic Energy Commission to serve as the local outpost of that agency. AEC employees are considered "official" and liaison, but, by the analytic methods used here, they are indistinguishable from University of California employees.

Once a youthful lot, staff members have aged perceptibly—a feature perhaps characteristic of well-settled research institutions.[32] Average age of all laboratory employees rose from 33.5 years in 1951 to 40 years in 1962. Staff members' average age was slightly lower, however, at 39 years. Termination rates have recently been 4.4 per cent annually for scientists, slightly over 8 per cent for all laboratory employees, and 15 per cent for clerical and administrative employees. Staff members who leave tend to go into research environments with universities or corporations holding research contracts, and are apt to have been with the laboratory for less than two or three years. (In stressing the permanence of the laboratory, Director Norris E. Bradbury has noted that in twenty years there he had presented over 2,000 ten-year pins, nearly 1,000 fifteen-year pins, and 100 twenty-year pins. Victims of the "mad scientist" stereotype may be reassured to know that chemists, physicists, and mathematicians beam as broadly as retiring salesmen or railroaders at the pin-awarding rites.)

A quite different organization, the Zia Company, has attended to the more mundane matters of housing construction and maintenance, and the chores attendant upon the provision of municipal services. Zia—a corporate offshoot of the Robert E. McKee Construction Company—had a roster in 1963 of about 1,300, of whom about three-fourths were union members. Most of Zia's custodial and labor forces live in the neighboring communities whence they are recruited, but about half of its skilled workers and the majority of its managerial staff live on the Hill. It is the Zia Company and its craftsmen, and the skilled workmen and technicians of the laboratory, which provide the hard core of Democratic voters in Los Alamos. Their precincts of residence now produce the most consistent Democratic voting.

As in the case of the Los Alamos laboratory, the activities of Oak Ridge National Laboratory lean toward the solution of problems critical to set objectives and technology—a stance ably advocated by its director.[33] The laboratory in Oak Ridge is a bit larger than that of Los Alamos, but its mission and the place occupied by its staff are less dominant in Oak Ridge than those of its counterpart in Los Alamos, for Oak Ridge is also the site of several production facilities employing about 7,000. The production plants, like the National Laboratory, are operated by Union Carbide under contract with the Atomic Energy Commission. The local AEC operations office employs about eight hundred persons, and Associated Oak Ridge Universities (formerly Oak Ridge Institute of Nuclear Studies) three hundred and fifty in providing staff functions and research facilities for its forty or so member universities. Since 1960, however, Oak Ridge has been becoming more like Los Alamos and somewhat less preoccupied with a strong sense of division into two community segments based on factory and laboratory. Only 30 per cent of its hourly-wage production workers live in the town, while 60 per cent of Union Carbide's salaried people are Oak Ridgers as are the great majority of the staff members of the laboratory. Scientists, engineers, and technicians increase in number while clerical and manual workers become relatively fewer. Overall, among Oak Ridge residents, the 1965 ratio of production to research and development, and administrative, employees came close to parity.

La Dolce Vita, R and D Style

The scientist equipped with a good new degree or an established research record possesses a wide range of choice and is prone to weigh the quality of the environment his wife and children will call home.[34] In consequence, the AEC has provided amenities in Los Alamos and Oak Ridge that are far beyond the capacity of most towns. Nor are other items blinked in recruitment calls and letters.

The upper valleys of the Rio Grande and the Tennessee present ecological contrasts sharp enough to penetrate the awareness of even the most casual observer. But, to the gratification of recruitment officers of both laboratories, each area has its own charms. Los Alamos clusters at 7,300 feet on canyon-cut mesas buttressing the Jemez Mountains and with a view to the east of the Sangre de Cristo Mountains. By day, to the great satisfaction of its residents, the town is nearly invisible to travelers of the valley highways; by night, as from Santa Fe's handsomely situated opera house, Los Alamos appears as a raft of lights floating along the black hulk of the mountains. Oak Ridge is in the gentler landscape provided by the wavelike ridges and woods parallel to the eastern slopes of the Cumberland Mountains, where rigorous land-use controls protect it from the shanty and junk-yard detritus so common to Appalachia. The towns themselves would please the run of city planners, in whose view they would be judged a blending of building and purpose, landscape and space happier than most, but their new private housing is a faithful reflection of current and regional tastes. Oak Ridge is developing a style in which a sub-urbanite of Atlanta would feel at home in its newer area; Los Alamos favors residences in the more daring modes of Santa Fe or Colorado Springs.

And, for those who struggle with the problems of providing munic-ipal and educational services in a host of frayed-white-collar suburban areas, the scale and quality of services in Los Alamos and Oak Ridge must excite the deepest envy, for these frequently meet even the stand-ards of the professional societies concerned about these matters. The disposal act for Los Alamos transferred to the city-county facilities costing $22,000,000 and provided that an additional $8,700,000 were to be expended before 1967. (New Haven, Connecticut, is spending about $1,000 per capita on its well-publicized renewal plan; the investment in Los Alamos is double that.) Oak Ridge municipal facilities are nearly as well endowed, but its aging primary school buildings became something less than the models of East Tennessee. Although visiting Los Alamos officials could once report with some satisfaction that Oak Ridge facilities "could not compare with school facilities and the library which the AEC has provided" Los Alamos,[35] the less magnanimously treated citizens of Oak Ridge have since voted $6.6 million in school and library bonds to repair the deficiency. Federal assistance payments and services equivalent to 20 to 25 per cent of municipal and educational costs have been provided Oak Ridge by a formula providing ten dollars for each eight raised locally through property taxes; Los Alamos has received grants-in-aid for services and education equivalent to $500 or more per family.

To aid cogitation about the meaning of these figures it may be useful to note that the 1960 median family income in Los Alamos was $9,269, while that of New Mexico was $5,371. It was $7,566 in Oak Ridge and $3,949 in Tennessee, but the per capita figure for Oak Ridge would be equivalent to that of Los Alamos were it not for the relatively large number of hourly-wage employees in the Tennessee town. Nearly 44 per cent of Los Alamos families and 27 per cent of Oak Ridge families had incomes in excess of ten thousand dollars. Of Los Alamos children of age fourteen through seventeen, 98 per cent were in school as compared to 87 per cent in the rest of the state. Tennessee's state average of 82 per cent in school at that age was thirteen points below the 95 per cent in Oak Ridge. These U.S. Census data about income, schooling, and ratios of subsidy to family costs for services may be summed by the observation that services available in Los Alamos and Oak Ridge (and the use made of them) are about on a par with those of a number of upper class suburbs of Chicago, New York, and Philadelphia in which median family incomes are nearly twice as great.

Other and more provocative implications are inherent in these and similar data. As befits these two towns (with the help of wives of laboratory members either town could staff a full-fledged college; together Oak Ridge and Los Alamos could staff a university), the feature which most makes them distinctive, and yet most indicative of the cultural drift of the nation, is their emphasis upon education. It is relevant to note, in this connection, that over 90 per cent of the personal income received by residents of Los Alamos is from wages and salaries, but other New Mexicans receive only 70 per cent of income from that source. (The figures for Oak Ridge and Tennessee show a similar relationship.) The standard of living is high but it is sustained out of current earned income, for few can point to a backlog of family fortunes rooted in other communities. A few slight increments in the level of taxation, any uncompensated-for inflationary drift, drastically affects the quality and quantity of spendable income —a matter of which these citizens are acutely aware. In the nature of things, few in these new towns will build a transmissible estate—some buy variable retirement equities or acquire other savings, but for the most part their wealth is strictly in their heads, for their earning capacity and status are largely resultants of training. Consequently, to bring those of their children who are adequate to it to their level of attainment can often be a formidably expensive task. (The genetically and statistically ordered occurrences of children not born adequate to this hard-to-acquire cultural inheritance is well understood in these towns; but, when it occurs there results much of the poignancy and sense of the inevitable of Greek tragedy.) Competitive attention becomes centered on the problem of getting offspring into colleges and graduate schools of quality and then the potentially expensive business of maintaining them there. Hence the great stress these citizens place upon local provisions for education, for this is the element essential to the only scheme of inheritance useful to them.

So what is developing out of the emphasis of these new towns upon abstract intellectual training is strangely reminiscent of the situation of ancient China when it nurtured a powerful and prestigeful literati. The Chinese sages and administrators could not lay claim to hereditary privilege, but by and large it was their sons who aspired to and qualified for the posts. Not of a caste, nor yet an endogamous group, the children of Oak Ridge and Los Alamos will nevertheless tend to marry others of similar background and prospect, and their parents will seek to reinforce lifeways and skills useful in maintenance of this new kind of culturally transmitted status. For example, in tracing the background and locations of students successful in national merit award scholarship competitions, Nichols found that an apparent aberration in his data could be explained by small states like Delaware and New Mexico, with relatively large proportions of scientific and technical personnel."[36] The fathers of thirteen of the twenty-eight merit finalists in Delaware were scientific or high-level management employees of DuPont; the fathers of seventeen of the sixty-two merit finalists in New Mexico were scientists at either Los Alamos or Albuquerque's Sandia Corporation. Similarly, a lecture by Margaret Mead on the education of Oak Ridge children was heard there by an intensely involved audience of over one thousand, while a lecture by scientist Jerome B. Wiesner on the virtue of voting for Johnson rather than Goldwater drew less than a fifth as many.

Voting and Representation

Although high incomes and education in the professions are ordinarily indicative of a stratum of active voters leaning to Republicanism, one segment of the learned sector is inclined to be Democratic. In Rossiter's summation, these are the people with "higher degrees in the sciences, humanities, and social studies."[37] The basis of this assertion is probably fully established in the main, yet science town's experience must either cloud its universality or require the differentiation of several aspects of conservatism.

One broad but useful indicator of political attitudes of well-educated, hence active, voters is party affiliation. By this measure, Los Alamos (and a number of similarly composed precincts in Albuquerque) has made a startling shift. Prior to the 1952 campaign, Democratic registration in Los Alamos was 70 per cent of the total, but it dropped to 58 per cent in 1958 and to 57 percent in 1964. Republicans and Independents profited about equally from a shift which was the sharpest in the state and which brought the county's percentage of Independent voters to 9 per cent—a trend reversing, and a proportion doubling, those in the state as a whole. When coupled with other attributes of science town, surely these are provocative data: Why, in view of the low rates of employee turnover, this erosion of Democratic strength? Has there been some selective principle at work in Los Alamos so that these people are recruited by a process and maintained in an environment rendering less likely the employment of the more academic or peripatetic types? Do a propensity for personal security and the phlegmatic capacity of adhering, more or less, to an eight-hour day lead some to be favorably disposed to the environments of the big laboratory and science town? Does the government's obsession with security lead inadvertently to the screening out of certain types of individuals?

Inadequate to the resolution of such intriguing questions but useful for the limited purposes at hand, there has lately occurred a sorting out of the voting elements of Los Alamos. (Oak Ridge has not yet so clearly distributed itself into class-ordered areas.) Barranca Mesa, the first area opened to private housing, is attracting the housing investment of a good many of the town's senior laboratory members. Its precinct (3E) is the only one in the county in which Democratic registration has dropped below 50 per cent of the total, but it is close to that point in White Rock (precinct 1D, a new area about ten miles out of town) where much of the housing is being developed or purchased by young and recent products of engineering and graduate schools, and in the Mountain School area (precinct 3B) which harbors some Zia employees and a broad array of laboratory staff. At the other end of the scale is a set of precincts whose inhabitants more frequently earn less at sub-technical or sub-professional employment, and more frequently register as Democrats. The twelve precincts of the 1964 election fall, in Table 16, into three distinct groups when differentiated by Democratic percentage of total registration.

TABLE 16. PARTY REGISTRATION IN LOS ALAMOS, GENERAL ELECTIONS, 1964.

Precincts	Range of percentage registered Democratic	Party registration in percentage		
		Democratic	Republican	Independent
1B, 1C, 2C	61-67	65.0	26.8	8.2
1A, 2A, 2B 3A, 3C, 3D	55-56	55.7	34.3	10.0
1D, 3B, 3E	47-51	49.1	41.1	9.8

Related to these data descriptive of shift and differentiation of party attachment and to similar data concerning customary differentials in voter turnout are the results of recent presidential elections. In its first election, when Los Alamos was still a precinct of Sandoval County, Truman received 54 per cent of the 382 votes cast. The Democratic candidates of 1952-1960 received there a vote ranging from 48 to 51 per cent for a mean of 50, while the mean in Oak Ridge was a point lower and the range of the Democratic vote a point less. Both towns, as Table 17 shows, were five or six percentage points more attracted

TABLE 17. THE PRESIDENTIAL VOTE OF LOS ALAMOS AND OAK RIDGE REFLECTS THAT OF THE NATION

Election	Democratic percentage of the two-party vote		
year	U. S.	Los Alamos	Oak Ridge
1948	52.3	53.9	...
1952	44.6	50.7	49.5
1956	42.2	47.9	48.2
1960	50.1	51.1	48.8
1964	61.3	66.5	59.6

by the Stevenson candidacies than was the nation, and the Kennedy vote in Los Alamos was a percentage point more and in Oak Ridge a point less than his share of the national vote. Both candidates attracted a dedicated local following, but neither the avowed liberalism of Stevenson and Kennedy, nor the dependence of these towns upon federal support and programs seems to have had any great influence upon the vote. Nor, in spite of vigorous and well-publicized efforts by the local chapters of Scientists, Engineers and Physicians for Johnson and Humphrey, did the 1964 contest evoke a shift significantly different from that apparent elsewhere. Johnson did five percentage points better in Los Alamos than in the nation, but his Oak Ridge vote was two points worse.

Johnson was the first of the four presidential candidates to draw in each Los Alamos precinct a percentage of the vote greater than his party's percentage of the total registration there, but it is strange that the vote in science town was not more pro-Johnson (or, perhaps, more anti-Goldwater) than it was, for factors contributing to Republican defection elsewhere should have been present in Oak Ridge and Los Alamos in even greater measure.[38] At any rate, as Table 18 indicates, the vote for Johnson and his fellow Democrats, Congressman Morris and Governor Campbell, was heavily pushed from the Democratic norms by Republican voters. The more ardent Goldwater partisans and the most unsinkable of congenital Republicans would scoff the claim, but, in all probability, the Republican defections of the top-drawer precincts of Los Alamos were moved, in this case, by a profoundly conservative impulse—to preserve the essential features of the science, war, and welfare policies of the nation.

Much more than various aspects of conservatism is needed, however, to approach differentials in the treatment accorded the candidates arrayed in Table 18. In all likelihood a ranking of the four Republican candidates from New Mexico on a scale of rigid to relaxed conservatism would place them just as they are in the table, but a panel of analysts would probably find Montoya out of place, for in terms of his activities, adherents, and avowed objectives he must be counted with Johnson as a stalwart New Frontiersman. Morris, Campbell, and Walker would frighten no bankers or bureaucrats but they are more middle of the road than right, and each has a capacity to synthesize a range of policy considerations. Yet Walker was beaten by conservative Redman in the more Republican precincts. Los Alamos voters have long displayed a marked capacity to depart in either direction from party lines in order to favor candidates who share their own social and intellectual characteristics, as in the case of Republican candidate Redman, an Albuquerque physician, or who have already demonstrated prowess in legislative or political undertakings of rele-

TABLE 18. Deviations of Percentage of Vote for Five Candidates from Percentage of Los Alamos Voters Registered as Democrats, 1964

Precincts grouped by percentage of registration Democratic		Deviations of percentage of vote for Democratic candidates from party registration percentages				
		President	Congress (Seat 1)	Governor	U. S. Senate	Congress (Seat 2)
		Johnson (D)	Morris (D)	Campbell (D)	Montoya (D)	Walker (D)
Precincts	Regis-tration	vs. Goldwater	vs. Sims	vs. Tucker	vs. Mechem	vs. Redman
1B, 1C, 2C	65.0	5.4	6.2	0.4	−3.1	−9.6
1A, 2A, 2B 3A, 3C, 3D	55.7	9.8	12.2	6.5	−4.3	−10.9
1D, 3B, 3E	49.1	14.9	9.3	6.9	−1.4	−10.2

vance to their town. U.S. Senator Clinton Anderson, one of the first
to see the implications of the current connections between science and
government, is a key element in that set of congressional activities and
a bona fide politician delegate to the science establishment. Anderson
is highly valued in Los Alamos and treated accordingly at the polls.
Congressman Tom Morris was badly beaten there in his first race when
he had the misfortune to draw as his opponent a liberal, ex-lawyer,
composer, and recent dean of the College of Fine Arts, University of
New Mexico—nearly a pure intellectual type. Morris has also become
a trusted congressional link who would be hard to beat in Los Alamos.
But, in the absence of specific and time-proven information such as
these voters have in the cases of Anderson and Morris, their vote has
repeatedly favored those candidates, whether liberal or conservative,
Democrat or Republican, who most nearly approximate the preferred
Los Alamos type—the "eggheads," and holders of academic and professional degrees. A candidate's place on the political spectrum is
evaluated, of course, but if a candidate is clearly not at either extreme,
if he can be judged capable, and if he be deemed diligently and
thoughtfully conservative of the institutions and processes of government, science, and education he has little to fear from these voters
regardless of the other tags he wears. If a candidate is not so judged,
the results can be disastrous. For example, John Burroughs, a former
governor whose 1959-1960 administration had been much criticized
in Los Alamos, was able to capture only 12 per cent of the county's
heavy vote in the 1966 Democratic primary.

The blow meted out to the former governor has frequent parallels in
the general elections where the party vote can show a wide range in
candidate preference. If the presidential and a few uncontested races
are left out of the accounting, twenty-three Democratic state and
county candidates received shares of the 1960 vote as follow: five
candidates received from 58.0 to 73.5 per cent, twelve received from
50.0 to 57.9 per cent, and six received from 28.0 to 49.9 per cent. The
vote for the Democratic candidate for governor in the six elections of
1950-1960 ranged through 30 percentage points in reaching lows and
highs of 32 and 63 per cent. The vote for state representative established the notable range of 50 points in varying from 28 to 78 per
cent. Other things being equal, in the fine shades of distinction Los
Alamos voters can make, partisanship may prevail, but a party's candidacies are separately and critically weighed.

And, as one might expect, the voters of science town are relatively free from ethnic bias. What has appeared to be a pattern of discrimination in Los Alamos against Spanish-American candidates is probably fortuitous and explainable by the other characteristics of the town's politics. If relatively unknown Hispanic and Anglo candidates run opposed to each other at general or primary elections, the Anglo normally will prevail. But if the Hispanic candidate can point to political or educational accomplishments, Los Alamos judges him vis-à-vis his opponent. Thus, Fabian Chavez, articulate and competent leader of the state senate, took 69 per cent of the 1964 Los Alamos Democratic primary vote to defeat Congressman Walker, but the incumbent corporation commissioner defeated his Hispanic opponent by the same margin.

Otherwise, in their voting, these citizens usually display those characteristics of activity and ranges in attitude to governmental policy and organization one might anticipate from studies of similar groups and individuals elsewhere, but some interesting differences appear.

Those precincts in Albuquerque in which reside people associated with Sandia Corporation and the university score good turnouts in school, presidential, and city elections, but their residents participate less frequently than those of Los Alamos in state and local primaries. Inclined for some years to cast a light primary vote, residents of Los Alamos are increasingly apt to be more actively engaged in all elections than other voters in the state except in general elections not held in conjunction with presidential elections, and then the Hispanic counties set the pace. In 1964, after several years in which it was recording irregular but incremental gains in primary participation, Los Alamos exceeded the statewide turnout, and apparently showed less than most other areas whatever inhibitory effects might have stemmed from the newly restored pre-primary nominating system (Table 19). Moreover, those Los Alamos precincts highest on Republican and socioeconomic scales voted in the primaries at a rate significantly higher than those at the lowest—again a reversal of the conventional pattern in Albuquerque.

School board elections in Los Alamos attract only 20 to 25 per cent of the registered voters—a rate lower than in Hispanic counties, but frequently above that customary in most areas of the state. The stable rates of turnout at school elections may be but the measure of voters' satisfaction with their schools, for the Los Alamos board has long

TABLE 19. REGISTRATION AND PRIMARY TURNOUT, NEW MEXICO AND LOS
ALAMOS, 1964
(The eleven Los Alamos precincts opened for the primaries are grouped
to reflect diminishing percentages of total registration Democratic.)

Area	Percent of registrants voting		
	Democrats	Republicans	Total
New Mexico	34	18	30
Los Alamos Precincts:			
1B, 1C, 2C	40	17	33
1A, 2A, 2B, 3A, 3C, 3D	51	23	41
3B, 3E	59	30	46

been dominated by ranking members of the laboratory and comprises
a regime highly successful in capitalizing upon every facet of state and
federal school law and financial assistance. (I have little doubt that
any fundamental change or threat to those schools would produce an
awesome uproar and some ardent grass roots political activity.)
Scientists are not as heavily represented on the Oak Ridge school
board as they are in Los Alamos. An M.D., a dentist, an insurance
man, a housewife whose husband is employed by the AEC, and one
member from the National Laboratory composed the board in 1965—
a pattern that had prevailed for some time. During the board's early
and critical years, however, an advisory commission largely composed
of AEC and laboratory staff members was highly influential.

From 1951 through 1955, a period in which no laboratory members
came forth as candidates, Los Alamos was joined with three other
counties for the nomination and election of a member of the state
house of representatives. Under authorization of an emergency law in
1955, the county commissioners appointed a physicist member of the
laboratory staff to the senate in time to serve for most of that session.
A reapportionment measure effective in 1956 permitted the county to
elect its own house member as well as a senator. Thereafter, from 1957
through 1965, a Republican sometimes held the house seat; and in
two sessions both seats were held by physicists. (Reapportionment
acts governing the 1966 and subsequent elections permit Los Alamos
to retain its seat but the county will share its senate seat with the

northern precincts of Santa Fe County.) Oak Ridge scientists, however, have not sought election to the Tennessee legislature. I am not at all sure why they have not, but I would guess a combination of several factors: Party mechanisms may not have the strength or traditions which would enable them to assist in recruitment or in the making of primary nominations; scientists are probably uncertain about the nature of the voter reception they would receive in areas outside of Oak Ridge; and the legislature is probably not visualized as a vital and independent policy-making agency.

Directed to the improvement of administrative and procedural arrangements as well as to matters indicative of a concern for social justice, the amount and quality of innovative legislation originating in Los Alamos has been high. Its scientist and lawyer legislators have consistently addressed themselves to statewide as well as to local matters, and the legislative and research files developed for Los Alamos legislators by the staff of the legislative council have been nearly as voluminous and complex as those assembled for the house and senate leadership. The county's legislators (and most of its other residents who have served on statewide party or governmental advisory bodies) have been actively engaged in efforts to develop the range of statewide services and have been associated with the liberal position on such matters as educational finance, fair trade or resale price maintenance, creation of public parks, prohibition of out-of-door advertising, and the like.

Issues, Solidarity, and Community Cleavage

Issue voting in Los Alamos brings out numbers of voters comfortably exceeding the state level. As in the case of candidacies, Table 20 indicates, the party alignments or socioeconomic characteristics of the precincts influence both the size and direction of the issue vote. (The four constitutional issues or referenda of 1964 used in Table 20 to mark some of the patterns of Los Alamos issue voting are arrayed in an ascending order from left to right in reflection of their relevance to the voters as determined by the total votes cast on each.) If issues are matters permitting a reasonably precise means-end analysis, the vote will normally result in very large majorities to accept or reject. If an issue is more difficult to evaluate or raises complex questions of political or administrative relationships, as in the 1964 highway commission amendment, the result is apt to be relatively close. Thus,

TABLE 20. Los Alamos and Statewide Voting on Four Referenda, 1964

		Vote on issues as percentage of vote cast for President			
	Percentage				
Precincts	*of registration Democratic*	*To repeal pre-primary convention*	*Highway Commission amendment*	*Bonds for University buildings*	*Los Alamos home rule amendment*
1B, 1C, 2C	65.0	50.3	51.2	57.4	59.9
1A, 2A, 2B 3A, 3C, 3D	55.7	66.0	67.3	74.7	80.2
1D, 3B, 3E	49.1	73.4	74.3	79.5	84.3
State		36.2	35.9	40.0	35.6
		Percentage voting favorably on issue			
1B, 1C, 2C		82.4	65.6	85.0	87.9
1A, 2A, 2B 3A, 3C, 3D		86.9	64.7	89.7	92.2
1D, 3B, 3E		85.4	65.5	88.9	92.5
State		75.0	46.3	72.1	70.3

twelve constitutional amendments voted on in a special election in 1961 were all accepted (within a range of 10 percentage points or so) by 82 per cent of those voting. Responses in 1964 to ten amendments and two other issues, when the county again led the state by good margins in percentage of turnout and degree of acceptance of the proposals, were much the same as in 1961.

On the evidence of Table 20, one can surmise that Los Alamos voting on issues occasionally reflects perhaps inadequate analysis or some deeply embedded conceptions about the nature of political processes and institutions. Although the town was less enthusiastic about the 1964 highway commission amendment (increasing gubernatorial and legislative powers over the commission and department) than it was about the others, its voters were, nevertheless, much more receptive than most in the state to the political-responsibility and administrative-efficiency arguments of the proposal's sponsors. Conversely, arguments voiced by their champion, Senator Anderson, and based upon similar assumptions, in support of the pre-primary convention were rejected out of hand, for 86 per cent voted to abolish the convention. Yet, with the aid of its legislators and congressional allies, plus its easy access to news media attention, the town could quite likely exert more influence over party nominations in a pre-primary convention than it can by its few thousands of primary votes. (In registering several dissents to my comments on the politics of his town, a Los Alamos reviewer took strong exception to this one, claiming that the "remark does not take into account the nature of New Mexico politics!" The statement makes one yearn for the opportunity to assess in depth the configurations and correlates of the political opinions and perceptions of the people in this and similar communities. I gather that many in Los Alamos are still dubious about the nature of the political system which has permitted them to enjoy an easy access and a high level of success wherever policy is made. Perhaps some of these scientist—but not always scientific—voters rely more than they know on the dogmas of their generation's civic textbooks.)

Although elections on the big and relatively clearcut statewide issues are apt to produce a clear decision and a fairly uniform precinct-to-precinct vote to accept or reject a proposal, the voting on purely internal issues of science town sometimes produces results indicative of underlying social and economic strata and divisions.

The Los Alamos city-county constitutional amendment of 1964 (which attracted 63 per cent of the county's registered voters and a majority of 91 per cent) resulted, in due course, in a proposed charter providing for a government which most academic specialists and many frustrated administrators of cities and counties would probably be willing to accept. Provisions for a broad ordinance power vested in a five-member commission nominated in the primaries and elected at large in the regular November election, an appointive executive, a merit system, a modicum of specialized boards, and a broad mandate for the provision of services (all in a well-written draft) indicate, if one accepts the administrative and political-responsibility premises involved, that the charter commission and its advisors had done their homework well.

Predictably, the vote of February 1966 on the charter referendum was large (60 per cent of the registered voters); unpredictably, the result was a "no" vote by 62 per cent to reject the charter. One precinct, marginally Republican and upper-crust Barranca Mesa, turned out 86 per cent of its vote to return a 61 per cent majority for the charter, but each of the remaining ten polling places rejected it with turnouts ranging from 39 to 81 per cent and with negative votes ranging from 56 to 79 per cent. The correlation of per cent "yes" to per cent voting was a firm .790, but reworking the precinct results to test the correlation of "yes" votes with percentage of voters registered Democratic produces a −.720, and the correlation of percentage of total registrants voting with percentage of voters registered Democratic a similarly sharp −.717. Opponents had little difficulty in making the matter a partisan issue and it is quite likely that the large turnout increased the margin of defeat. In the face of specific reservations expressed about the charter, its proponents stressed its potential for producing logical and administratively sound policy and organization; opponents stressed that abolition of elective positions was a diminution of democracy. The latter argument struck home. (A negative vote of this magnitude may indicate that the arguments of the charter's draftsmen and proponents stirred up some latent antagonisms among many voters. To work in the ranks is not readily productive of affection for large organizations; and, although the proposed new government would not have been large as such things go, its internal logic and organization may have seemed to reflect those of Zia, the AEC, and the laboratory itself.)

With due allowance for variations traceable, for the most part, to differences in electoral systems and population components, Oak Ridge has set patterns of political activity much like those of Los Alamos and much different from those prevailing in the remainder of Anderson County or Tennessee. Oak Ridge normally tops the state and county turnout in national and statewide elections, and its municipal politics is also characterized by a relatively high level of voting and activity. In primaries and elections for sheriff and other county officers, other areas of the county will match or surpass Oak Ridge, but in most referenda the level of participation elsewhere in the county is normally lower by a half or more. Oak Ridge is less engaged, however, in county primaries than is Los Alamos—a difference probably related to the relatively complex and irrelevant system of county government in which Oak Ridge is situated—and governmental issues sometimes attract little attention. For example, a novel and potentially far-reaching amendment greatly increasing Oak Ridge's representation on the county court (the county governing body) attracted only a quarter of Oak Ridge's voters but less than a tenth of those in the rest of the county. Oak Ridgers voted 91 per cent yes; county residents voted 81 per cent no. But, in a melancholy series of six referenda to permit the operation of liquor stores, Oak Ridgers saw their heavy turnouts and 65 to 70 per cent majorities matched and countered by voters of the county.

Issues sometimes arise within Oak Ridge which are indicative of stresses similar to those Los Alamos showed on the charter issue. When the Oak Ridge hospital was to be disposed of, the question became: "To whom?" Numerous officials and upper-bracket citizens, plus the Negro voters of the Scarsdale precinct, favored some form of public or non-denominational ownership and control; the opposition coalition favored a church-supported hospital and easily carried the issue.

Local Politics and Problem Solvers

The Los Alamos and Oak Ridge laboratories are predicated on the conception that if a problem can be clearly stated, its statement implies or carries within it some recognition of the operations that must be used to solve it. A problem may involve the creation of new scientfic knowledge or aim at solutions to intervening but unresolved problems that basic (i.e., not oriented to problems of application or development) research might attempt, and if the task requires a team approach, the requisite talents are brought together without any particular tenderness to going concerns, disciplinary boundaries, or similar limits. Members of both laboratories are fully convinced of the efficacy of their way of defining and resolving problems.

This same sort of thing (if at a less organized and sophisticated level) goes on when these science towns are confronted with a problem in the schools or city government. Given a discrete question of organization, of financing, or of conflict of objectives, many (if not always a majority) of their voters will entertain little doubt that concerted attention to it will yield some proximate results that will ameliorate, if not solve, the difficulty.[39] But this variety of systems analysis for system maintenance is radically different than its parallel would probably be in a more conventional setting. In the perspectives and values of numerous citizens of Los Alamos and Oak Ridge, problem solving looks less to the maintenance of particular and traditional ways and institutions than it does to the maintenance of process and change.

Whether the problem involves a long and complex series of legal and political steps as in the creation and rejection of the charter of the proposed city-county government of Los Alamos (few groups anywhere have been able to bring it off) boot-strap efforts to develop a college in Oak Ridge (hopefully, by 1968), the disposition and use of federal facilities in both towns, the overhaul of the county court of Anderson County, or the gathering and dissemination of data and analyses to illuminate a host of public issues, these towns can call upon the resources of numerous groups or agencies or quickly devise an ad hoc effort. They process and act upon a large amount of information, yet neither town gives evidence that it has approached the limits of its skills or resources. The science community in Oak Ridge is less pervasive, less the obverse of the whole structure than is the case in Los Alamos, and so is more apt to act as but one of several community components. Nevertheless, scientists and their wives are present in Oak Ridge affairs with much more frequency than their numbers would suggest. When groups heavily weighted with scientists are beaten on an issue they are sometimes simply outnumbered, but when the issue was the public management and control of the hospital, religious groups in town also outmaneuvered and out-politicked them. In the view of many Oak Ridge scientists and their civic allies, the town's single-member, councilmanic district system lacks the virtues of simplicity and cohesiveness, but most of the twelve precincts vigorously opt for their version of direct representation. But even on these losing issues, the cohorts from the laboratory stay in the fray.

So it is that Los Alamos and Oak Ridge are places to liven the hearts of political scientists or sociologists. Their residents have faith in functional agencies with defined roles, and each specialty appears to respect the knowledge and expertness of the others, and to give credence and weight (assuming their academic or social respectability) to other varieties of specialized knowledge. Legislators and school board members are regarded as specialists in public problems and information, and so are groups like the local chapters of the League of Women Voters. Conversely, other groups and agencies appear to feel slight compunction in calling early and late upon the policy specialists for help and advice. Indeed, the ethos of science town, and the makeup and style of its mode-setting groups are apparently quite different from those where scientists are scattered among populations not so composed, as in Boston's environs, and in which: "In instances where scientists have been involved as neighbors and friends in local controversies, the public's respect for their judgment is more likely to hinge on evaluations of personalities than on deference to specialized knowledge."[40]

Of group clients generally, the policy specialists surely have a sufficiency, for there are available to the residents of Los Alamos more than 150 civic, service, and religious organizations supplying, a recruitment brochure states, "an outlet for every kind of activity." Oak Ridgers can choose from 245 groups whose interests range from child care to metallurgy. There is an organization to every 100 residents of Los Alamos; the ratio in Oak Ridge is one to each 110. (It is possible, in a wild moment, to imagine these towns, beset as their citizens are with organizational claims, coming one day to a condition of complete, quivering, cross-pressured immobility.)

These and related data indicate that what we see in science town is a convergence of forces, attitudes, and activities which produce an extraordinary degree of political socialization of a type suggested by Almond and Verba.[41] In their view, a pluralism of voluntary associations, whether they are politically oriented or not, plays a major role in developing civic competence, and if groups and associations are close to the political system, as so many are in science town, that effect should be enhanced. Almond and Verba also stress that "politically competent, aware, and active women seem to be an essential component of the civic culture," and that the family open to discussion of political issues enables its children also to develop "a sense of political competence and obligation, and to learn to tolerate the ambiguities of politics and political controversy."[42]

It is here, in the roles and activities of the women, in the intensity of a family life which emphasizes the utility of learning, that science town gets much of its flavor. Its politics is by no means an exclusively feminine avocation, but a few observations of the role women play in the definition and debate of community issues, the scrutiny and evaluation of policy statements and candidates by groups like the League of Women Voters, and the activity of women in party organizations leave no doubt that women are becoming coequal guardians of these polities.

And it is largely here, in the status and activities of their women, that Los Alamos and Oak Ridge have so successfully and spontaneously bridged the "two cultures," that the question seems never to have been of any more significance than an additional topic of conversation. Few wives are scientists, but many have educations or intellects that rival their husbands', and their interests have the range one might expect. Libraries and bookshops do a brisk trade in current materials relating to social and economic matters, but patrons draw most heavily upon fiction, history, the arts, and the other components of the humanities. Nor, on other scores, do these towns live by chalk and instrument alone. Residents of Los Alamos subscribe heavily to the Santa Fe Opera, local paintings are preferred to ancestral photographs and portraits, many have acquired an eye for the genuine in Indian stuff, and when the superintendent of schools starts his springtime shopping for teachers, he advertises in the columns of the *Saturday Review*. Comparable indicia are evident in Oak Ridge where professionally directed orchestras and dramatic groups compete for an extraordinary range and amount of amateur talent.

The Civic Culture

By these rough measures, it seems clear that science town writes large those political and social characteristics of upper income and highly educated, elite citizens precisely traceable only by intensive or sample survey research. How otherwise, though, do these towns and voters comport themselves as components of larger polities? Do their self-conscious elitism and, more important, the characteristics of their science activities seem to make a difference?

Just as in other communities, there is, or so it seems to me, a strong (but not necessarily prevailing) impulse to hold at arm's length other social groups and obligations, and to create and then keep inviolate the cosiness of a highly satisfactory way of life. Witness the following suggestive, if not probative, items: In response to the question whether "physical scientists are aware of the social implications of their work," Weinberg has stated his impression that "scientists can be divided into two groups, those who have time, or take time to concern themselves with social consequences (this group tends to be the administrators) and those who have their bellies so close to the bench that they can't or won't take time to consider broad issues . . . They are busy people and they are not generally given to thinking in these terms."[43] Many of the women of each town and a good percentage of ranking laboratory members strenuously resisted when the AEC announced actions to open the towns and to remove the barriers of passes and security gates. Some in Oak Ridge "actually bought guns" to protect themselves from anticipated hordes of wild-eyed hillbillies,[44] and some in Los Alamos, I recall, publicly protested that they did not want to be bothered by tourists, the curious, and peddlers. Oak Ridge has maintained a small Negro ghetto for years, and residents of two of its neighborhoods long fought off attempts by a thoughtful minority to transfer Negro primary grade students to their schools. In remarks to city council, a deputy director of the Oak Ridge laboratory has stressed the bargaining leverage, in their search for new industry, of towns with large numbers of scientists, suggesting that what Oak Ridge " 'should be trying hardest to do is make this city an attractive place for scientists to live.' "[45] A New Mexico political columnist has expressed a widely held conviction in referring to a proposed city-county home rule amendment sought by Los Alamos: Approval would "move the county a step deeper into its insulated isolation from the rest of New Mexico."[46] (One frequently hears similar judgments by Tennesseans of Oak Ridge.) The skilled administration so useful in the logistics of big science is also highly prized in science town for its capacity to generate the material underpinnings of the good life — matters alluded to by Eugene P. Wigner in the observation that twenty years ago the administrator was looked down on "as a necessary evil. But now all I hear is how important it is to be or have a good administrator."[47]

To say all this is perhaps merely to note that, like the rest of us, scientists are only human. But there is probably a sense in which they are more rational, and hence more human, in the large, than the rest of us. In view of a host of community, political participation, and attitude studies, it is quite likely that many citizens of science town are more aware, or can more quickly see, than most, just what it is they and others do when they create a closed polity (by definition, all communities are "closed" in some degree). True, some of these attributes of science town have been quite conclusively demonstrated to be the attributes of most well placed, well educated, and high income people who vote, who are active, and who think their actions make a difference. The presumption is strong, however, that the political style of science town has some of its roots in the laboratory. That is to say, the sense of political efficacy prevalent in these towns is nourished to some substantial degree by the operationalist conceptions dominating their problem-solving science as well as by their strong sense of community.

It appears, in sum, that as a result of their educations and life experiences, residents of Los Alamos and Oak Ridge have developed a code and system of participant behavior that serves as an efficient and highly complex, but necessarily selective, communications network.[48] These citizens are more frequently able than those of most communities to have access to, and use, a broad array of abstract cultural symbols — the code which gives perceptual order to a complex environment.[49] Much that would be of relevance to a traditional society, or an agricultural community, will be screened out as noise of little utility, but of those elements relevant to current social and political discourse where change is generated and reacted to, towns like Los Alamos and Oak Ridge are more attuned, and consequently, more efficient in the developing cultural milieu, than is the older or modal community. It is quite possible, however, that their very success in utilizing this mode of abstracting experience may serve increasingly to differentiate them from conventionally organized and oriented communities.

By and large, the residents of Los Alamos, and those of similar vocation in the university and research establishments down the valley of the Rio Grande, are a lively group of citizens whose contribution to New Mexico's political and social systems will doubtless be as significant as their demands upon the state's policies and institutions. That the state's political system has so successfully bridged the communities and social systems of Spanish Americans, Texans, and scientists is no small accomplishment.

INDIAN PATHWAYS TO POLITICS

In view of group diversity and the survival power of deliberately maintained cultural forms and attitudes, it cannot be forecast with unqualified assurance that Indian political participation will soon become universal and a pragmatically utilized means of goal attain-

ment. Yet, the institutions and process which, in the sixty years preceding statehood, so efficiently enrolled New Mexico's Spanish Americans as active members and contributors to the political system may
be operating in a similar manner to incorporate Indians into the
larger polity. By its competitive and open nature, the logic of the
state's political system provides clear pathways to participation, and
the recent record indicates that many of New Mexico's Indians are
taking them.

If the political strength of a group were determined solely by its
relative size, New Mexico's Indians would more clearly be a factor
of occasional importance in statewide elections and a real power in
several localities. Indians number nearly sixty thousand, about four
times as many as the residents of Los Alamos, or about 6 per cent
of the state's total population. Twenty thousand are concentrated in
three counties, so that they comprise 28 per cent of the total in Mc-
Kinley, 13 per cent in San Juan, and 21 per cent in Sandoval. The
state's Indians are not a group, however, whether described in the
terms and frames of reference of an anthropologist, a politician, or
any self-aware Indian. The two largest Apache tribes live in far-
separated mountain or upland areas — the Mescalero in Otero County,
and the Jicarilla in Rio Arriba County. Eighteen pueblos — of a
highly distinct but non-tribal group which includes identifiable sub-
groups — constitute villages spotted down the Rio Grande from Taos
to a few miles south of Albuquerque, with a western extension through
McKinley and Valencia counties. Some thirty-three thousand Navajo
are scattered throughout McKinley and San Juan and the adjacent
portions of Valencia and Sandoval counties, as the eastern portions
of a somewhat inchoate tribal group of more than eighty thousand
extending through the northwestern quarter of Arizona and a portion
of adjoining Utah.

Involvement of reservation and pueblo groups in the electoral politics of the state was delayed until 1948 when a three-judge district
court struck down constitutional barriers to Indian enfranchisement.[50]
Since then, Indians have moved toward participation in politics at
varying rates limited, in the main, only by the attitudes and structures of the various Indian groups and communities. All are cautious,
none has been in a hurry, and four or five pueblos have largely re-
frained. The Navajo and, to a degree, the Apache, are least characterized by a social organization which contributes to resistance to

competitive and individualistic activities and have shown the greatest tendency to involvement in white man's politics.

The individual pueblos of the 1960's are still apt to be governed internally by their ancient theocracies — systems in which majoritarian voting on issues or personalities would be highly out of place.[51] An All-Pueblo Council provides a limited means of external representation on broad matters of joint concern and a forum for the discussion of common issues, but its constituents are towns, not individuals, and these have yielded no federal charter.[52] Each pueblo appears to accept or reject as a group the politics of the external society, and pueblo members no doubt come to that decision with an eye to its implications for their own highly organized community and social life. Taos Pueblo, for example, was still far from persuaded in 1960 or 1964 that it should take the step, but introspective and enigmatic Zuñi turned out a vote and developed an interest in political issues that may have astonished some anthropologists.

The pueblos are not only highly successful in protecting and maintaining themselves as groups, but they appear to achieve their stable systems by holding in balance traditionally intersecting sets of partially conflicting, partially congruent, dual organizations which provide overlapping roles for individuals.[53] This complex system of social control apparently sets clear limits to individualistic activities, but it may not bar the incorporation of major feaures of the white man's politics into the pueblo social and political system. Almost invariably, in the matter of acceptance or rejection of aspects of white culture and technology, the principle of duality permits a division which aligns liberals against conservatives and traditionalists[54]— a phenomenon which leads Pauker to speculate that the secular aspects of pueblo government are becoming more dominant than the sacred and traditional, and becoming so in a manner in which various factions may provide the segments available for alignment with the major parties.[55] Whether many members of the pueblos will soon become classified as Democrats or Republicans is still conjectural, but the development of personal identification with party may well be on its way among the Navajo, for, in their case, a relationship has recently emerged between tribal factions and external party organizations. Appropriately enough, the tribal conservatives — the Longhairs or Old Guard—favor the Republicans; those oriented to more rapid change support Democrats.

Traditionally a people whose systems of social control required neither a hierarchy of command or representation, nor an area-wide organization in which clans or camps formed a governing network, the Navajo did not begin to develop as a political unit until 1923, when the federal government established a small tribal council elected from the areas associated with Navajo and Hopi Agencies of the Bureau of Indian Affairs.[56] (The federal government had long been baffled by the problem of dealing with the tribe as an entity when no tribal organization could be found that could so represent it. Who, for example, could legally sign an oil lease in the name of the tribe?) A constitutional assembly was called in 1937 under the terms of the 1934 Indian Reorganization Act, but, after the tribe rejected the resulting constitution in a close vote, the Secretary of Interior resolved the governmental impasse by issuing regulations creating a seventy-four member council of delegates elected for four years from election districts or communities. The tribe is still without a constitution, for, in spite of the inducements advanced by the Bureau of Indian Affairs, its leaders and counsel appear to favor a strategy of proceeding as if the tribe had ample residual authority to develop new offices and programs as opportunities arise.[57]

The development of Navajo political institutions proceeded rapidly after World War II. The council still meets only at quarterly sessions, but its advisory committee has emerged as a full-fledged executive board whose sessions occupy about two weeks of each month. Standing committees concern themselves with health, welfare, education, law and order, resources, and the like, and there is no hesitation to designate ad hoc groups. Budgets approached thirty million dollars a year by the end of the 1950's and reflected policies and considerations debated throughout the tribe. At the local level, nearly a hundred tribal Chapters provide a grass roots means of administration, and a community forum which is an integral part of government and the essential link connecting the traditional society with the modern council system.[58] The Navajo have also moved with assurance to develop improvement and training programs under the Area Rehabilitation and Economic Opportunity Acts, for they have had no difficulty in meeting the criterion that projects reflect plans which the poor have helped draw up!

And the tribal politics that is developing is reassuringly like that of the larger society. As in the case of the state legislature, some 30 to 50 per cent of council delegates are not re-elected or decline to run again. Voters complain that councilmen forget their constituencies, delegates that they are unfairly criticized. Some delegates rewarded or punished for their alignments with council factions, are thought to be too conservative, others are thought to be too young or too progressive. Tribal and council factions strenuously compete for positions of institutional leverage, and the institutions themselves are redefined or changed to confer or confirm tactical positions, for the Old Guard, still in possession of a council majority after 1963, has acted to restore to council the young chairman's authority to appoint committees and their chairmen. The Bureau of Indian Affairs strongly protests the Old Guard's tactics, but it too, at last, has caught the self-government principle and permits the tribe to settle these matters on its own.

In the larger polity, a few signs indicate that the state's Indians may be able to achieve a political and cultural accommodation unprecedented in the United States. As LaFarge puts an aspect of the matter:

Neighboring [New Mexico's] Indians is an unusual zone of non-Indian acceptance extending along the Rio Grande Valley from Taos to Albuquerque, and including Los Alamos . . . They and the communities are ready for intermingling without talk of "assimilation." As a result the Indians are no more segregated than is anyone having the choice of either living on the farm or going to the city.[59]

Another observer has noted that in 1956 over 80 per cent of the Navajo who voted were resident in New Mexico, although only 40 per cent of the tribe were inhabitants of the state, and attributed the relatively high voting rate of New Mexico's Navajo to the state's encouragement of voting by the establishment of necessary precincts, aid given by local officials, and the absence of a literacy test.[60] A civic altruism probably plays a significant part in this capacity of the state to admit new groups to participation and the sharing of power, but a weightier factor is doubtless the openly competitive structure of a party system in which (unlike some of the one-party, one-class systems in the deep South) office is won by soliciting support from all groups willing and able to impose obligations.

However reluctantly, the Department of Interior did approve the council action that stripped the Navajo chairman of his appointive power, but it coupled its action with a directive to the Bureau of Indian Affairs to revive its efforts to seek Navajo agreement on a tribal constitution. The Commissioner of Indian Affairs went a few weeks later into the reservations with state and congressional candidates to seek Indian support in an election thought to be critical to two major candidates. The state administration acceded to Zuñi and Navajo requests that a liquor license at a location near Zuñi be denied. Tribal leaders all over the state were invited to appear on an Albuquerque platform with campaigning President Johnson, but what in the past had been ceremonial appearances was this time related by Indians to the Administration's policies. One set of Navajo in opposition openly endorsed Goldwater. Aided by a state legislative apportionment requiring election by districts in counties with more than one state representative, Navajo candidates in 1964 won a legislative seat in San Juan County and another in McKinley County. And the New Mexico Cattle Growers Association inadvertently confirmed the Navajo's new political status when it unsuccessfully petitioned the legislature to refuse to seat the Navajo members on the ground that they would be enacting legislation to which the Navajos' tribal status gave them immunity. Twenty-five years ago, the cattle growers would have been successful.

Whatever its other merits, the point raised by the cattle growers has the virtue of clearly posing the critical problem which must be solved if Indians are to become part of the fabric of state and local government and politics. The loss, too soon, of the services and protections accorded Indians by their tribal organizations and the specialized agencies and programs of the federal government which assist in the support of Indian cultures and communities could be brutally inhumane. But to continue those policies unchanged will tend to deny to individual Indians the right to acquire the capacity to opt for whatever life and roles they seek. Indians probably will, as they desire and must do, seek more positively than did New Mexico's Spanish Americans to retain their group identities and cultures, even to the point of retaining for several or many generations the legal capacity to develop, maintain, and define their own tribal governments. The Navajo have learned to operate a tribal corporation. What is needed, and what may be developing, is a new perspective for and application of the familiar legal concept of municipal or county home rule. It should not be beyond the wit of a demonstrably inventive state legislature to devise governmental instruments which vest in groups of Navajo communities a set of corporate powers and capacities similar to those joint city and county powers recently vested in the residents of the county of Los Alamos. Entities similar to municipal corporations could also be slowly developed to fit the radically different needs and traditions of the tightly knit city states of the pueblos. Meanwhile, the dimensions of the Indian vote have already attracted the courting of its segments; and, for the moment at least, Indians are reflecting local patterns in their reactions to state and national politics. The Johnson candidacy was even more successful among Indians than among New Mexico's scientists in providing a large Democratic majority.

Precise enumeration and location of the vote of the various Indian groups is difficult, but enough scattered precincts in which theirs is the predominant voice can be identified to provide a profile of certain reactions to primary and general elections. The vote in twenty-three precincts scattered throughout the major regions of Indian settlement is set out in Table 21 for the 1960 primary elections and the general elections of 1960-1964 on a scale determined by the percentage of the vote going to the gubernatorial primary winner in 1960, a year in which the primary was strongly contested.

Of the precincts heading the list on the scale of factional dominance in the primary, only Torreon's Navajo — a scattered group on the extreme eastern range of the area of Navajo settlement — would seem to give much cause for alarm for the state of their political health. The area has been notorious for several years among white politicians as one of a manipulable vote (I know of little in Torreon's recent history to support the idea that its votes have been the outcome of intragroup discussion leading to a consensus, but a little research on the scene, sans reference to local politicians, might refute this armchair conclusion). Near the bottom of the scale, the fact that the Mescalero Apache in Otero County disrupts the symmetry of the relation of primary factional strength and general election vote is probably evidence of a social and political condition related to that of the Navajo of Torreon.[61] The widely dispersed people of the vast Apache precinct have few opportunities for extensive discussion of politics, and the area is extremely difficult for campaigners

TABLE 21. RELATION OF DEMOCRATIC FACTIONAL AND GENERAL ELECTION
STRENGTH IN TWENTY-THREE PRECINCTS IN WHICH A MAJOR-
ITY OF VOTERS ARE INDIANS

County, tribal group, and number of precincts	Percentage to winner of three-man gubernatorial primary, 1960	Percentage to Democratic candidate in three general elections		
		1960	1962	1964
SANDOVAL (1)				
Navajo: Torreon	97	82	97	89
VALENCIA (1)				
Pueblo: Laguna	78	57	60	85
McKINLEY (11)				
Navajo: Wingate, Thoreau (2), Ambrosia, Rehoboth, Tohatchi (2), Hospah, Crownpoint	59	54	52	68
Pueblo: Zuni (2)	56	48	37	64
RIO ARRIBA (1)				
Jicarilla: Dulce	58	55	51	67
OTERO (1)				
Mescalero: Mescalero (Bent, in 1960)	78	63	52	84
SAN JUAN (8)				
Navajo: Sanostee, Blanco, Shiprock (2), Toadlena, Chaco, Naschitti, Crystal	45	44	44	63

in the primaries. The tribal group has no marked history of highly effective internal mechanisms of social control; hence its voters, too, are exposed to vote buying, external pressures, and the influence of dominant factions of the white community.

The voters of the pueblos of Laguna in Valencia County and Zuñi in McKinley County, on the other hand, give evidence that they are taking the game of white man's politics in stride and fitting it into their highly integrated communities. Both pueblos have been the object of strenuous activities of the two parties and their factions to register voters and to secure their loyalties. The scores posted by these pueblos, just as in the cases of the San Juan and McKinley county Navajo, indicate that their partisan alignments, and Democratic and Republican intraparty factional divisions may reflect those of the counties in which they are situated, for the patterns of the Indian voting do not depart significantly from the modes set by the white voters of their counties. In 1960, the twenty-three Indian precincts surveyed here posted a range of 29.7 to 79.8 per cent in the Democratic share of their vote for president; in 1964, the range extended from 43.6 to 88.1 per cent. If the precincts are lined up in an order determined by the increasing sizes of the Democratic percentage for president, the half in the middle set a range in 1960 of 44.0 to 58.0 per cent. In 1964, the range of the middle half was from 63.2 per cent to 72.9 per cent — a notable shift, and one indicative of voters willing to use their votes for policy objectives.

New Mexico's Indians are not yet highly sophisticated voters, however. Their voting on constitutional issues that could be of significance to them is still far below the level of the state and only at a ratio of an eighth or so of the vote cast by the citizens of Los Alamos. The gubernatorial vote of Indians in 1960 and 1964 was normally within a percentage point or two of the vote cast for president, and never were presidential and gubernatorial candidates of the same ticket separated by more than four or five percentage points. Only in voting for local offices has a limited capacity so far appeared to indulge in ticket splitting of a sort indicative of a practiced intent to reward friends and punish enemies. Slow progress, perhaps, but what most acculturating communities can accomplish only after a generation or two should not be expected of the Indians in less.

MAIN STREET AND SMALL BUSINESS

New Mexico's economy has come increasingly, in the post-war shift from agriculture, to rely on secondary or derivative businesses and small industries; but these, in turn, rely heavily upon investment and employment in governmental agencies and defense installations. Some 88,000 persons, or 26 per cent of all employed, work for governments, and of these well over half are with federal old-line and research agencies or military installations. Clovis and Roswell in Little Texas and nearly all of the major towns and cities along the Rio Grande have experienced periodic or continuing growth stemming in large part from federal activity.

Probably in consequence of the rapid growth of Albuquerque, a significant change has occurred there in the organization of political activity. A bifactional rivalry for legislative nominations in the primaries of 1940-1944 was succeeded by a continuing period in which three or more individuals are apt to contest for each Democratic nomination. Both parties have had to make room for new groups of political activists so that the dominant factional organization of each is now considerably larger and more amorphous than it had been in the period preceding the war and the direct primary. Relatively few of the newer groups and neighborhoods are dependent upon state-level politics for employment, and the level of activity and participation is far higher in the presidential than in the off years when the old-line factions are more effective in controlling nominations.

Organized labor is of considerable importance in the politics of the mining communities in the peripheral areas of the state, but in Albuquerque and the defense and research towns along the Rio Grande its importance is largely limited to activity in the Democratic primary. And there its structure and membership is such that it can be of weight only when it is aligned with the dominant local faction. The place occupied in many areas by medium and heavy industry, and the corresponding organized trades, is largely filled by government in New Mexico.

The blending of group and counter-group, the mixture of laboratory employes with those of main street, and the influx of new people have produced a politics still very much in flux. The balance struck in recent elections seems to be productive of a conservative result at both national and local elections, but it is perhaps a balance easily disrupted and one apt to terminate with a heavy movement to one or the other of the parties.[62]

There are countervailing forces at work which are reviewed in a later chapter, but one aspect of New Mexico's current urban politics serves to contribute to federalization of the community and its economy, and to a denigration of state and local government.

In recent years the perecntage of the vote in most of the growth areas going to Democratic congressional and senatorial candidates has increased; the percentage of the urban vote going to Democratic gubernatorial and presidential candidates has been decreasing. The awareness of residents of these areas of the implications of federal policies and national politics is apparently acute, and there is a marked capacity to judge the members of the congressional delegation by their ability to obtain helpful appropriations and to deal with those who make governmental decisions of importance to New Mexico. In the short run, such a voting pattern is more rational than schizophrenic, but it may be disruptive of the health of local politics and government.

New Mexico's Two-Party Blending of the Groups and Issues of Politics

The two great group and regional elements of New Mexico's politics when statehood was gained in 1912 were the long-native Spanish Americans and the relatively recent settlers of Anglo-American extraction. In part, the groups were antagonists, separated by their regional and cultural interests; in the main, the parties served to conquer and use them both by achieving an operational but somewhat unbalanced division of the two segments, so that a reasonably strong group adhered to the party in the minority in either area.

In the course of time, the Hispanic element of the state lost in relative power, to be superseded in the statewide balance by a rapidly growing urban strength after 1940. The weight and consistent voting habits of the Hispanic counties preserve them as a regional power so that the division the parties must now contain is of three principal units.

Certain of the broad assumptions so far employed involve the effect on party balance of urbanism, and the sensitivity of various groups and areas to issues.[63] Table 22 provides a measure of the relative attraction of an abstract issue to the voters of the areas and groups described. The order in which the extent of voting on the issue ranks the areas is essentially identical with rankings determined by urban density, level of educational attainment, and personal income.

TABLE 22. VARYING ATTRACTION OF A CONSTITUTIONAL ISSUE TO VOTING GROUPS AND AREAS IN THE NEW MEXICO GENERAL ELECTION OF 1960

County or area	*Vote cast on amendment as percentage of the total vote cast for governor and the total registered vote*	
	Governor's vote	*Registered voters*
Los Alamos	68	53
Bernalillo County	49	37
State	40	29
"Little Texas"	39	28
Five Hispanic counties[a]	33	23
Three "Indian" counties		
McKinley	27	18
San Juan	27	24
Sandoval	27	19
Fifteen Indian precincts		
Apache (4)	25	n.a.
Pueblo (2)	14	n.a.
Navajo (9)	11	n.a.

[a]Mora, Rio Arriba, Taos, Santa Fe, and San Miguel.

Urban areas and those affected by governmental enterprises have attracted residents of relatively uncertain party adherence whose voting reflects a concern with issues. The more strongly Democratic areas, such as Little Texas, are also becoming urbanized and retaining their capacity to cast a variable and issue-oriented vote within the broad confines of a still-durable party allegiance. An increasing proportionate importance of two issue-sensitive areas, a weakening of party strength and influence stemming from or related to urbanism, and the influence of national politics among the newer voters provide the ingredients for a sensitive and uneasy party balance. Scientists

and technicians recently coming into the state are an increasingly
important subgroup. Their penchant for an issue politics in a period
of a tight party balance gives them a weight greater than their number would otherwise accord them. Indians are increasing their voting
participation sufficiently to win for themselves a significant influence
in local areas, but their regional, cultural, and two-party divisions will
probably prevent them from being a bloc. Issue commitment or orientation of Indian voters is still largely nascent or unformed.

The relative weight of the three chief regional components and
some of their political characteristics are summarized in graphic form
in Figure 9.

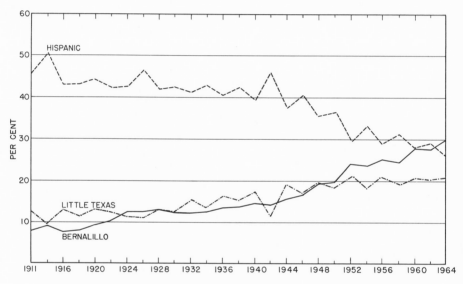

FIGURE 9. Percentage of total state vote cast for governor, 1911-1964, by
10 Hispanic counties, Bernalillo County, and 6 Little Texas counties.

Although Little Texas and the Hispanic counties do not comprise
two group entities, they maintain the distinct characteristics of voting
behavior which have set them apart from each other and the rest of
the state. Bernalillo County has recently become a significant entity,
made so by its relative size, rapid growth, and political characteristics.
Considered as three political units—the Hispanic counties, Little
Texas, and Bernalillo County—they have always together cast a bit
more than 60 per cent of the state's total vote. But *vis-à-vis* each other,

the position of each of the three is now greatly different from that existing as late as 1936, as Figure 9 portrays. The graph line representing the total vote of the Hispanic counties shows a marked sawtooth profile just as does the line representing the Little Texas counties; but each dip of the Little Texas line invariably corresponds to a simultaneous peak in that of the Hispanic counties. The Little Texas counties, and recently Bernalillo County, tend to permit their non-presidential election year vote to drop heavily; in such elections the vote of Hispanic counties drops also, but it varies relatively little whatever the type of election, and so in off-year elections comprises a larger percentage of the state's total. Hence, in a period of tight elections, the decisive vote may now come in one year from the Hispanic counties and those several of the remaining counties sharing their preference; but in the next presidential election the decisive vote changes are apt to come from Bernalillo County or Little Texas.

FOUR

The Course and Measure of Levels of Party Combat

STATEWIDE party strength in New Mexico's gubernatorial elections was remarkably stable for a half century. Democratic majorities of 1911-1964 varied through a range of only 14 percentage points and the trend line of party gains and losses went up only two points from its 1911 mark of 51 per cent. But beneath this placid-seeming horizon the counties and cultural regions of the state have displayed sharp reactions to events, candidates, and campaigns. The several counties and regions display two sets of characteristics productive of substantial effects in over half of the counties and more limited and indeterminate results in the remainder. Little Texas and recently urbanized counties evince an acute sensitivity to the campaigns and candidacies for presidency and governorship. Their two-party vote is highly variable. Half of the state's counties have also shown a marked secular trend toward one party or the other with the result, however, that they approach a common norm or center in gubernatorial and presidential politics. Since the vote of these counties is also likely to be highly variable regardless of the direction of their secular trend, there can be frequent alternations in presidential and gubernatorial party majorities, while at the local or legislative level of candidacies the range of party margins is narrower.

This capacity of many of the state's counties and areas to respond heavily to presidential and gubernatorial campaigns while they hold fast to their ancient party allegiance at the local level indicates that New Mexico's citizens may be dividing into two constituencies, or two electorates capable of forming two majorities. The one is that group of voters most likely to be called periodically into activity by the pull of presidential politics; the other, smaller and more stable, attends consistently to the issues and mechanics of state and local politics as well as those of presidential or national politics. There is, says Key, the question "whether a different constituency, a different shade of opinion, may not tend to be dominant in state affairs from that which moves the national government."[1] If two electorates are present in New Mexico, and there is considerable evidence to that effect, then, perhaps, a "new kind of relation" between the parties and the social structure is causing the parties to yield to a realignment of their adherent groups.[2]

It is clear, however, that the influence of national politics is discernible in New Mexico when it is measured by direction and extent of long-term drift of the counties. The campaigns and episodes of the state's politics are seldom the climactic events they may appear to be to the voters and observers of any moment, for underlying the votes and issues of campaigns are movements which persist in spite of, when they are not reinforced by, the occurrences and outcomes of particular elections. Hence, although some elections like that of 1928 or that of 1936 may be critical in that they induce greater breaks or more lasting shifts than do others, the cumulative effects of change are such that "election returns merely provide periodic readings of the relative magnitude of the streams of attitudes that are undergoing steady expansion or contraction."[3]

Trends and Variations in Regional and County Voting Patterns

The bare record of the statewide electoral majorities of twenty-six elections for governor, or of those for the presidency, or of the clean sweeps by which the state tickets lost or won, shows little of the significant changes in partisan attachment of various areas or communities.

The tables and charts immediately following describe the long-term changes which the thirty-two counties have made, and show those changes of the counties in relation to each other and to the state. Two sets of data are used. In the one, counties and regions of the state are arranged in reference to each other according to the amount by which each has moved, over the fifty-year period, toward increasing or decreasing Democratic percentages in the vote cast for

TABLE 23. LONG-TERM SHIFTS IN STATE AND COUNTY VOTING AND PARTY
     STRENGTH
(Counties ranked by order of trend line percentage points gained or lost
by Democratic gubernatorial candidates, 1911-1964, and relation to total
vote cast, 1924 and 1964)

County or area	Area symbol	Democratic percentage points gained—lost	Regression line values		Area vote as percent of state vote	
			1911	1964	1924	1964
1. Valencia	*	39.2	19.5	58.7	3.7	3.6
2. Rio Arriba	*	18.0	39.3	57.3	6.1	3.0
3. Socorro	*	16.7	38.0	54.7	3.2	1.3
4. Taos	*	14.8	40.0	54.8	3.7	1.9
5. San Miguel	*	14.5	40.4	54.9	7.7	2.6
6. Los Alamos (1948-1964)		14.1	44.8	58.9	. . .	1.8
*TEN HISPANIC COUNTIES		14.1	40.4	54.5	(43.0)	(26.9)
7. Santa Fe	*	13.3	40.5	53.8	5.9	5.7
8. Sandoval	*	12.1	44.0	56.1	2.5	1.4
9. McKinley		11.8	47.9	59.7	2.8	3.0
10. Grant		9.5	55.7	65.2	3.9	2.2
11. Doña Ana	*	8.7	46.1	54.8	4.2	5.5
12. Torrance		6.5	43.6	50.1	2.8	0.8
13. Guadalupe	*	6.3	46.9	53.2	2.2	0.8
14. Colfax		5.0	49.1	54.1	6.3	1.5
15. Luna		0.7	56.7	57.4	1.4	1.2
					56.4	36.3
16. Sierra		−1.5	50.1	48.6	1.1	1.0
17. Otero		−2.1	55.1	53.0	1.8	2.9
18. Hidalgo		−3.2	67.7	64.5	0.8	0.5
19. Catron		−5.0	51.0	46.0	0.9	0.4
20. Lincoln		−5.4	49.0	43.6	1.9	1.0
21. Mora	*	−6.3	50.3	44.0	3.7	0.8
22. Union		−7.1	55.7	48.6	3.4	0.7
23. Bernalillo		−8.1	54.0	45.9	12.6	30.0
24. Harding		−10.9	53.6	42.7	1.5	0.3

County or area	Area symbol	Democratic percentage points gained—lost	Regression line values		Area vote as percent of state vote	
			1911	1964	1924	1964
25. Eddy	#	–12.0	75.4	63.4	2.0	5.5
26. Quay		–12.5	68.9	56.4	2.7	1.3
27. San Juan		–17.3	59.4	42.1	1.7	4.2
28. De Baca	#	–18.8	69.1	50.3	0.9	0.4
#LITTLE TEXAS COUNTIES		–19.7	75.3	55.6	(11.5)	(20.7)
29. Chaves	#	–23.1	67.7	44.6	3.3	5.2
30. Lea	#	–27.9	87.4	59.5	0.6	4.9
31. Curry	#	–28.7	80.3	51.6	2.8	3.1
32. Roosevelt	#	–29.1	83.4	54.3	1.8	1.7
					43.5	63.9
State		2.3	50.7	53.0	99.9	100.2

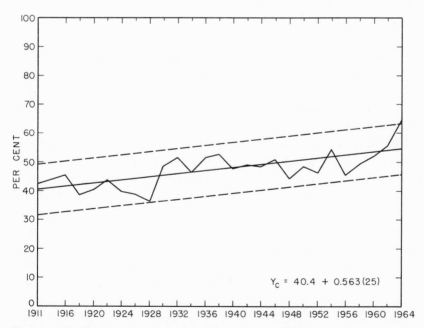

$$Y_c = 40.4 + 0.563(25)$$

FIGURE 10. Percentage and variability of vote for Democratic candidates for governor, ten Hispanic counties, 1911-1964.

governor. In the other set, the counties are ranked by the degree to
which the Democratic percentage of the two-party vote of each has
varied.[4]

The same trend and variability measurements are also applied to
two groups of counties considered as units. These are the six counties
of the southeastern corner of the state—Little Texas—and the ten
counties which traditionally have been the core of Spanish-American
voting strength.

The Long-Term Movement of Counties and Areas

When the counties are placed on a scale such as that in Table 23,
measuring relative shift and place during the fifty-year period, fifteen
counties have moved toward increasing Democratic majorities and
seventeen have moved away from the Democratic position. (A similar
switch in the placement of the counties of the ancient lineup was found
in Wisconsin. The movement of the counties there had been related
to the switch of some of the old Progressive areas to the Democratic
party. Ten of the twelve New Mexico counties most affected by the
Progressive and Farmer-Labor votes of 1912 and 1924 are in this
group of counties registering Republican gains. Although the parties
of the newer attachment are reversed in New Mexico, the phenomenon
they represent seems to be of a type with that described in Wisconsin.)[5]

If the data of Table 23 are read in conjunction with the composite
for the Hispanic counties represented by Figure 10, the diversity
underlying the state's pattern and that of the Hispanic counties is
made apparent.

The trend vote shown for the group of Hispanic counties in 1911
is about 40 per cent for the Democratic candidate for governor, and
by 1964 the ten counties had moved 14 percentage points to produce a
group trend line "majority" of 55 per cent. The five Hispanic counties
heading the list of Table 23, however, have registered Democratic
gains ranging from 15 per cent to 39 per cent. The movement of this
half of the Hispanic counties has been so steadily toward the Democratic party's candidates that there is some likelihood that they may
march past the border of a 45-55 per cent electoral range well into
the province of that party.

Mora is to be found as the sole anomaly among the Hispanic
counties—a stranger two-thirds of the way down the list. But Mora's
drift toward the Republican end of the scale of Table 23 is exceeded

by that of each of the six Little Texas counties. These range from Eddy, which has registered a twelve-point Republican gain, to Roosevelt, which has moved closer to the Republican position by twenty-nine percentage points. But, like Valencia County, which moved across the political horizon by thirty-nine points from her extreme Republicanism, Roosevelt County had a great distance to go. Another, Lea County, started in 1918 as a newly formed county from a Democratic regression line "vote" of 87 per cent, so that now, after forty-six years, it is still a potent, if much less salient, Democratic stronghold in its current 60 per cent margin. The Little Texas counties as a group have moved twenty points toward Republicanism, but only two—De Baca and Chaves—are readily capable of delivering a majority to a Republican candidate for governor.

Little Texas has nearly doubled its contribution to the state's total vote, as Table 23 indicates, by going from 12 to 21 per cent of the state's total. This alone would make the area a prize worth seeking; but as candidates have learned, its extreme tendency to vary its vote makes it nearly as capricious as New Mexico's summer rainfall.

Political Mercury: The Tendency of Counties to Vary their Vote

The several counties are by no means alike in their reactions to campaigns and candidates. Variations in the percentage of the vote to a series of a party's gubernatorial candidates are quite limited in some counties, but others have consistently shown a disposition to make relatively radical shifts in the percentage of the vote going to a party's candidates. The six counties of Little Texas are among the more changeable, and collectively provide an illustration of the uses of Figures 10 and 11 and Table 24.

Although the Little Texas counties are no longer the homogeneous group they once were, they still show the same broad reactions to candidacies and political currents. Hence, while they tend individually to a high degree of political changeability, they also usually change together to produce the results shown in Figure 11. The graph shows two parallel, broken lines at a distance of 14 percentage points from the regression line. The broken lines are consequently 28 percentage points apart (equivalent to plus and minus $2S_y$), a distance which may be read as representing the approximate limits of the range of the Little Texas vote to the Democratic candidates.

Such measures may be read for each of the thirty-two counties of

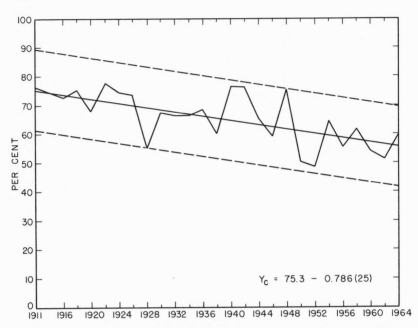

FIGURE 11. Percentage and variability of vote for Democratic candidates for governor in six Little Texas counties, 1911-1964.

TABLE 24. VARIABILITY OF PARTY VOTING IN COUNTIES AND CULTURAL
AREAS
(Little Texas, Hispanic, and individual counties ranked in order of range from trend line of party vote for governor, 1911-1964; with proportion of total)

County or area	Area symbol	Variability rating ($2S_y$)	Area vote as percentage of state vote	
			1924	1964
1. Los Alamos		18.7	...	1.8
2. Roosevelt	#	18.6	1.8	1.7
3. Curry	#	17.5	2.8	3.1
4. Luna		16.9	1.4	1.2
5. Chaves	#	16.9	3.3	5.2
6. Quay		15.7	2.7	1.3
7. Doña Ana	*	15.7	4.2	5.5
8. Hidalgo		15.5	0.8	0.5

County or area	Area symbol	Variability rating $(2S_y)$	Area vote as percentage of state vote	
			1924	1964
9. San Juan		15.0	1.7	4.2
10. Valencia	*	14.3	3.7	3.6
11. Grant		14.3	3.9	2.2
12. Sandoval	*	14.2	2.5	1.4
#SIX LITTLE TEXAS COUNTIES		(14.0)	(11.5)	(20.7)
13. Eddy	#	13.8	2.0	5.5
14. Lea	#	13.3	0.6	4.9
15. De Baca	#	13.2	0.9	0.4
16. Bernalillo		13.1	12.6	30.0
Totals—most variable counties			44.9	72.5
17. McKinley		12.8	2.8	3.0
18. Santa Fe	*	12.4	5.9	5.7
19. Socorro	*	12.0	3.2	1.3
20. Rio Arriba	*	11.8	6.1	3.0
21. Union		11.6	3.4	0.7
22. Catron		10.9	0.9	0.4
23. Taos	*	10.9	3.7	1.9
24. San Miguel	*	10.8	7.7	2.6
25. Colfax		10.4	6.3	1.5
26. Mora	*	10.1	3.7	0.8
27. Sierra		10.1	1.1	1.0
28. Guadalupe	*	9.8	2.2	0.8
29. Otero		9.5	1.8	2.9
30. Harding		9.1	1.5	0.3
*TEN HISPANIC COUNTIES		(8.8)	(43.0)	(26.9)
31. Lincoln		8.6	1.9	1.0
32. Torrance		8.4	2.8	0.8
Totals—least variable counties			55.0	27.7
State		7.7	99.9	100.2

Table 24. Examination of the different results posted there by the counties at the opposite extremes reveals that Los Alamos and Roosevelt, at the top, have demonstrated that over the years each is apt to vary its electoral margins through a range more than twice as great as that of Torrance County at the bottom of the list. Even De Baca, the least changeable of the Little Texas counties, has moved its vote through a range of ($\pm 2S_y$) of 26 percentage points by the measure used in the scale.

That the reactions of the ten Hispanic counties are quite different may be seen in a comparison of Figure 10 with the arrangement of the data of Table 24.

The variability score of the Hispanic counties as a group is only nine points. Yet these counties differ greatly in their individual ratings of variability—from 16 percentage points in the case of Doña Ana down to 10 in the case of Guadalupe—measures indicating that the several counties of the Hispanic group have frequently evinced differing reactions to candidates, issues, or campaign tactics. The 1948 and 1950 elections illustrate the matter. The Democratic gain from 1948 to 1950 for the ten counties was 4 percentage points. The party gains in nine of the ten counties ranged from 4 to 14 percentage points; but in Doña Ana, the largest and most variable, local issues brought out an imposing vote and the Democratic margin there declined by 20 percentage points, a factor sufficient to limit the change for the group. Seven of the Hispanic counties are among the sixteen least variable counties, however.

CORRESPONDENCE AND DIVERGENCE IN NATIONAL AND LOCAL POLITICS

In 1912, in their new statehood, New Mexico's communities were often fiercely partisan and some were strongholds devoted to one or the other of the major parties. Local majorities ranging from 60 to 90 per cent were not at all unusual, but they would be balanced by opposing majorities in other areas. Over the years, however, most of the old one-party salients have come to lose their prominence and to slide to the center in presidential and gubernatorial politics; while, perhaps not too strangely, the electoral and organizational base of the Republican party is inclined to deteriorate.[6]

Table 25 provides a measure of the extent to which New Mexico manifests within its borders the increasing homogeneity of presidential and gubernatorial politics the states appear to be producing in the nation.

The now narrow range of the majorities the counties give the candidates for governor is comfortably exceeded, however, by the range they have recently posted for president. The 1948 campaign of President Truman produced a 43-per-cent increase in the total vote over

TABLE 25. EROSION OF ONE-PARTY SALIENTS AS COUNTIES MOVE TO CENTER

(Quartile distribution of counties by percentage Democratic of two-party vote for governor in three periods, 1911-1958)

	Range of mean Democratic percentage		
Counties	*1911-1928*	*1930-1948*	*1950-1958*
Top 7-8	63-84	63-75	54-64
Middle 16	46-61	49-62	47-52
Lower 8	22-44	42-48	42-46
Total range	62	33	22

that of the previous midterm election, to result in a party-vote range among the counties of thirty-nine percentage points; the 1960 Kennedy-Nixon campaign so aroused the electorate that the vote jumped by 100,000 for a 49-per-cent increase, and the Kennedy percentage of the counties' vote extended through a range of thirty-five points.[7]

Divergence of the long-term party-voting for president and governor from the voting for legislative and county candidates; sharp periodic increases in the vote brought on by the presidential candidacies; and the peculiarities of the counties characterized by extremes of one-party attachment may stem from a common root. There appear to be two electorates: One group of voters is relatively undisturbed by the issues, policies, and mechanics of state and local government and makes its presence felt in the increased voting of presidential election years. The other group apparently attends to the issues and candidacies of statehood and local politics almost as diligently as it does to those involved in presidential politics. In the short run, the interactions of the two groups contribute to the vagaries of state politics, but over the long pull the presidential electorate may be producing a realignment of the more durable factions.

Sectional and Party Division of the Two Electorates

In spite of a registration about a third of that of their opposition, Republicans captured control in 1952 of the state house of representatives; a Republican won four of the eight 1950-1964 elections for governor; and after a narrow miss or two, the voters gave a hairline majority in 1960 to the Republican candidate for lieutenant governor. But the same decade witnessed a doubling of the percentage point spread between candidates for governor and the bulk of the ticket, and a slow erosion of Republican legislative and county-courthouse strength. The even party balance prevailing at the level of governorship and presidency disappears in half of the counties, and in the others a rigid majority-minority conflict, or a long-standing and extreme party attachment permit but slight variations in the local vote.

A hint of the effects of the capacity of the electorate to divide regionally as well as between the parties may be gained from the two divisions of Table 26, in which the counties are grouped by their degree of one-party attachment and then by a related sectional grouping. The remaining columns of the table indicate the direction of secular movement of the counties in their vote for governor, and give a measure of the propensity of the voters to split their ticket rather than permit their vote for president to affect their vote for legislative candidates.

Variations appearing in the two groupings of data of Table 26 parallel, to a degree, the findings of Miller and Press. In a sample-survey, interview study, it was found that voter identification with party was more determinative of voting behavior than the attraction of issues or candidates; hence, it is a factor not likely to encourage carrying a vote for the other party's candidate for president very far down the line.[8] In a related study of election data, it was found that in areas of weakness on the congressional level, the president runs ahead. But where the party is traditionally entrenched locally, congressional candidates lead the presidential candidate.[9]

Factors determinative of the spread between the vote for president, governor, and legislators apparently vary from region to region in the state and produce different effects at various degrees of political

TABLE 26. RELATION OF LEGISLATIVE AND PRESIDENTIAL VOTE TO 1958
PARTY REGISTRATION AND THE COUNTIES' DIRECTION OF
SECULAR MOVEMENT, ELECTIONS OF 1952-1958

Percentage of registration Democratic	Number of counties moving		Percentage of vote Democratic		Difference
	Dem.	Repub.	Legislature	President	
80-90	2	7	69.3	48.1	21.2
70-79	1	2	54.1	38.7	15.4
60-69	9	4	52.8	43.5	9.3
40-59	2	4	49.2	39.2	10.0
Little Texas (84.5)	0	6	68.4	46.4	22.0
Bernalillo (59.7)	0	1	50.3	37.8	12.5
Hispanic counties (59.7)	9	1	52.2	44.8	7.4

balance or imbalance. As Table 23 made clear, the counties of the
state are not climbing political slopes of the same gradient, nor have
many started from the same place.

The Hispanic counties were early commanded by rather narrow
but consistent majorities which persisted throughout the state and
county party tickets. Those counties, plus the four or five tied to them
by mutual inclinations or the system of multi-county legislative districts, once provided the majority of Republican legislative member-
ships as well as many of the county officials and other political activists
relied upon by the party. The 60-40 percentage balance enjoyed by
Republicans of 1920-1930 in the Hispanic counties was nearly reversed by 1960, but the process (which took about thirty years)
showed early and decisively in county-level elections. In the ten Hispanic counties and four others often allied with them (Colfax, Lincoln, San Juan, and Torrance), the biennial Republican percentages
of the vote for governor varied through a range in the five 1940-1948
elections of 5.3 percentage points, and through 8.8 points in the
1950-1960 elections to set the means posted in Table 27. The differ-

ence between the largest and smallest Republican biennial percentage of the fourteen-county vote cast for legislators was only 1.9 points in 1940-1948, but the high-to-low difference was 9.5 percentage points in the elections of 1950-1960.

TABLE 27. FADING REPUBLICAN STRENGTH IS ANTICIPATED AND AMPLIFIED IN LEGISLATIVE ELECTIONS IN TEN HISPANIC AND FOUR ALLIED COUNTIES

Series of Elections	Mean Republican percentage of 14-county vote for		Republican-held seats as percentage of		Republicans from 14 Counties as percentage of all GOP members
	Governor	Legislature	14 county delegation	all seats	
1940-1948	51.8	49.3	48.6	30.6	90.6
1950-1960	51.5	46.4	29.7	21.2	63.6

Table 27 suggests that increments of party strength in the Hispanic and allied counties were often established by legislative or other local candidates rather than by gubernatorial candidates, and that small additions to local party strength in these areas of intense partisan activity were often seized and retained (a result probably reinforced by the long-term direction of change in the voting for president and governor, and the organizational strength engendered by the even party battle). If so, the sequence is unusual, for elsewhere in the American scene, and elsewhere in New Mexico, a party shift affecting local candidates is normally led, and by good margins, by national and state candidates. In any case, and in spite of the close party margins, as Table 27 shows, the Republican party lost all but a tiny portion of the legislative representation of the Hispanic counties. A repectable percentage of seats held by Republicans in the 1940's dropped sharply when the average vote dropped only three points. Replacements that might have come in the 1960's from other areas awaited an uncertain progression of more counties to a much higher point on the line of Republican percentages.

Bernalillo County, in which the voting balance is also tight, returned Republican legislative delegations in 1952 and 1956, and narrowly missed in 1960 when the Nixon majority there was relatively slight. (A legislative reapportionment, effective in 1964, requiring counties electing several legislators to nominate and elect members from districts has also doubled the size of the Bernalillo County delegation. Since the electoral strength of the parties tends to be concentrated in certain areas and neighborhoods, each party is now almost assured of a share in any legislative delegation.) The county's registration is about 60 per cent Democratic, but its 1911-1964 direction of movement was toward the Republican party. The coattail effect counts in Bernalillo County, for its periodically increased voting group usually exhibits a relatively strong inclination to refrain from ticket splitting, and so it carries the momentary party preference far down the ticket — a characteristic by which Bernalillo County must be ranked a little below the Hispanic counties and far above those of Little Texas.

The counties heading the two segments of Table 26 — whether the nine-county group in which Democratic registration was over 80 per cent of the total, or the six counties of Little Texas — present the other facet of these anomalies of time, extent, and direction of change. Their vote for legislative candidates is a measure of a one-party dominance complete enough to indicate a political subculture. (If the data of Table 26, concerning the vote for legislative candidates, are plotted against Democratic registration in a scatter diagram, three-fourths of the counties fall into a loose three-to-one progression, but the counties in the 80 to 90 per cent registration area then pull the upper range into a sharp J-curve.)

These counties of a one-party dominance have not lost their capacity to render a highly variable total vote in the sequence of presidential and off-year elections and to make marked shifts in party percentage majorities—attributes which become of greater significance as the other and more closely balanced counties of the state tend to come to a common norm. The response of the heavily Democratic counties to stresses and conflict is less inhibited by party, their top-of-the-ticket vote frequently reflects those stresses, and their party-vote differentials in vote for governor and legislators, or governor and minor state officers are far greater than in the Hispanic counties. In the counties of Little Texas, and several others with a similar politics, the minority position in the 1920's of the Republican party was much inferior to the strength maintained by the Democratic group in areas of Republican dominance. Tables 23 and 26 indicate that the direction of movement of Little Texas and similar counties in the guber-

TABLE 28. THE TWO ELECTORATES: EFFECTS OF VARYING VOTER TURNOUT AND THE PRESIDENTIAL COATTAILS IN MAJOR VOTING AREAS IN THE GUBERNATORIAL ELECTIONS OF 1958 AND 1960

County group	Area percentage of total state vote		Increase in vote turnout		Winning margins				1960 net gain by party benefiting
					1958		1960		
	1958	1960	Number	Percentage	R	D	R	D	
10 Hispanic counties	31.4	27.9	20,964	32.7	840	.....	.....	3,432	D: 4,272
Bernalillo County	24.3	27.7	34,621	69.4	10,605	.....	9,252	.....	D: 1,353
6 Little Texas counties	19.1	20.7	24,194	61.9	.....	9,131	.....	5,223	R: 3,908
15 Remaining counties	25.3	23.7	20,715	39.9	.....	4,228	1,391	.....	R: 5,619
Totals and margins	100.1	100.0	100,494	49.0		1,914	1,988		R: 3,902

natorial elections is Republican, but the presidential and gubernatorial electorate there is apparently but slightly more disposed than formerly to upset the existing local arrangement of power.

Some measure of the varying extent and consequences for party of the division of the regional electorates into presidential and gubernatorial components on the one hand, and those also effective or active in off-year elections on the other, may be seen in Table 28.

The tug of presidential politics in 1960 and 1964 brought out numerous additional voters, and the largest increases were in metropolitan Bernalillo County and in Little Texas. But the impulses of the elections were in the direction of the long-term movement of every area save Bernalillo County and there they tended to preserve an existing balance. So some portion of the gains and losses of the gubernatorial (and lesser) candidates is no doubt traceable to the impact of the presidential elections.

Occurrence and Characteristics of the Two Electorates

The variations in voter turnout and party margins measured in Table 28 are merely tokens of profound and controlling differences in the politics of the different areas of the state—differences not altogether evident in the data of the table.

That the periodic increase in the vote of Bernalillo County and in Little Texas is so marked stems in part from a relatively large number of new residents at each presidential election. But, the styles of political participation in the various areas of the state are highly affected by the kinds of political organizations obtaining and the differing uses made of them. The relative presence or absence of two electorates in an area is a factor.

A portion of the background of these differing styles of political activity shows up in the data of Table 29. The groups of counties are arranged on a gradient determined by population growth; the remaining columns outline the degree of periodicity of political participation.

Table 29 is not as definitive as it might appear to be, however. (The historic continuity, in its regional dimensions, of the presidential-year increase in the size of the vote is better approached through Figure 9 of the preceding chapter.) The sharp periodic increase has always been highly marked in Little Texas and other border counties, and it is a relatively new thing in Bernalillo County (Albuquerque) where it

TABLE 29. AREAS DIFFER IN INCREASE IN SIZE OF VOTE IN PRESIDENTIAL
ELECTIONS

County or county group	Population increase in 1950-1960 per cent,	Percent increase in vote for governor from non-presidential to presidential elections		
		1950-52	1954-56	1958-60
10 Hispanic counties	18	9	13	33
15 Remaining counties	33	27	27	39
6 Little Texas counties	38	55	49	62
Bernalillo County	80	60	42	69
State	40	33	30	49

began to appear in 1944, coincident with the city's rapid growth. Perhaps the presidential-year increase in Little Texas is now augmented by recent population growth, but its cause lies elsewhere. The phenomenon has never been significant in the Hispanic counties, for in the off-year election their vote (while it does not then increase) drops but little, so that it has always comprised an increased percentage of the state's total.

A better measure of the problem may be found in its reflection in local politics, although the typology of community politics set out here is a casual one and employed with some trepidation.[10] (There is, I am persuaded, a kinship or a linkage between what is described in these jottings and the operations of the state's politics.)

Political affairs in the Hispanic counties are almost entirely affairs of party. Consequently, if the citizen wishes to influence the activities of almost any type of governmental entity, he must do so through the parties; for non-partisan political agencies like chambers of commerce and citizens' leagues are few and of small authority. The conduct of village and municipal governments, the issuance of bonds, and often the slating of candidates for land grant and school boards are determined by the conflict between the political parties or their factions.

These are not, however, communities of a monolithic power structure. Although voluntary associations are few, public office and the political system provide an avenue to personal advancement and power.[11] To borrow Janowitz' conception, politics in these towns is anything but "diffuse in its goals and in its penetration into the social fabric." Although these communities are more rural than industrial-urban, political organization is highly developed. Theirs is not, in any conventional sense, a politics in which "working-class elements" prevail.[12] The typical municipal government is of the mayor-council variety, and city managers or any of the various devices of non-partisan control are rare indeed. The voting in the spring municipal elections in the Hispanic counties normally brings out percentages of the electorate that would be deemed phenomenal in many other areas of the state.

An indication of the attention voters of the various areas pay to municipal politics is provided by results of the April 1962 elections available in the daily press. Table 30 reports the percentage of the

TABLE 30. PERCENTAGE OF POTENTIAL ELECTORATE OF GROUPS OF CITIES AND TOWNS VOTING IN THE 1962 MUNICIPAL ELECTIONS

Area and towns	Percentage of electorate voting
Albuquerque	24
Little Texas (Carlsbad, Artesia, Roswell, Portales)	28
Other—Western Border (Farmington, Gallup, Silver City)	40
Spanish American (Socorro, E. Las Vegas, W. Las Vegas, Belen, Santa Fe)	49

SOURCE: Press wire service reports in *Albuquerque Journal, Albuquerque Tribune,* and the *New Mexican* (Santa Fe). The same ratio of persons of voting age was presumed to apply in all areas. (Wire service data for many of the small towns was inadequate.)

potential electorate voting in major towns and cities representative of the county groupings used in other tables of this chapter.

If the Hispanic towns of Table 30 are a fair sample, the behavior they represent indicates a high level of attention to municipal politics, and a relatively low degree of separation of the electorate into sub-electorates called into being by particular types of elections. In sum, these voters have not yet divided themselves into two electorates of which one responds chiefly to issues of national politics while permitting the other to control matters state and local. That they have not may be a resultant of their historic division into two highly competitive parties. (In this connection it might be pointed out that one-partyism is not typically associated with small towns in New Mexico. It shows up strongly, of course, in Little Texas and a few similar areas, and it is characteristic of some ranching areas of widely dispersed populations associated with small core towns in Luna and Hidalgo counties. But in the ranching areas, the two-party division of sentiment concerning national politics can be rigorous.)[13]

The towns of Little Texas and Albuquerque are now much alike in their attention to municipal politics; but again, the low level of participation is historic in Little Texas, and recent in Albuquerque.[14] Both areas, it will be recalled, now distinguish themselves by a high rate of increase in voting at the presidential elections.

Albuquerque's domestic politics long had a close relationship to state politics. Its city-manager charter dates from 1917, but not until the mid-1940's was city hall effectively removed from partisan control.[15] The long-dominant series of slates that appeared in the 'forties was fostered by a citizens' association narrowly representative of the peak interests in the city, and, until 1966, factional candidates in opposition to the slates of the Citizens' Committee were unable to develop an organization which could muster the support of new interests and associations striving for recognition in City Hall. In 1962, the sixteen candidates opposing the three-man Citizens' Committee slate shared 49 per cent of the vote, and the leading opposition slate received 23 per cent of the total, but the April elections four years later produced a decisive margin for the candidates of a group based upon a broad range of formally organized and mature community associations. (Some had tired, it seems, of their customary role of petitioners.) Albuquerque's recent history indicates that the town may be developing a local two-party system parallel to but separate from the

Republican and Democratic organizations. The conservative Citizens' Committee long functioned as a party, i.e., as "a group that coheres for electoral purposes," and it had a definite policy orientation.[16] The successful opposition coalition of 1966 could also readily become equivalent to a party if it aims, as it probably must, at a broad base of support.

The counties of Little Texas present a perhaps more interesting variety of a local politics in which the two electorates are present. In this case, their presence seems somewhat more clearly related to the structures of power, and the type of involvement in state politics of those communities.

In the years of 1940-1960 (and in sharp contrast to Albuquerque's experience) there persisted a notable longevity of service of legislative members from Little Texas, and it is in these counties that the uncontested legislative primary and general election were most frequent. Both are matters probably indicative of centralized structures of local political authority in a one-party environment. There was no withdrawal of economic leadership from local politics.[17]

The rate and kinds of popular involvement in local and legislative politics convey the impression that individuals and groups dominating the towns of Little Texas are somewhat akin to presidential Republicans, but they have found the key to an economical maintenance of local conservatism. With a Democratic registration of four to one, there is no problem in controlling local government affairs, since county office tickets are easily arranged; municipal elections are of the non-partisan variety and as easily managed as they are lightly attended.

In the Little Texas environment that thin crust of the politically active comprising some 10 to 20 per cent of the electorate can readily control simply by their activity and cohesion, if not by force of numbers, municipal, school board, and bond elections. They also operate the Democratic party as one of their civic enterprises. In areas of this kind, the one-party system comes as a heritage that can be made to support a highly integrated structure of community power. Those who would oppose that structure are apt to find that the minority party is a most inadequate instrument for their purpose, a matter which doubtless contributes to the light attendance of off-year and local elections.

The majority of the electorate of Little Texas is undeniably attracted by the economic and social issues of national politics. About half of the numerous voters at the recent presidential elections felt constrained by party ties or personal objectives to vote for Stevenson and Kennedy, but some must have been attracted by the liberalism those candidates represented. A good many of the more politically active and influential citizenry of those areas are not so attracted, and the political apparatus of their communities is carefully insulated against the heat and pressure of state and national politics. As a result community influentials can readily manage the local part of affairs. They can, and do, retain their own sensitivity to issues and candidates; but they remain registered Democrats while they vote Republican, if necessary, at that level where the vote has an effect on policy which might otherwise be made away from their sphere of control.

In sum, the presence of two electorates is far more obvious in Albuquerque and Little Texas than in the Hispanic counties. Some part of the voting shifts described in the next section dealing with the elections of 1928 and 1960 may well be the measure of the growth of the newer nationally oriented electorate rather than the shifting of the old.

FROM ALFRED SMITH TO JOHN KENNEDY: THE MEASURE OF
POLITICAL CHANGE

The memory of the debacle of Alfred E. Smith and the 1928 campaign lies deep in New Mexico, and John F. Kennedy's presidential nomination in 1960 was regarded with anguish by a sizeable bloc of Democrats who failed or refused to grasp the stubby Kennedy coattails. Yet Kennedy carried the state—not handily, but he won—while Governor John Burroughs and the candidate for lieutenant governor lost by the narrowest of margins, and the remainder won easily.

The measure provided by the two campaigns is good, but not entirely unequivocal. Yet, it is clear (when the votes of 1928 for Catholic, liberal Alfred Smith are compared with those for Catholic, liberal John Kennedy, so that those votes become details in a greatly altered pattern) that the two campaigns are the span and measure of a broad change in the state's politics.

The religious issue was of importance in both campaigns, and so it becomes a sort of statistical constant by virtue of the persistent pattern of religious affiliation in several areas of the state. The wet-dry or prohibition issue was probably as important in some of New Mexico's areas in 1928 as it was in several other states, but it was not associated in New Mexico with the urban-Catholic, rural-Protestant division that began to show in the 1928 and 1932 elections, for here both the Catholic and Protestant areas were then predominantly rural.

That whole set of conflicts of attitudes or values, and economic leanings which may be so handily summed up in some states, in the 1960's and for some years past, as the liberal-Democratic-urban grouping versus the rural and small-town-conservative-Republican grouping is difficult of application in New Mexico. Yet, it must be said that underlying the political changes of New Mexico is a complex set of economic and social changes. The eastern and southern counties, which once warmly embraced the New Deal, moved in the 1950's with amazing speed to embrace (and perhaps to cherish for some years to come) economic and political attitudes akin to those of Dallas and Houston. The graph line of Democratic majorities in the Little Texas counties breaks most sharply in 1928 (Figure 12). Kennedy did nearly

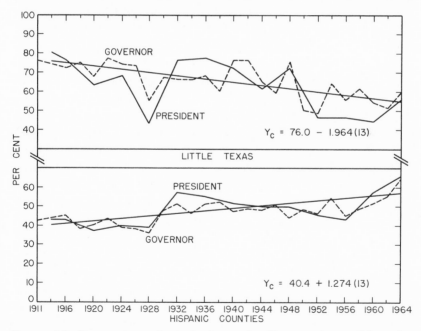

FIGURE 12. Percentage and trend of vote for Democratic candidates for president, and relation of vote for governor, Little Texas and Hispanic counties, 1912-1964.

as badly there as had Smith; yet, and perhaps most significant, the Kennedy defeat there in 1960 was but little worse than those of Stevenson in running against Eisenhower in 1952 and 1956. Meanwhile, the Hispanic counties (which granted a few more points for Smith than they did for his gubernatorial running mate) moved sharply to Roosevelt and, until Eisenhower, remained well attached to the liberal position (as that term is now used)—an attitude perhaps reinforced when their Catholic background also disposed them to find an appeal in Kennedy, yet they liked Protestant Johnson even better.

Smith carried one county of the day's thirty-one. Kennedy carried eighteen of thirty-two and in only six of the thirteen he lost did Kennedy do so by a percentage vote smaller than that obtained by Smith. (Johnson carried twenty-nine.)

The vote of 1928 and 1960: From Aberration to Normal

In nearly every area of the state the vote that moved so sharply against Smith was a sizeable departure from the normal Democratic percentage of that day; the vote that went to Kennedy thirty-two years later was in close correspondence to the 1960 statistical expectations in most areas—a conclusion derived as follows:

The regression lines described in connection with Figures 2, 10, and 11, showing the percentage of the vote Democratic in various areas, give a value for any election which may be likened to the "normal" for that election. The actual vote for a candidate in any such election may thus be read as a deviation from that normal vote. Most deviations were large in 1928. The actual vote by counties or areas in 1960 usually represents a much smaller deviation, in percentage points, from the norms as represented by the 1960 value of each area's regression line. If the results are presented in tabular form as in Table 31 they express, in percentage points, the extent by which the Democratic candidate fell below or exceeded the vote he "should" have received as a statistical expectation in a group of counties. Kennedy and his gubernatorial running mate failed by small margins to reach their anticipated vote.

The County Shift

When the Smith-Kennedy electoral changes are contemplated, the question occurs whether the principal areas of the state reacted to the 1960 presidential campaign simply by accelerating a bit a movement

TABLE 31. Smith Receives an Abnormal and Kennedy a Normal
    Party Vote
(Percentage points by which Catholic candidates exceeded or fell short, in
1928 and 1960, of Democratic trend line of 1911-1964)

Type of vote by election	Hispanic counties		Little Texas counties		Bernalillo County		State	
	Pres.	Gov.	Pres.	Gov.	Pres.	Gov.	Pres.	Gov.
1928 Trend line vote	47	45	66	68	51	51	52	52
Actual vote	39	36	43	55	43	50	41	44
Discrepancy	-8	-9	-23	-13	-8	-1	-11	-8
1960 Trend line vote	56	54	52	56	49	46	53	53
Actual vote	58	52	45	54	48	45	50	50
Discrepancy	2	-2	-7	-2	-1	-1	-3	-3

they had long been making. And it does appear that those counties
tending to move toward the Democratic side of the scale and those
moving in the opposite direction must have found little in the campaign to cause them to halt or reverse their movement.

Alfred Smith drew a better vote than his gubernatorial running
mate in only eight counties, and seven of those were of the Hispanic
and Catholic tradition. Kennedy led his running mate in nineteen
counties (including Los Alamos) and received 50 per cent of the
state's vote, while Smith had been granted but 41 per cent of the vote.

The parallel scattergrams of Figure 13 describe the voting position of thirty-one counties by their 1928 vote for the Democratic
gubernatorial candidate and for Smith, and by their 1960 vote for
Kennedy and his local running mate. The Little Texas counties, the
Hispanic counties, and the remaining counties are each designated
by symbol so that they may be identified in relation to each other
and to the whole. If Smith and his gubernatorial running mate, Dow,

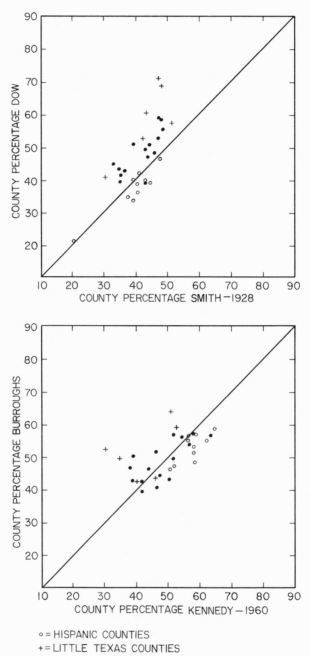

○ = HISPANIC COUNTIES
+ = LITTLE TEXAS COUNTIES

Figure 13. Disparity of county vote for president and governor in the elections of 1928 and 1960.

had received the same vote in any county, that percentage point
would be represented by a dot falling at the appropriate place on the
diagonal line. If the two had run about equally well or badly in all
the counties, then the whole set of dots would have paralleled the
diagonal line. Where the mark falls above the line, Smith led Dow;
where it falls below, then Smith trailed Dow by the number of points
indicated.

The group of symbols for the 1928 election falls in a broad and
nearly vertical band, and in only a dozen or so counties is there a
fair correspondence between the gubernatorial and presidential vote.
The Hispanic counties responded with a reasonable degree of con-
sistency, but seven showed a preference for Catholic Alfred E. Smith
over his running mate. All but Mora, however, gave a rather small
minority of their votes to the two Democratic candidates. In 1960
Mora moved a few points, horizontally, to give Kennedy a slight
majority; but the remaining nine Hispanic counties moved upward
a considerable distance to pass Mora. All gave Kennedy a majority
as great or greater than that given his running mate, although only
seven of the ten gave a majority to the gubernatorial candidate.

In the main, the counties of the state brought their votes for president and governor closer together in 1960 than they had in 1928,
although the divergence—much of which results from the continuing
ability of three Little Texas counties to disassociate sharply their
votes for president and governor—remained wide.

Whether or not the issues of the Smith campaign were more divisive in some objective sense than those of 1960 is impossible to
determine, but it is clear that those of 1928 cut more sharply across
customary political patterns than those of the Kennedy campaign.
The marked divergence in 1928 between presidential and gubernatorial vote in the typical county is the measure of the break in the
traditional voting. The direction and extent of movement of the
counties across the political spectrum in the years since 1928 have
been such that the Kennedy vote generally confirmed or accentuated
long-prevailing trends.

The Economic Alignment and the Voter Shift Across Party Lines

When the votes for Kennedy and the gubernatorial candidate were
examined above in relation to the direction of movement of areas
and counties to or away from the Democratic position, the figures

appeared to be quite normal resultants of the direction of change. But in another context—the relation of the Kennedy votes to the long-term Democratic registration of the counties—the results are far more chaotic, and probably indicative of extreme stresses besetting the parties. In 1960, some 68 per cent of the state's voters were registered in the Democratic party, and, except for Mora County where Democratic registration was only 41 per cent of the total, the range of Democratic registration in the others was from 57 to 89 per cent. Yet there is no relation between the percentage of Democratic registration of the counties and the percentage of the votes cast for Kennedy; for the coefficient of correlation is -.166, although it had been .897 for Truman.

If there be any pattern at all in the vote for Kennedy, it obviously must be found in some other context or set of determinants than those implied in registration data. The factors that most readily come to mind are those relating to economic position, such as income, welfare payments, and area growth rates. Table 32 utilizes the familiar grouping determined by the counties' long-term movement toward increasing or decreasing percentages of their vote to the Democratic candidates for governor. The percentage of the vote going to the 1960 Democratic candidates for president and governor is then placed in relation to welfare payments, per capita income, and population growth in the county groups.

Although the generalized data of Table 32 obscure the sometimes aberrant behavior of individual counties, the pattern is clear enough. Kennedy led his gubernatorial running mate in those counties (often Catholic) of lowest per capita income and highest welfare payments, and the lowest rates of population growth. In the counties of a Republican tendency, Kennedy did less well than his local running mate. It is these counties which have gained most rapidly in population and which have the highest per capita income and the lowest per capita welfare payments.

The abrupt movement of voters across party lines induced by the Smith campaign moved most of the counties then Democratic in their later direction of travel. Franklin D. Roosevelt's first two campaigns served to deter or deflect the movement of the eastern and border counties, but all save three or four have long since resumed their march toward the Republican end of the scale. The Hispanic counties were measurably attracted by the Smith candidacy, greatly

TABLE 32. The 1960 Vote for Democratic Presidential and
Gubernatorial Candidates in Relation to Population
Growth, Income, and Welfare Payments

Counties' range of increase or decrease in percentage of vote Democratic, 1911-1964	Number of counties[a]	Percentage of vote		Population increase, percentage, 1950-1960	Per Capita	
		Kennedy	Burroughs		Welfare payments[b] (1959)	Income[c] (1960)
10 to 39	8	59.0	53.4	17	$37	$1,318
0 to 9.9	6	55.4	52.2	13	20	1,806
0 to -7.7	7	47.3	48.1	31	20	1,594
-8.1	1[d]	47.7	44.5	80	12	2,231
-10 to -29	9	43.0	51.4	48	13	1,828
State	31	50.4	49.7	40	$20	$1,810

[a]Los Alamos is excluded from these calculations.

[b]Ralph L. Edgel and Vicente T. Ximenes, *Income and Employment in New Mexico, 1949-1959,* "New Mexico Studies in Business and Economics," No. 8. (Albuquerque: Bureau of Business Research, University of New Mexico, 1961), Table I, p. 18.

[c]Ralph L. Edgel and Peter J. Lalonde, *Income and Employment in New Mexico, 1960-1962, ibid.,* No. 14, (1964), pp. 15-30.

[d]Bernalillo County (Albuquerque), containing 27.6 per cent of the 1960 state population.

moved by those of Roosevelt; they matched their 1932 Roosevelt vote with their vote for Kennedy, and in 1964 they found a powerful attraction in Johnson.

In the main, the realignment of voters taking place in New Mexico reflects the ancient conflict between those who have more and those who have less, for the resulting division of the counties is quite "congruent with lines separating classes, religions, [and] other social groups."[18] Generally, it is the relatively poor Hispanic and Catholic counties, those heavily engaged in the extractive industries, and the other counties of lower income which have moved toward an increased Democratic vote. The New Mexico result is not a universal one, however. Fenton found that low-income counties in the Border States often tend to be Republican, and they have been for a long, long time. He found in them Republican organizations that dominated politics and a monolithic power structure.[19] It may be that the bivariate organization of the politics of New Mexico's Hispanic counties frees them to follow their bent in the 1960's just as it did fifty years earlier. And it may be that the structure and processes of New Mexico's society elsewhere are not so restrictive, not so culture bound as one finds them in the towns of the rural midwest and the northeast, for the sifting of populations as they moved west may have deposited in the state a highly individualistic lot.[20]

Whatever the merit of the foregoing speculations, the 1950-1960 decade was marked by a high degree of ticket splitting that differentiated between president and governor, with a second level of splitting between gubernatorial and other state and local candidates. Findings of similar but less pronounced patterns in Illinois were read as suggesting the inference that "the new cleavage resides more in national affairs (issues and candidates) than in state politics and that the overall reorientation was more pronounced for the presidency than for statewide candidacies."[21] The inference seems suitable also for New Mexico. And the conclusion suggests that groups of voters making the periodic switch for president or governor may be holding the state in a rather lengthy transitional period while they mark out the route for a more conclusive realignment of the electorate. Yet, if the factors contributing to the formation of two electorates — the presidential and the local — persist, the calculations this chapter contains may be simply differentiating unique from shared characteristics of the two groups pending some future critical election.

PARTY BALANCE, SECULAR CHANGE, AND
VARIABILITY OF THE VOTE

New Mexico's post-war politics incorporates an uneasy and perhaps fragile arrangement of the components of the two parties. The degree or range of variability of voting margins of a half or so of the counties' vote for governor is inversely related to the extent and rigor of locally organized, two-party competition. In those counties where Republican registration is higher than in the state as a whole, and where reasonably effective county organizations are most apt to be found, the tendency (if one excludes Bernalillo and Los Alamos counties) to cast widely fluctuating majorities has been low. The remaining and more Democratic counties, and those of most rapid growth, have usually reacted the most sharply to presidential politics.

Preceding discussions have also emphasized long-term changes in party adherence in gubernatorial and presidential elections. By the accounting in Table 23, fifty-year trend-line gains for Democratic gubernatorial candidates ranging from 14 to 39 percentage points were scored in five counties, but were balanced by Democratic losses in nine counties of 10 to 29 points. Similarly, Democratic registration in Los Alamos County dropped from 70 per cent in 1952 to 57 per cent in 1964. About half of the thirty-two counties made marked secular changes in the gubernatorial and presidential races, but at this level neither party gained much more than it lost in the transaction.

The counties of a reasonably even party balance are usually highly competitive, and, except for a few like Bernalillo and Los Alamos, most were once in the Republican camp or periodically allied with it. The most strenuous campaign efforts are apt to be met there with strong, countervailing activity and to be rewarded, if at all, with a minute percentage-point gain; for, except for a few like Doña Ana, the old two-party counties are usually not inclined to vary their vote much. Although a winning or a close campaign in the traditionally competitive counties is requisite to Republican successes, it is no longer sufficient, for their voters are too small a part of the state's electorate.

The result is a forced strategy in which support from the more Democratic and more variable counties (as measured in the data of Table 24) is essential to Republican victories. The variability in the size of the total vote, plus the wide range of the two-party margins in these counties, periodically becomes the Republican salvation, for the counties of a strongly Democratic registration are nearly uniquely capable of drastically shifting their vote at the presidential or gubernatorial levels, and hence to reward additional campaign efforts by the minority.

To measure the extent to which the counties split their vote away from their Democratic registration in 1960, Table 33 groups the counties into three units determined by their decreasing variability rank (Bernalillo and Los Alamos counties are considered separately). The dependency of the Republican candidate upon voters registered as Democrats in the counties of variable vote is shown in relation to the Democrat for whom the "firmness" of his party's registration is highest in the least variable counties. In the seven most variable counties, the Republican received a number of votes twice as great

TABLE 33. Counties of High Democratic Registration and
Variable Electoral Margins Give Aid and Comfort
to Republican Candidate for Governor

Counties ranked and grouped by variability of party vote (2S_y rating)	Republican percentage of total registration	Vote to each gubernatorial candidate as a percentage of party registration		Republican percentage of 1960 vote
		Republican	Democrat	
7 most variable (15.5-18.6)	18.8	200.4	44.6	52.2
15 of mid-range (10.8-15.0)	25.6	125.8	54.1	46.1
8 least variable (8.4-10.4)	32.8	108.1	58.3	49.4
Los Alamos (18.7)	32.2	135.9	58.7	56.5
Bernalillo (13.1)	32.9	128.0	56.6	55.5
State	27.1	134.0	53.1	50.3

as his party's number of registrants; the Democrat received there a
vote only 45 per cent as large as his party's number of registered
voters. Party regularity of voters — a firm Democratic vote — showed
up much more strongly in the least variable counties. Similar differentials, if not always so large and orderly, have shown up in each
election since that of 1950.

The relation of the proportionate vote of the fifteen Democratic-
tending counties of Table 23 to that of the sixteen most variable
counties of Table 24 is diagrammed in Figure 14. The 1964 positions
of the two groups of counties in relation to the state's total vote are
the reverse of those occupied in 1924, and a much greater distance
separates them although the rates of divergence decreased slightly
after 1948.

Even at the level of gubernatorial and presidential elections, however, the Republican prospect is less pleasant than Figure 14 might
make it seem. In its measures of the extent and direction of partisan

change of the counties, Table 23 indicates that of the fifteen counties which have produced a 1911-1964 trend line favoring Democratic candidates only Torrance has failed to put its 1964 trend-line terminus above the 50-per-cent mark. These fifteen counties now cast only 36 per cent of the vote. The seventeen counties of the lower half of the scale cast 64 per cent of the state's ballots, but a third of the vote of these Republican-tending counties is cast by eight or nine whose typical majority is still Democratic, and in three cases strongly so.

Although varying rates and directions of movement of the counties have operated to preserve a party balance at the level of presidential and gubernatorial elections, various factors have led to sharp

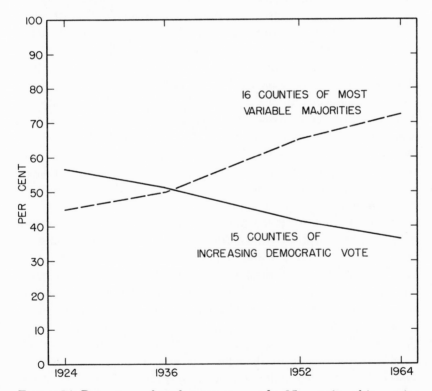

FIGURE 14. Percentage of total state vote cast by 15 counties of increasing Democratic majorities, and by 16 counties of most variable vote. (Six counties, casting 16 per cent of the state's total vote, are common to both curves.)

differentials in rates of change lower on the tickets. The shift from Republican to Democratic in the Hispanic counties, and from strongly to marginally Democratic in Bernalillo County occurred nearly simultaneously at all levels of the ticket. But in most of the old Democratic strongholds moving toward a Republican vote for president and governor, relatively little change has taken place in the balance of local partisanship. In consequence, the statewide Republican position has deteriorated considerably more than is indicated by the loss in the gubernatorial fifty-year trend-line vote of a little more than 2 per cent.

Movement of the counties described in this and the preceding chapter on the level of gubernatorial and presidential politics rather strongly suggests an accumulative impact of issues upon party adherence.[22] Yet, the failure of a significant group of New Mexico's counties to produce a two-party vote at lower levels of the ticket is perhaps the reflection of a profound separation there of national, state, and local politics. Chances are that the erosion of New Mexico's one-party salients stems primarily from the long series of issues and policies identified with the national parties. These policies are apparently infrequently associated with local politics in the several counties whose voters are most prone to be called to the polls only by national personalities and issues. In areas of a consistently tighter party balance, the impact of national politics upon local candidacies is greater, and perhaps more consistently accumulative in spite of their relatively small party shifts.

Secular movements at the top of the tickets produce a horizon of politics quite sharply separated from the more purely local-state voting underlying it. So it is quite likely that the complementary predispositions of voters in New Mexico's areas of a one-party dominance have most strongly militated at lower levels of the tickets against "a redressing of the political balance and a revival of two-party competition."[23] Whatever the cause, the currents of secular movement which the parties manifest at the top of the ticket are rather effectively reduced to eddies when the offices concerned have few functions substantially affecting opinion or state operations. Even at the lower levels of the ticket, however, there is probably a significant potential available to exploitation in some areas by the long-term minority.

Table 34 describes changes in the aggregate percentage vote for five statewide candidates lowest on the ticket. In each group of coun-

TABLE 34. Shifting Base and Trend of Votes for Republican Candidates for Five Minor State Offices[a]

Area	Area's percentage of total state vote		Percentage of area vote to 5 minor candidates		Republican gains or losses	
	(1) 1940-48	(2) 1950-60	(3) 1940-48	(4) 1950-60	(5) In percentage points[b]	(6) In index points[c]
Hispanic counties	39.7	31.1	48.3	44.3	−4.0	−535.6
Little Texas counties	17.1	19.5	29.2	34.5	5.3	173.6
Bernalillo County	16.0	24.6	45.6	48.8	3.2	471.9
Other counties	27.2	24.7	43.0	40.7	2.3	163.8
State	...	...	43.1	42.6	−0.5	−53.9

[a] Auditor, treasurer, attorney general, land commissioner, and secretary of state. Percentages of cols. 3 and 4 are calculated from sums of votes cast for the five offices for each period.
[b] Entry of col. 4 minus that of col. 3.
[c] Calculated from col. entries: (2) x (4) — (1) x (3).

ties except "Other," the gains or losses in the second decade are consistent with the gains or losses of the Republican party as measured in the governors' elections. (The category of "Other" counties includes three mining counties which have moved toward Democratic increases.) The Little Texas counties have produced a significant switch at the presidential and gubernatorial elections, but there (see Table 26) the gulf between levels of the ticket is widest. The most damaging loss to the Republicans occurred in the Hispanic counties where party voting is most consistent — a loss of votes not compensated by the larger percentage-point gain in Little Texas where relatively less of the political gain was realized for those lower on the ticket.

The other facet of this matter is that the compelling exigencies of meeting the competition in the close areas have probably drawn a disproportionate outlay of Republican effort there, for the party has consistently made its maximum efforts in the northern counties. Only in 1950 and the campaigns of 1960-1964 did the emphasis shift so that Little Texas and similar counties, as well as Bernalillo and the North, became objects of intensive campaigning. The maxim of highest effort in areas of strength has been adequately tested in New Mexico; but the North-county trend has nevertheless been adverse for minor Republican candidates, for impulses of the party vote there are visible far down the ticket.

In the North few electors are called out only by the presidential elections; in the eastern and southern counties relatively little attention is paid to minor candidacies by the augmented presidential electorate, and it is probably this factor which is most damaging to the minority party's cause. In spite of such limiting circumstances, Table 34 indicates, the movements of the parties at one level tend eventually to induce some movement at the next. The 60-40 balance of the 1920's in the Hispanic counties against Democratic candidates at all levels of the ticket has about been reversed. Several Hispanic counties have made a spectacular shift to a Democratic attachment, while one reversed the field and moved from Democratic to Republican. Seven or eight counties of other areas have moved away from strongly Democratic positions. It appears, therefore, that the movement of New Mexico's counties would seem to justify Miller's tentative observation that there is "some small evidence, that . . . more change in party identification may take place in defiance of the community environment than takes place in accord with that environment."[24]

FIVE

Party and Factional Organization, 1900-1934

ELECTORAL and oganizational activities of New Mexico's parties in the period 1900-1934 provide a classic example of two-party politics. In this era of intense and, on the whole, even competition, the balance of party strength was appreciably shifting from Republican to Democratic. The nature of the party balance contributed to the formation of U. S. Senator Bronson Cutting's bipartisan faction, and the actions of the parties and of Cutting's Progressive faction were profoundly conditioned by the convention system of nominations. Conversely, activities of the Cutting-Progressive group contributed to a growing strength of the Democratic party; and, in the Republican party, to the eventual replacement of the "Old Guard" by the Progressive wing.

THE BASE AND SHIFT OF THE PARTY BALANCE

With the end of the second Cleveland administration in 1897, Republicans of New Mexico Territory entered upon a decade when every success seemed but to lead to another. Party and administration were operating under the mantle of Marcus Hanna's enlightened capitalism; in the territory, Miguel A. Otero, Sr. was beginning a nine-year term in the governorship. With the exception of territorial secretary and the judiciary, every appointment was "Gillie" Otero's to make. A simple and lucrative patronage system enabled corporate and private contributors to assist the treasury of the national party; for strategically located around the territory were a score of mounted patrolmen, and the one office of coal oil inspector sustained the party's faithful with $40,000 per year.[1]

When Theodore Roosevelt succeeded to the presidency, many New Mexicans of Democratic areas who had served in his regiment promptly made themselves his local allies, publicly joining the party which, it is said, became "a political machine so powerful that even the appointment of notary public was considered in some localities a great favor."[2] Albert Bacon Fall, one of the more effective and flamboyant of the Democrats of the southern counties, turned Republican in 1906, explaining years later: " 'I know when to change horses.' "[3]

Margins in the elections for delegate to Congress were scanty, but Republicans estimated with calm assurance that they would dominate the constitutional convention of 1910 by a two-thirds majority—a claim that fell below the seventy-one seats attained to the twenty-nine of the Democrats and the one Socialist.[4] Yet, in the first election a year later, the party lost the governorship, one of two congressmen, and five other state offices. And in the next eighteen years, the party lost about as many statewide contests as it won. Albert Fall did not, in fact, know when to change horses.

Tardily appearing electoral results of the post-1900 shift and growth of population began to run strongly against the Republican party after 1910. At the beginning of the decade, nine principal Hispanic counties central to the Republican hegemony contained 67 per cent of the population; by 1910 their population was only about half the total. Succeeding increments of population were smaller, but again most marked in the more Democratic areas.

Habits of voting participation in various areas maintained the precarious party balance for a time, for where the Hispanic counties took rather full advantage of their voter increments, the Little Texas and border counties did not. The state's 1920-1930 increase in voter turnout from 106,000 to 118,000 amounted to only 11 per cent, while the population increased by 17 per cent. During the ensuing six years the population increased by about 65,000; but, as Figure 15 indicates, the advent of the New Deal attracted an additional 50,000 votes in the three elections of 1932-1936. This 42-per-cent increase in the active electorate bent steeply upward the curve of Democratic strength.

Eight counties leading in percentage of gain in voter turnout during the three elections of 1932-1936 were Lea, Roosevelt, Eddy, Curry, Catron, Doña Ana, Bernalillo, and Chaves. Catron, as it still is, was a huge but scantily populated ranching area. Doña Ana is the only county of the group central to the Old Guard Republican organization.

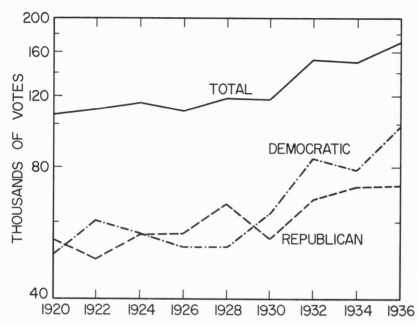

FIGURE 15.—Democratic voters account for two-thirds of gain in voting for governor, 1920-1936.

Five of the counties are of the six Little Texas counties of the heavily Democratic east side.

The eight counties went from 34,000 votes to 59,000 votes for governor in the three elections for a gain of 74 per cent. They gave a 59-per-cent Democratic majority in 1930 and one of 65 per cent in 1936. Conversion of voting margins and gains to ratios indicates that the Democratic party may have received 74 per cent of the new votes; if so, the Democratic percentage of the total "new" votes received in those areas registering marked increases in voter turnout was perhaps higher by about ten points than it was in the state as a whole.

The previously high voting levels of the ten Hispanic counties of the Republican coalition permitted their 1930-1936 voting to increase by only 37 per cent, while in the six counties of Little Texas the total vote increased by 90 per cent. The rate of increase in the northern and Hispanic counties was not significantly greater than the rate of population increase; the 90-per-cent jump in the vote of Little Texas and several similar counties indicates that a substantial proportion of their increase was cast by an electorate which had not been voting before.[5]

ORGANIZATIONAL AND VOTING BASE OF REPUBLICAN POWER

The political framework of the new state was the reflection of an old organization. Long prior to 1900 there had developed a political establishment of considerable skill and permanence based on the dominant counties of the Rio Grande and Upper Pecos valleys. If Colfax be included there were eleven key Republican counties and within each there were one or more individuals of political energy and acumen who could direct the local work necessary to win elections, act in concert with other politicians, and work successfully at the higher level of strategy and abstraction required by state and national politics.

At the time of statehood the dominant Republican group included such political notables as T. D. Burns, Ed Sargent, and B. C. Hernandez of Rio Arriba County; Malaquias Martinez of Taos; Charles and Frank Springer of Colfax and Santa Fe; Tom Catron and George Armijo of Santa Fe; Holm Bursum of Socorro; Felipe Hubbell of Bernalillo; Charles Spiess and Secundino Romero of San Miguel; Albert Fall of Doña Ana; and Solomon Luna, Sylvestre Mirabal, and Eduardo M. Otero of Valencia. Their counties, with Mora, accounted for fifty-five members of the constitutional convention; and, with the several counties within the area of their political dominance, they accounted for a full two-thirds of the membership of one hundred. It was these Republican *políticos* who were known throughout the state as the "Old Guard."

The Old Guard's power was inherently a fragile one, however, resting as it did upon an increasingly restive base of Hispanic votes. With Mora and Guadalupe counties (but excluding Colfax) the counties listed with some of their political leaders are those ten whose populations as late as 1950 were still 50 per cent or more Hispanic. The eleven counties cast 55 per cent of their vote in 1908 for the Republican candidate for delegate to Congress, and 54 per cent in 1906.[6] It was on such slender majorities as these that the party dominated the state, and it was these counties which enabled it to hold for so long to its power to set legislative policy.

With the shift of population running strongly against areas at the base of Republican strength in the period 1900-1920, organizations at the county level enjoyed a lop-sided voting strength in one county, a strong but not unquestioned majority in five or six others, and a marginal and easily lost majority in nine or ten. Republicans were drastically outnumbered in the remaining eight or nine counties. In consequence, the pattern of competition and the attitudes and alignments of voting groups in the counties were by no means set by the Republican organizations alone. In every county, not excepting Valencia where the then badly outnumbered Democrats maintained only a nuclear but active organization, there was a vigorous and highly visible Democratic organization that consistently fielded a full county and legislative ticket, and sent full delegations to the state convention.

Factional disturbances were frequent in both parties in the Hispanic counties, and, since they could not be settled within the nonexistent direct primary, they frequently resulted in the overt shifting of small factional or "fusionist" groups, as they were called, to the opposition party. This maneuver could be drastically punished if it lost, but the ease of creation and frequency of factional groups tended to make the local leadership of both parties acutely sensitive to local groups and demands. Hence, although the operation of state-level politics (in the Republican party particularly) was strongly hierarchical, it was so in a rather contingent fashion; for the county base of each party's state organization required it to engage endlessly in the type of bargaining and concession granting that Dahl and Lindblom have called polyarchical control of leaders.[7] And from 1912 to 1934 the Old Guard was compelled to bargain with the increasing strength of the Cutting faction or face defeat—the latter a consequence it was at last willing to accept. So, in their mutual association in state politics, the Old Guard could not always act as a unified system of power responsive to one center or person of authority. In consequence, the party leadership was frequently compelled to act as an internally controlled polyarchy. By and large, there could be no necessary unity or apex of political power in the Republican party system, based as it was upon party organizations marginally dominant in from ten to a dozen key counties.

There was, however, the always present need to work to a concert of action in which a reasonably clear consensus would prevail. The Old Guard, composed as it was of a dozen or so principal figures and a few score experienced local politicians, was a stable but flexible organization. Disruptions could and did occur, but they were doubtless regarded as costly and foolish. In spite of occasional schisms in the hustings, unity of the Old Guard was usually achieved at the policy-making levels—it was the most economic means of maintaining the concert of interests welding party and legislature into a functioning organization. Effective though it proved to be, the Republican system of political management never approached the condition of oligarchy held inevitable in Michels' "Iron Law." The Old Guard was subject to numerous checks by the party membership as well as by the opposition. The toughest of them would no doubt have been astonished and disbelieving of the claim that "in the history of party life it is undeniable that the democratic system is reduced, in ultimate analysis, to the right of the masses, at stated intervals, to choose masters to whom in the interim they owe unconditional obedience."[8]

The New Mexico state senate is described in the following chapter as the pit in which the Republican Old Guard conducted its concert of interests and attitudes. The senate was also the cellar to which the faction retired when the winds of politics were adverse. But, although the legislature was a redoubt costing but little to maintain, the Old Guard and its affiliated interests could not well remain entrenched there indefinitely. Party leaders were fully aware that the loss of any element of strength would contribute to the loss of others, and so they were constrained to do more than rely upon legislative brokerage— they were forced to undertake the far more expensive operations and forays of aggressive party operations designed to capture the govership and seats in the U.S. Senate.

Four electoral defeats in the period 1911-1924—after a rapid increase in the size of the electorate—compelled, in the mid-twenties, a more elaborate organization which might better bridge the gulf between the economic interests central to the party, and the county organizations. There was also a need to fill a gap in party organization in the rapidly growing Little Texas and southern counties. For this purpose there was created a position best described as "party manager."

The new position was long identified with Ed Safford, who was, in fact, its only occupant; and who later became state chairman and in 1946 the party's candidate for the governorship. Mrs. Safford was for some years county clerk of Santa Fe County, or employed there when she was ineligible to run, as she was deemed a good politician in her own right. With this backlog of security for the family fortunes, Safford was enabled to serve the party as its manager or executive assistant at a salary that was usually $250 per month plus a somewhat limited expense account—a sum deemed to be ample, for "Ed was also a very sharp poker player."

Safford's salary and expense fund was made up principally by Ed Sargent, Charles Springer, George Kaseman, and the "Chino Copper Crowd," and for years he got his check from an official of the Chino Division of the Kennecott Company. The Phelps Dodge Corporation and W. A. Hawkins, its counsel, tax and legislative agent, could always be relied on for additional funds if needed, and so could the Santa Fe and Southern Pacific Railroad Companies.

Several leaders of the party have described Safford's role as being limited to organizational matters, and one stressed that he "had to consult on policy." Another stressed that Safford was a good politician who knew both sides of his role. That is, he was constrained to consult on policy in those instances when policy was still unformed, but he was otherwise expected to put policy into performance. In addition, it is said, Safford was a "walking delegate," one of whose prime functions was to keep other party chieftains informed of those matters essential to their own role in the party. He served, therefore, as party intelligence agent as well as its organizational representative.

Another instrument deemed indispensable at the time was the press, which the leadership of both parties strove mightily to control, own, or influence. (In the early years, the *New Mexico Blue Book* regularly listed newspapers by their party affiliation.)

McNary has written that when he bought the Las Vegas *Optic* in 1903 it was "with the co-operation and financial assistance of a number of prominent Republicans of the state."[9] The friends who helped buy it were Holm Bursum, W. H. Andrews, and H. W. Kelly. Governor Otero then appointed McNary public printer after taking the job away from M. L. Frost of Santa Fe.[10] Albert B. Fall for a time owned the *Mesilla Valley Democrat,* and author Eugene Manlove Rhodes was employed briefly as editor of the Roswell *Daily Record* to give that sheet a proper Democratic tone.[11] In 1919, Governor Larrazolo informed Lieutenant Governor Ben Pankey that he was writing party chieftains about securing control of *La Revista de Taos*[12]— a venture that was undertaken, for Charles Springer wrote Holm Bursum four years later:

The Revista de Taos, Taos Valley News and Boletin Popular are consolidated and conveyed to three trustees: Hon. Ramon Sanchez,

Hon. Malaquias Martinez and myself. The papers have been running behind about $100 per month average. Don Ramon has contributed about $200. I have put up the balance. I have paid the interest on the $6,100 note and about $3,500 expense of the papers. You paid $300. None of the others paid anything except $440 pd. by Mr. Kelly. . . . Hon. Frank Hubbell, D. J. Leahy, N. W. Kelly and Geo. Craig signed the old note. Ed Sargent and W. G. Sargent and Ed Otero should have signed and they should sign the new note.

Please see Cap't W. C. Reid about this. The RY co. ought to help us out on this. They are surely interested in having a Republican State Senate and Republican U.S. Senate elected next year. . . .[13]

The Taxpayers' Association took an inventory in 1924 indicating that Democrats were slightly ahead in this field of political operation:

There are 87 newspapers in New Mexico, of which 11 are printed in the Spanish language. As to political affiliation, 30 are Republican, 33 Democratic, 8 Independent, 3 Independent Republican, 6 Independent Democratic, 2 Progressive and 5 unknown affiliations.[14]

To be able to subsidize at public expense the friendly segment of the press was one of the highly valued attributes of electoral victory, for the party which controlled state and local official printing was thereby relieved of a considerable burden. In the 1926 campaign, for example, Bronson Cutting is said by responsible party leaders to have put $19,000 into the Republican campaign fund for the sole purpose of acquiring news space and friendly editorial policy for the Republican ticket. M. L. Fox, an able journalist, was employed by the party to write its material and the party sought agreement with as many papers as possible to print all or part of it at regular advertising rates, whether or not the material appeared as news copy. A good many papers, particularly the smaller weeklies, took advantage of the opportunity.

After the 1924 defeat of the strong but predominantly Old Guard ticket, the Republican central committee was reorganized in the spring of 1925 and later undertook a campaign of continuous pledge financing among party notables while it sought to build up some sagging county organizations. A dinner meeting in Santa Fe of the more active of the party faithful was presented with:

a plan for raising subscriptions in the amount of $15,000 a year for three years. . . . [We were] successful in securing subscriptions for a large part of the total fund proposed, which we later supplemented by further solicitation among prominent Republicans over the state who were not present at the meeting. We finally were successful in securing pledges for the total amount.[15]

In addition to this fund for the maintenance of state headquarters, approximately $50,000 was raised for the campaign of 1926.[16] For money and organized effort the 1926 Republican campaign was not to have a rival until the Dewey-Lujan campaign of 1948.

THE DEMOCRATS—FROM OPPOSITION TO MAJORITY

The story of the Democratic party in New Mexico from McKinley's day to the New Deal can properly be told as an essay on the uses of adversity. From the beginning of the century, New Mexico's Democrats were forced to play the game on a field they did not lay out, by rules they did not write, and, except for 1912-1920, subject to the refereeing of a Republican national administration. Their problem was that of marshaling the forces of agrarian discontent and new population elements into a stable voting base, and retaining stronghold areas and finding breeding places for political talent while they sought the means of breaking the Republican coalition; if not in all of its parts, then in enough so that some of the river and mountain communities could be induced to shade their normal Republican majorities.

Democrats achieved a strength nearly equal to that of the Republicans, but, in spite of strenuous efforts for the first twenty-five years after statehood, the politics of the period may be characterized as one of stasis. The conservative legislative program of the Republicans, the continuing inability of the Progressive faction of Bronson Cutting to do much more than march across the county and convention battlegrounds, the lack of stirring issues in national politics, and, perhaps, the even party balance, had dampening effects upon New Mexico's politics—full of sound and fury though it was.

The stalemate persisted until the forces which created the New Deal had their full impact also in New Mexico, but the long period of closely balanced and vigorous politics had permitted the development of an experienced and able group of Democratic political leaders and operators. The party that National Chairman James Farley came to inspect prior to the elections of 1934 was a tough, going concern which he could safely counsel to throw out the Cutting Progressives.

Changes occurring during the era were amplified and confirmed by the advent of the New Deal, and it is probable that the New Deal released tendencies which had long been present.

When Octaviano Larrazolo ran as the Democratic candidate for congressional delegate in the last two elections before statehood, his losing margins were only a few hundred votes; and in those elections he and his fellow candidates commanded a significant support in all but a few counties. Except in Valencia, and perhaps Sandoval County, Democratic organizations throughout the territory were substantial groupings. Democratic conventions in the northern Hispanic counties were not attended, as the Republican meetings were, with available candidates "three deep," but on balance it appears that the Democratic party of the day had a better organizational system of local party groups across the state than the Republicans had developed. In the border counties of the southeast, Republican candidates for state office could count on 30-35 per cent of the vote; in the Hispanic counties the Democrats could count on 40 per cent or more, and in most elections Democrats could win in one or several of those counties. In the southeast, the Republican organizations were of the nuclear sort needed to make local nominations and find convention delegates; in the north, the Democratic groups were more extensive, and although they had no manpower to spare they customarily had fully staffed precinct organizations. The northern Democrats, moreover, were more apt than southern Republicans to find their following augmented from time to time by organized groups of dissidents from the majority party. And the Democratic state organization was fully as active as the Republican in attempting to further the local factions.

Since no man active in the politics of 1920-1928 was apt to have foreseen that the forces which were to lead to the New Deal would have the effect of bringing out a sizeable new electorate in those counties most committed to the Democratic party, it was as inevitable as it was political wisdom for Democratic leaders of the time to expend great efforts in the Hispanic counties.

Those who sought to break the Hispanic-Republican attachment were fully aware of the necessities of the strategic situation, but their tactical tasks were not always easy. The Texas attitude to New Mexico's native Hispanic population was always apt to be tinged with folk memories of the Alamo, and Hispanic leaders and voters were, and are, sensitive to any real or fancied slight of their own group pride. Thus, in ending in 1911 his long attachment to the Democratic party, Larrazolo stated his conviction that the party had failed to make a due place for Hispanic citizens residing in strongly Democratic counties and raised the question whether such conduct manifested "any disposition to fraternize and do equal justice to all." There was, he noted, "an element of intolerance that should not be countenanced or encouraged."[17]

Friction between Democratic party groups was apparent at several of the early conventions, as in 1918 when:

> the delegates . . . disregarding the advice of their party leaders, proceeded to nominate a ticket in their own happy fashion and twice at least permitted a straight line-up to get in the record between the native counties and the "Texas Democrat" counties in which the latter ran the steam roller over the former on each occasion without so much as splitting a delegation.[18]

Hispanic candidates sought five and received three of the twelve nominations of the 1918 convention. Ten years later, the Republican convention met a week after the Democratic, a circumstance which enabled Republicans again to take advantage of the same situation:

> There were differences between the Spanish-Americans and the Anglo element throughout the [Democratic] convention. The difference was largely due to the formation of the state party ticket. The Spanish-Americans were demanding six positions on the state ticket and threatened to leave the convention unless their demands were met. . . . George Armijo . . . after much compromising, was able to restore harmony and the rebellious 200 delegates returned to the convention.[19]

The convention finally succeeded in nominating three Hispanic candidates while the Republicans placed six, and the matter became of considerable importance in the campaign.

The Democratic party was only slightly less successful over the years, however, than the Republican in making a place for Hispanic members. During the period 1910-1930 Republicans gave forty (35 per cent) of 113 biennial convention nominations to Hispanic candidates; Democrats gave thirty-five (31 per cent); but in nominations for U.S. senator, congressman, and governor there was a greater difference. Republican Hispanic candidates received two nominations for senator, eight for congressman, and two for governor for a total of twelve places at the top of the ticket. Democratic Hispanic candidates received one senatorial nomination, three for congress, and two for governor, for a total of six during the period.

Throughout the period of tight electoral balance, leaders of the Democratic party were consistent and diligent in their efforts to capitalize on factional disturbances in the northern counties.

Most notable of the organizational and tactical specialists of the Democratic party was Arthur Seligman who, in the territorial period, was a wholesaler supplying many of the little stores in the north. Seligman began attending conventions as early as 1904 and, in the words of an Hispanic Democratic leader of Taos County, "helped us a lot." An intelligent, active man who knew a host of people, Seligman became a banker who kept himself poor in a succession of political assignments ranging from county chairman, state chairman, and national committeeman, and finally, to the governorship.

Seligman was not alone as a party agent. There were other good ones, but he was outstanding; and the obituary written by his close friend and business associate records that before and during his governorship Seligman was tireless in traveling about and making arrangements for state and local tickets.[20] He was "a great one for building fusions"[21] — a political technique as old as party politics in the state. Seligman, in his unpaid role, performed many of the same functions as Ed Safford performed as a paid professional for the Republican party.

Seligman's capacities did not go unremarked, for as Miguel Otero remarked in one of his chatty letters to Senator Cutting:

Arthur [Seligman] will certainly make the best chairman for the Democrats; he is great on stirring up Independent moves, and should he take hold, I look for an Independent movement.[22]

In fulfilling his gubernatorial obligations to the Cutting faction,

Seligman awarded them numerous patronage posts, a matter which caused some dissension among the party regulars. He explained the strategy:

"Elections are so close in New Mexico that the result usually depends on which way the independent vote swings."

Governor Seligman added, however, that he does not believe the recognition given the Independent Republicans has been out of proportion.

This was the first public statement made by Governor Seligman on this phase of the administration's appointments since the names of Independent Republicans now holding office appointively were announced shortly after the first of the year.

The Independent Republicans are generally interpreted to be the political followers of United States Senator Bronson Cutting.[23]

Party splits and fusions with one or the other of the parties were frequent at the local level of politics in the north and seem often to have been related to contests over local positions of control and patronage. For example, in the 1922 elections, although Bronson Cutting was ostensibly committed to Hill, the Republican gubernatorial nominee, as well as to Democrat Jones seeking the U.S. Senate seat, he and Seligman worked quietly to build the fusion ticket in Taos County aimed at Republican county chairman Malaquias Martinez.

The Independent Republicans are estimated to have a voting strength of 900 in Taos County.

At the 1922 election five Democratic candidates were elected . . . with majorities running up to 800. This was credited to the Independent Republicans.[24]

In the 1924 elections, fusions of Democrats and disgruntled Republicans were made in Taos, San Miguel, and Valencia counties, but only in San Miguel were more than a few score of votes on the state ticket affected. Each switch left, however, a residue of party members or workers who would stick with their new affiliation, and each tended to build new nuclear groups for future factional activities.

Factions served also to augment the Democratic supply of high-level political talent, as did the formation of Progressive blocs during the period 1912-1924.

When the Democratic state convention followed in Santa Fe,
October 2 [1911], it was announced that "Independent Republicans," headed by Herbert J. Hagerman and Richard H. Hanna,
Santa Fe lawyer, wished to join in forming a fusion ticket and
the offer was eagerly accepted by the Democrats.[25]

Hagerman soon returned to the Republican party as a member in
good standing, but Hanna became the unanimous choice of the 1920
Democratic convention as its nominee for governor.

It was typical of Democratic politics of the era that its leadership
echelons were more open and fractious than those of the Republicans.
Nominations in the Democratic conventions were more often made
after sharp contests, and the major positions more often attracted
numerous candidates. Both Seligman and Cutting were not only several times in the field for nominations to senate and governorship,
but they actively sought party control. They got neither until 1930,
nor did any other group achieve an unequivocal ascendancy in the
party until Hannett was able to use his gubernatorial office to dominate the 1926 convention. Even Hannett, however, was to lose the
support of a strong Albuquerque faction which joined with the Cutting forces to support the Republican ticket. And, in 1924, it had
been the convention and its Little-Texas-oriented factions rather than
nominee Hannett who chose the new state chairman. In the main,
the more numerous and raucous of the factional support garnered
by Seligman and other party operators was more apt to respond to
the Cutting spurs than to party curbs.

The parties differed, but those differences were more subtle, and
party leadership more pragmatic, than a simple conservative-
progressive division would indicate. The first two governors, Mc-
Donald and C de Baca, Democrats both, were liberal enough to cause
some apprehension among the Republican guardians of the legislature. McDonald reflected the surge of Progressive sentiment stirring
Little Texas in 1912, and even Larrazolo, after his conversion to
Republicanism, was by no means immune to the leanings of his past,
but it was Cutting who articulated the premises and provided the
liberal leadership goading both parties. Highly competitive, each
party sought strenuously to avoid disruption of the mixed array of
interests confronting it, and each tended to make the same adjustments to group demands and in about the same terms.[26]

Governor Merritt Mechem, Republican, was more representative of the interests and attitudes of the southern and eastern areas of the state than previous nominees and his liberalist, but unsuccessful, legislative program reflected that attitude. His two Democratic successors, Hinkle (1923) and Hannett (1925), each sought (and gained little of) a legislative and administrative program paralleling much of Mechem's. (Liberal planks frequently turned up in the platforms of the party currently enjoying Cutting's support.) But, although Democratic legislators were more apt than Republicans to support items like direct primaries, increased aid to schools, and public health expenditures, the differences were not significant. Both Hinkle and Hannett were later to emerge as key members of the conservative wing of the Democratic party, and none of the three saw fit to disturb the arrangement which permitted the Taxpayers' Association to construct the state's budgets.

Within the geographic strongholds of the Democratic party, Hinkle and Hannett represented much the same group and social interests that the Republican Old Guard represented in their legislative and party activities. The Republicans, operating within a framework of powerful local party organizations, incorporated spokesmen of many of the dominant interests of the state in their leadership. Hinkle and Hannett, and other Democrats of the time, operated within a somewhat more fluid and dispersed political organization reflecting social attitudes of rapidly growing Bernalillo County and the counties of the south and east. Democrats represented interests of farm and municipality rather than ranching, transportation, and mining. The differences were not sharp, but they were indicative of the strivings of new groups.

Party differences were those of style, technique, and organization as much as they were of group affiliation or intellectual outlook. To the Republicans a governor was a lieutenant in the line, not the commander; but when Hannett was asked who was in command of the party and its convention during his governorship the quick reply was: "Why, dammit, I was."[27] Others who should know confirm that Hannett did indeed make his mark on his party as no Republican governor had done. Although Hannett's unequivocal attitudes about party leadership and policy gained the support of his Little Texas and border county colleagues, they brought a bitter break with Bronson Cutting.

BIPARTY FACTIONALISM AND DESTRUCTION OF THE REPUBLICAN
OLD GUARD

"Faction," in the current terminology, usually designates a party
element "whose purpose is to control the personnel and policies *of
the party*."[28] In a description of New Mexico's politics of 1912-1934
the term properly refers also to a biparty group, well financed and
ably led, whose object it was to control both parties. The situation
then obtaining was precisely that described by Leiserson in his finding
of party cycles sometimes productive of periods

> of extremely close competition between the parties when their
> strength is so evenly balanced that the shift of a small minority
> holding the balance of power can throw the government into oppo-
> sition and vice versa. This situation almost approximates that of
> a multi-party parliamentary system, and accentuates internecine
> factional party strife.[29]

This "third force" was the reflection and instrument of Bronson
Cutting, friend and associate of notable mavericks like Wisconsin's
Robert LaFollette the younger, and Hiram Johnson of California.[30]
It is notable that Cutting duplicated the feat of the elder LaFollette
and Johnson, "prominent . . . advocates of the primary," in attain-
ing power through the "convention system, which established that
their brand of politics was not completely blocked off by that procedure."[31]

To a substantial degree the Cutting faction was *sui generis*. It
relied heavily also upon a segment of the Spanish-American vote.
For these reasons Cutting's mode of operation is worth describing
in detail sufficient to permit the reader to discount, perhaps, the
weight here accorded it.

The Cutting Faction: Biparty Third Force

Bronson Cutting was reared in the patrician tradition of his contemporaries Theodore and Franklin Delano Roosevelt, following hard
upon the heels of FDR to Groton and Harvard. Tuberculosis forced
his removal to Santa Fe in 1910 where his wealth, considerable talents, and the acquisition of a good daily newspaper permitted his
easy entrance into politics. There is little doubt that his entrance into

politics was deliberate or that Cutting intended to exercise on his own terms whatever power he could summon.

Dissident Republicans, in 1911, formed the core of the Progressive Republican League, which was to become the Progressive Party of New Mexico in the following year. The League successfully sought defeat of the Republican Old Guard leadership and passage of the "Blue Ballot" amendment. In the 1912 congressional and presidential elections, Cutting became an officer of the Progressive Party and energetically sought Roosevelt's election; perhaps, as has been said, to achieve a third party. "Whereas in 1911 Cutting was interested in the idea of a reforming wing within the Republican Party, by 1912 he was anxious to accept a third party—an idea he never completely relinquished."[32]

Cutting was not destined to supplant the leadership of either party until 1934 and relied, instead, on a personally led and financed third force or independent faction—an alternative presciently described by his father as available to him when Cutting was considering whether to join the Democratic party or to continue his Progressive association:

It may be, of course, that your little band of so-called "Progressives" may be able to keep up an organization that will hold the balance of power, and be able to compel the nomination of the best men of either party to buy your support, but it is not easy to hold together any political body on a basis of pure altruism. . . . The nomination of good men is not the only demand such a body must make; it must frequently demand the nomination of its own good men, and so, to an extent, weaken its reputation for altruism, and gradually draw near to the machine condition.

It may also be that you, personally, may prefer to play with Democrats for a while, or permanently.[33]

In the elections of 1911-1934 no candidate, other than Republican Merritt Mechem in 1920, was elected governor who was opposed by the Cutting faction. But not until 1932 did the faction strenuously attempt to capture control of local conventions in order to secure control of the state conventions. Meanwhile, however, Cutting had sufficient strength in both parties to veto a good many potential nominations as he did in 1924 to force the withdrawal of Democratic

Governor Hinkle. Hinkle had lost favor with Cutting and Hispanic leaders, and,

a strong faction spearheaded by a solid Santa Fe delegation opposed the renomination of Governor Hinkle. This element claimed 277 of the total of 606 votes and supported the recently converted Cutting for governor. Moreover, they threatened to bolt if Hinkle were renominated, and the Cutting faction had demonstrated its capacity to do just that.

. . . . .

In the end the choice was made without serious disagreement. With Hinkle out Cutting also withdrew.[34]

Within a few months, "Cutting, as was his custom, broke with the administration," and in the next campaign became Republican again to support Dillon.[35]

In 1927, Governor Dillon appointed Cutting to the United States Senate where he promptly became a member of the Progressive bloc. Cutting stayed "regular" during the remainder of Dillon's first term and won election to his seat in 1928. Thereafter, however, he publicly supported the Democratic gubernatorial candidacies in 1930 and 1932 of Arthur Seligman, that of Roosevelt in 1932, and by 1930 had accomplished a wholesale wreckage of the Republican party.

As the summer passed the Republican organization was torn to shreds. One county convention after another staged factional fights. In some cases the Cutting faction was strong enough to seize control; where they were not they bolted.[36]

Cutting's Method

Cutting's *modus operandi* is perhaps not unique, but on a stage as small as that provided by New Mexico the scale of his political operations was of imposing proportion.

The New Mexican, in 1910, had a circulation of about 500 and was kept alive, under Paul A. F. Walter's editorship, as a Republican organ, principally by its receipts as the official publication of state, city, and county. A former associate of Cutting states that the paper broke even for only two years under Cutting's ownership, and that in the early part of the period it was losing as much as $12,000 per year and in the later about $40,000.[37] Among the assets of Cutting's estate after his death in 1935 were listed fourteen miscellaneous notes, not of record, from the publishing corporation to Cutting for a total of $185,622. There were an additional thirty-two notes of record of $2,500 each for a total of $80,000, so the paper apparently accumulated a minimum total loss of $265,622 during the twenty-two year period, or an average annual loss of over $12,000.[38]

Cutting also made personal loans of which most were not of record to at least eleven newspaper men and women of the state.[39] According to reliable sources of the newspaper fraternity, Cutting also assisted several individuals in acquiring or maintaining four other newspapers in the state. Cutting's *New Mexican* reported without comment allegations that Cutting had bought or controlled a large part of the press of New Mexico.[40] As early as 1929 one of Cutting's Old Guard enemies in the state senate asked:

Are we a group of free men or a group of legislative vassals who are permitting a man that speaks through the press in this state that is owned and controlled by one distinguished private citizen . . .?[41]

A remark by Cutting is perhaps indicative of an attitude:

Many thanks for your letter of May 25th, enclosing the dodger from the Las Vegas Optic.

Personally, I think that this kind of attack, from the extreme reactionaries, is the most valuable kind of publicity. . . . As long as the Optic adopts this kind of policy, I should certainly not want to do anything to stop it. If, through any calamity, it should come out for me, I should feel that self-interest would prompt its suppression or purchase.[42]

The editor of the *Optic* had earlier made reference to "the Cutting newspapers.[43]

Factional alignments of various elements of the press contributed to an open squabble among editors and publishers in 1934, and the *New Mexican* reported of the 1935 press association meeting after Cutting's death that only "about a score of the nearly one hundred members of the newspaper and printing industry of the state" were

present at the convention. "Whether the organization will continue
to thrive as it did in 1933 . . . seemed to be a moot question."[44]
The *Albuquerque Journal* laconically reported that: "Stringent efforts
were made by the elements present to prevent political considerations
from entering into the proceedings of the convention. It appeared
that politics would be relegated to a back seat."[45]

Cutting was a prime mover in the formation of the national and
state American Legion, and until his death was to rely heavily on
the Legion in his political activities. Prior to the Legion's first national convention in 1919, Cutting became temporary state chairman.
He paid many of the early expenses of the state Legion and subsi-
dized the organizational work of Miguel Otero, Jr., Henry Dorman,
and Donald Blevins, the latter " 'an Irish K. C.' who had impressed
him as secretary of the Organization Committee in St. Louis."[46]
Thirty-one posts were established in the state by September 1919.
Cutting was to break with the reactionary directorship of the national
Legion in the 'twenties, when the Legion was supporting the Americanization Commission: "Alvin M. Owsley, assistant director of the
Americanization Commission, refused to permit deviation from the
national program and wrote that he could not understand how Cutting could condone the continuance of Spanish as a language of
instruction."[47]

> The veteran vote so closely supported Cutting's policies that
> the national organization of the American Legion later charged
> that the New Mexico Legion was a Cutting political machine and
> gave this as the official reason for a threatened revocation of the
> State Charter.
>
> . . . . .
>
> There is no doubt that the American Legion in New Mexico
> was actively engaged in politics.[48]

Former Governor A. T. Hannett has observed that Seligman and
Cutting "tried to high pressure me into creating a labor department
and a veteran's bureau. . . . I refused to go along on it. Their argument was that whoever controlled labor and veterans could control
the politics of the state.[49]

A good literary friend and admirer of Cutting has stated:

It is true that Cutting is not a frantic partisan, but a wise man. It is true that he is an influence in the councils of both parties in New Mexico—It is not true that any dollar of his has been used with his knowledge, consent, desire or connivance—or convenient blindness—to buy any man's vote.

Cutting encouraged, if he did not actually organize—the Spanish-American Society. Not a partisan affair . . . it insists that half of the candidates on each ticket, shall be Mexicans.

. . . . .

Senator Cutting has given his money freely to non-partisan, or more accurately, bipartisan societies—and to American Legion posts, a billiard table, a tennis court. . . . Also legitimate travel and hotel expenses of candidates, committee men, etc., in actual campaigns. A thousand details to be told by the moonlight alone. . . .

I'm for him. God knows that I'm no Republican, but then, neither is Cutting.

. . . . .

Note well! Cutting's Santa Fe *New Mexican* is the only paper or magazine in the U.S. that has *courage enough to let me say my say*. As my opinions are invariably the opposite of Senator Cutting's—as in the matter of John Barleycorn, D. H. Lawrence and sich—well, that's the kind of man I want. Not a retrograde, a progressive, a progressing along. . . .[50]

Tales told in New Mexico of Cutting's long-famed largesse seem prodigal, but are, none the less, scarcely exaggerated if the disposition of his estate is a fair indicator.

Probate proceedings after Cutting's death in 1935 dealt in part with a list of 500 notes representing $500,000 in personal loans made by Cutting over a twenty-year period. All but a few were in arrears; but, so far as is known, no attempt had ever been made to collect them. Notes of individuals ranged in size from $25 to $36,000, but the typical loan was from $350 to $500 while most of the larger loans were to those associated with Cutting in political campaigns as candidates or principal supporters. During the last five years of his life, when Cutting was fighting for control of Republican county organizations, he made 164 loans totaling $170,000 — a rate considerably higher than in the earlier years.

Cutting's will is also a roster of his political and American Legion associates. A casual review of the list of 183 legatees sharing $1,100,000 turns up the names of forty-odd who were politically active during some portion of the Cutting period.

Legislative Faction

Of legislators of the sessions of 1925-1935, thirty-six were borrowers or future legatees of Cutting, with the number identifiable by such means ranging from six to eleven per session. Several served through several sessions and one, R. L. Baca of Santa Fe, served as speaker of the house in the fractious session of 1929.

Cutting's adherents serving in the legislature only slowly developed a pattern of voting setting them apart from other legislative groupings. Much of the program Cutting impressed upon state conventions and leadership of the two parties never appeared in recognizable legislation. And much of Cutting's program was doubtless irrelevant to any needs felt by Hispanic legislators. Some Progressive items like woman's suffrage and the direct primary were anathema. Until Cutting obtained local strength sufficient to influence the convention-made nominations, the high rate of legislative turnover doubtless hindered development of a consistent session-to-session faction. Sessions of 1919-1927 present only occasional incidents in which men associated with Cutting were able to take action relevant to Cutting's known aspirations or pursue objectives reflected in the columns of the *New Mexican.*

Cutting's legislative bloc took substantial and continuing form in 1929.[51] Governor Dillon's legislative message had asked for a prohibition enforcement bill, "an adequate, fair and just workmen's compensation law, and the creation of the office of state commissioner of labor." Dillon also asked for a procedural speedup so that the legislature could conclude its work "in thirty days." On January 30, two weeks after the opening of the session, Senator Cutting appeared on the floor of the house and made a speech in which he called upon the party to redeem its platform pledges. By a previous Old Guard move, the labor commission bill had been recommitted from the floor to committee by a vote of 30-15. After the Cutting talk it was recalled and passed the house by a vote of 31-15. Hispanic Republican members split 14 to 10 for Cutting and left Old Guard strength confined to only three or four of the Hispanic counties. The split in the house was to persist. Republican legislative cohesion dropped sharply on the remaining handful of votes on which a reading was possible, and but little of either party program was enacted.

In the senate, the matter became a protracted and bitter stalemate to split both parties on much of the remaining legislation. Cohesiveness of both parties dropped precipitously. In most previous sessions of the senate, the parties had managed to adhere to party lines closely enough to give themselves "cohesiveness scores"[52] in the 70 and 80 range on those votes setting the parties in opposition; in 1929 the Democratic score dropped to 56 and the Republican to a 28 index of cohesiveness score for the regular and special sessions. (Here, again, the reader is owed an explanation of a phrase and numbers whose meaning is less than obvious, for, if he persists, he will encounter them again in similar contexts: If the agreement of a party's members, when voting in opposition to a majority of the other party, is perfect, with all members voting the same way, the party's "index of cohesion" is 100. If there is the widest possible disagreement within a party's membership, i.e., half the members voting one way and the other half the other way, then the party's index for that vote will be zero. If the vote divides three to one, the resulting index expression is 50.0 rather than the 75.0 the reader might expect, and not until the intra-party vote reaches a ratio of seven to one will the index go to 75.0.)

Ten Republicans and a Democrat became the Progressive, or Cutting, senate faction with the parliamentary backing of Lt. Governor Woodward. Eight Republicans and five Democrats became the Springer, or Old Guard, faction. The Old Guard included only one Hispanic member—Republican Gonzales of Rio Arriba County; the Cutting group was based primarily on the counties of McKinley, Santa Fe, San Miguel, Bernalillo, Mora, Chaves, and Quay, and included three Hispanic members. The factional alignment became evident half way through the session. Thereafter, thirty-five roll call votes were made that found a majority of one faction in opposition to a majority of the other. Cohesiveness scores of these two factions during the regular and special sessions were: Springer-Old Guard, 66.2; Cutting-Progressive, 67.9.

Although a game commission bill was also in the party platform, Governor Dillon pleaded in vain to the house to lay aside the labor commission bill and get to work on other business:

The house of representatives has recently defeated a platform
pledge by refusing to pass . . . the game commission bill and I
should be glad to see the house reconsider its action.[53]

The Taxpayers' Association then noted that some of the men who
were trying to fulfill one pledge were opposing the game commission
bill. "They became issues irrespective of their merits."[54]

House and senate groupings of 1931 and 1933 resulted in an out-
right alliance of Republican Old Guard members and a conservative
Democratic faction from the southern and eastern counties. Republican legislators of the Cutting persuasion held the resulting factional
balance of power in the 1931 legislature and determined which items
of Governor Seligman's program became enacted. The critical votes
in 1933 were again not those differentiating the parties, but those
reflecting a cross-party division similar to that of the senate of the
1929 and 1931 sessions.

In the 1932 campaign Maurice Miera, Socorro County Republican leader, was openly in the Cutting camp and state chairman of
the Progressive party which had withdrawn its ticket to support
Seligman. Miera was then in Santa Fe for the 1933 session, "in charge
of pushing the Progressive [Cutting] platform."[55] Seligman, Cutting, and Miera were then successful in organizing house and senate
in 1933 by the same means and in the same manner that the alliance
had organized the 1931 house—an arrangement in which the Cutting
influence seems to have been dominant. The 1933 legislature, however, contained a new senate of twenty Democrats and four Republicans, and the Democratic majority in the house was forty-one to
eight—a situation drastically changing the capacity of the Cutting
faction to act as a balance of power. (Seven of the eight Republican
house members were staunchly "Old Guard;" several Cutting Republicans of the previous session had turned Democrat, and those who
did not failed of election.)

Cutting quickly became acutely dissatisfied with the results of the
session. A bipartisan movement for tax and fiscal changes, for relief
of property owners from increasingly high millage levies, unexpectedly became the dominant concern of a legislature beset for the first
time in years with strong pressure from a good many communities
and groups. Cutting and Seligman yielded to the demand for a limitation on mill levies; both opposed imposition of a sales tax, Cutting

violently and Seligman with some reluctance. Factional alignments were reflected in roll call votes, and the Seligman program found hard going. The majority floor leader in the house opposed Seligman's highway debenture proposal, and a caucus "called by administrative leaders for the purpose of going over administrative planks and severance tax measures failed to reach any settlement."[56] Most of the items passed, but only after bitter altercations.

Immediately after adjournment of the legislature, Seligman came under a cross fire from both factions of the party. Cutting's reaction to his ally, Seligman, underwent the customary change. Said one fuming editorial in Cutting's *New Mexican:*

> Grotesquely provincial and incompetent, the eleventh New Mexico legislature will go down in history as the Two Per Cent Rubber Stamp Assembly.
>
> It sat as a Democratic state machine caucus, legislating for that institution under daily personal direction of the governor and the state chairman or Kingfish.
>
> . . . . .
>
> It made its chief politician the government, with dictatorial powers over finance, education, highways, industry and public employment, to be used for building its own political fences and disposing of opposition.
>
> . . . . .
>
> Its chaotic, disorderly, confused proceedings and the bedlam of its windup, with vital measures rushed through without reading, have brought public convulsion throughout the state.
>
> . . . . .
>
> We strongly favor a constitutional amendment abolishing the state legislature, as one of the principal evils of our governmental system and setting up a legislative board of a few non-politicians with brains and vision to draft laws voted upon by the people at the polls.[57]

Not noted in the editorial was the notable contribution the Cutting faction had made to the "bedlam" of the lamented session.

The impasse to which the Seligman administration had come was ironic. The man who, more than any other, had built the Democratic party through shrewd use of factions was bound by factions. He,

who as party manager or chairman, could superbly coach and direct
a legislative group, was unable to assume a clear gubernatorial command of his legislatures. The alliances which had put Seligman into
office prevented the banker-businessman, as governor, from developing or enacting the legislative-fiscal program the times demanded. It
was reported in April, 1933, that the state board of finance had not
met in nearly six months.[58] Levi Hughes, Seligman's banking associate, and J. O. Seth, who acquired a lasting reputation as a gubernatorial adviser, had both resigned. Banker-historian P. A. F. Walter
was appointed, only to resign very promptly. There is little doubt
that the terms of the Cutting-Seligman alliance prevented the advisory and policy-making functions of the board of finance and its
well-endowed members from operating. The bankruptcy of the administration was intellectual as well as financial. Cutting had forced
the administration into a condition of stasis, and Seligman's party
group was unable to summon the capacity for making policy that
the Republican party had formerly displayed and which, though
differently organized, was later to be the endowment of several Democratic governors.

ELECTORAL FACTION AND THE DESTRUCTION OF PARTY

It has been said that "to lose an election is a temporary thing; to
smash a party is an appalling disaster."[59] New Mexico's Republican
party had come to a division in which both sides willingly took
the risk.

Cutting was maneuvering, early in 1934, for a Democratic endorsement or nomination for U.S. Senator, but he was having some
trouble. Republican chairman Ed Safford was quoted to Cutting as
saying, " 'I hope to God that Cutting runs his Progressive ticket.' "[60]
Otero warned Cutting that Progressive Maurice Miera was "strongly
against the Democratic party, and that if you went with the Democrats again, he would join with Bursum and the Old Guard."[61] Cutting was for the gambit, however, and his paper published several
statements by Democrats who endorsed him. The Associated Press
reported that James A. Hall of Clovis had endorsed Cutting and
seconded Clinton P. Anderson in so doing: "State Treasurer Anderson recently announced he had advised Postmaster General Farley,

Democratic National Committeeman, to put the support of the Democratic organization behind the Progressive-Republican Senator."[62]

At least two other party leaders, Jake Floresheim and Ceferino Quintana, Cutting men both, scored failure of the Democrats to recognize Cutting. Quintana, of San Miguel, was critical of the "powers vested in the east side Democrats who have been placed in charge of state institutions in our county."[63]

But the Democratic central committee met early in July with one item barred from the agenda—discussion of the possibility of a formal Democratic-Progressive alliance.[64] Congressman Dennis Chavez and State Chairman John Miles refused to permit the group to work to such an agreement, and the party awaited a scheduled appearance of National Chairman James Farley.[65] An eight-man Republican group including several Cutting men met with a like number of Progressives, and with Senator Cutting, just prior to the Democratic meeting. Eight of the sixteen were to be listed a year later as legatees in the Cutting will.

> After the R and P [Republican and Progressive] conference, the Democrats filtered in 1100 strong Monday apparently unaware of the meeting. They stepped to the firing line and loosed a few shots here and there but tendered no peace pipe to the Ps.[66]

After the meeting Cutting wrote to Otero:

> It seems to me obvious that since the meeting of the Democratic state central committee last Monday, that there is absolutely no self-respecting way in which we can play ball with that organization. This at least clears the air, even though the other alternatives may not be any too agreeable.
>
> Under the circumstances I do not believe that Jim Farley can influence the situation in any way.[67]

Cutting had hoped, and apparently believed, that Farley's visit would result in a Democratic endorsement or invitation to join formally with the Democratic party. It was not only not forthcoming, but the result of Farley's meetings with New Mexico Democrats was a clear decision against Cutting. Farley's public references to Cutting, on July 17, were noncommittal and included a declaration that the national administration and the party would keep out of the matter. But,

Farley's declaration of "home rule" and his hands-off policy was taken to mean that the Democrats would select an out and out Democratic ticket this fall and make no overtures to Senator Cutting who gave the party his support in 1932.[68]

In the meantime, Chairman Ed Safford of the Republican party had called a central committee meeting, as he was required to do by the rules, and resigned. The two central committees met at the same time and the Progressives had

before them an invitation of the Republican central committee to join with them on a 50-50 representation basis on the central committee. . . . Party platforms and policies, should a fusion occur, will be determined after the consolidation has taken place.[69]

The fusion was made and Peter Rapkock, Progressive chairman, became chairman of the Republican party with the authority to name two commitees. One, an executive committee of ten to fix time, place, and apportionment of the convention, and the other a committee of five to "purge party of irreconcilables."[70] It was later stated that "adoption of a platform containing Progressive principles at the Republican state convention in Santa Fe September 24 will determine whether Sen. Bronson Cutting will be a candidate for re-election in the fall campaign."[71]

The New Mexican reported that a group of "die-hard" Republicans, meeting in Albuquerque, had made plans to bolt the party in opposition to Cutting. The five at the conference were Bursum, Safford, Captain W. C. Reid, J. M. Harvey of Roswell, and Lem White of Raton. "The sixth, who was an observor, if not present at the meeting, was John Miles, Democratic Central Committee Chairman."[72] At the same time Bursum released a statement to the Associated Press:

A conference was held Sunday . . . by prominent Republicans who have interviewed a large number of the rank and file of Republican voters through the state to ascertain sentiment and reaction to the Cutting group in Santa Fe—through capture by the Cutting office and job-holding brigade of the control of the state Republican central committee—which brigade has been on the payroll of the state Seligman administration since 1931.

At the conference it was pointed out that Mr. Cutting was the nominee of the Republican party and was elected United States Senator in 1928 by virtue of which he became the titular leader of the Republican party. That while holding such office and trust at each election thereafter, namely to wit, at the general election of 1930 and the general election of 1932, Mr. Cutting combined with the Seligman forces to defeat the Republican ticket. In the opinion of the conference and also the reported opinion of a large number of the Republican rank and file this sort of leadership is not conducive to good political morals, party integrity and solidarity, and also constitutes a serious menace tending to hinder a proper solution of vital problems confronting state and county governments.

In view of these premises, the conference expresses the opinion that there is no reason apparent why any Republican should cast his vote for Mr. Cutting. The conference definitely determined that there will be organized opposition to the re-election of Mr. Cutting.[73]

Shortly thereafter there were formed the Chavez-Tingley Republican Clubs. "We took the whole organization into the Democratic camp. We wrecked the GOP organization but we were willing to do it to bust Cutting. We nearly did it, too, but we were counted out."[74]

The agreement was honored. Bursum was named in April to the Interstate Streams Commission, other Republicans and Chavez Democrats were named to policy positions, and many of the county tickets had made room for local Republicans.

Cutting won in nineteen counties, including eight of those central to Republican power since 1900. Miller, Progressive Republican gubernatorial candidate, carried eleven, including six of the traditional Republican counties. It was an impressive performance, for, in the traditional Republican counties, the Old Guard-Tingley alliance prevented only Rio Arriba and Socorro counties from going for Cutting and only Rio Arriba, Socorro, Doña Ana, and Santa Fe from going for Miller. The total state voter turnout was only slightly below the number recorded in 1932. Hence, the Democratic-Republican realignment of voters which occurred in so many states in 1932 was postponed in New Mexico until 1936, when Democrat Clyde Tingley was re-elected governor by a majority (57.5 per cent) that stood until 1964.

Cutting died in the early spring of 1935. A number of his followers attempted to run the Republican party, but after the election of 1936 the Democrats of his faction returned to their party where they were found generally aligned with the Chavez faction: "The Cutting crowd are now [1960] mostly with us." The Republican Cutting followers who did not become Democrats of the Chavez wing stayed in the Republican party as a factional group which took twenty-five years to lose its identity.

By the time of Hinkle's administration, each party was constrained always to be aware of the Cutting faction, and from 1923 each legislature and each party's conventions had to reckon with it.

Most of those items from the Progressive inventory of proposed policies or governmental improvements which showed up now in the Democratic agenda, now in the Republican, failed of enactment; and they perhaps contributed to some confusion. In the circumstances, neither party could be firmly enough committed to the proposals to undertake the sometimes painful task of enacting or financing them. Cutting had pre-empted many of the appealing issues as they emerged, and neither party could yield to them or enact them into law without running the risk of submerging party identity and all that it implied for party chieftains.

SIX

Republican Party-Government, 1900-1930

Working models of "party government" closely akin to the parliamentary versions can scarcely be approached in the American states. A variant, acommodated to the institutional framework, in which party was responsible for the formulation and execution of policies, the selection of its nominees, the staffing of policy positions, and the direction of legislation is provided in this era of New Mexico's history. A principal, and typical, disparity in New Mexico is that the system was not constructed to permit a ready shift in legislative majorities—a factor enabling the Old Guard to dominate policy-making.

The state's retention of the convention system of nominations until 1939 and the organization and mode of operation of its parties, in particular the Republican party until 1930, provide a rare test of the model. It also makes relevant a number of the observations, and their underlying assumptions, of Key's examination of the role and capacity of the parties in state government, in which he reviews evidence of the need for "more adequate systems of political management and leadership within the states."[1] The agency of government essential to the purposes and mode of operation of the party during the era was not the governorship, however, but the legislature.

THE OLD GUARD: BRIDGE OF PRIVATE AND PUBLIC INTERESTS

That membership of the Republican Old Guard incorporated men active in the dominant business and commercial interests of the time was apparent to all who cared to look; the opposition brought it to the attention of all who did not. Old Guard unity in the policy-making echelons was a concert of interests welding party and legislature into a functioning organization described as follows by a banker-historian-politician of the era:

> Contemporaries, still living, ascribe the prosperity of the period
> [1900-1910] . . . to the wisdom of Otero in surrounding himself
> with strong men who worked hand in hand with him in controlling
> legislation, influencing capital to build railroads, founding new
> towns and encouraging the basic industries of the Southwest by
> thrift in public finance and low taxes. These men included Solomon
> Luna and Holm O. Bursum representing the livestock industry; H.
> L. Waldo and W. A. Hawkins representing great railroad systems;
> Charles and Frank Springer, representatives of the coal mining
> industries . . . who with their satellites controlled elections and
> wrote the laws passed by subservient legislatures.[2]

The observation that Otero "surrounded himself" with these leaders of the Old Guard gives the wrong impression, however. Like his elected successors, Otero was surrounded by the party group whether he willed it so or not.

It is doubtless significant that the more outstanding of the Old Guard were often key individuals in other civic and business enterprises. Unlike their contemporaries, the Fergusons and allies who dominated Texas politics during the 'twenties, but who failed to "develop an organized politics capable of ruling the state with decency and decorum,"[3] the Old Guard produced a workmanlike government. Except that New Mexico's Republican organization of 1900-1930 was much more closely pressed by faction and the opposition party, its manner of conducting its joint enterprise of business and government bears a marked resemblance to that of the Democratic oligarchy Key found in North Carolina.[4]

Republican leadership was quite willing to make its bias explicit. Holm Bursum, then chairman of the central committee, made clear prior to the constitutional convention that his party's orientation was conservative, and its intent was to govern as vehicle and arbiter of the interests of the day. A statement, paraphrased but duplicated in substance by official party pronouncements, declared concerning the forthcoming election of delegates to the constitutional convention:

> With reference to the selection and election of delegates to the

constitutional convention, it is the desire and efforts will be made by the Republicans, to select the very best material available. . . . The line of cleavage will hinge more on politics as advocated by what has become commonly known as conservatives and radicals or progressives. *The dividing line will be whether or not the constitution should contain prohibitions and limitations as well as providing for definite politics with reference to various interests.* The majority of Republicans seems to be of the opinion that the constitution should not contain legislation. . . .[5] (Italics added.)

In the main, those who comprised the nucleus of the Old Guard were men who had achieved a measure of independence from politics. Politics was complementary to their livelihood, not essential to it, and they represented overtly a union of business and similar groups with government, an arrangement that now tends to be more clandestine than acknowledged. Charles Spiess, the "Black Eagle" of San Miguel County, president of the constitutional convention, and lawyer-lobbyist for a number of mining and railroad companies, several times served as state chairman. He was in consistent attendance at legislative sessions, where he served as lobbyist, bill-draftsman, and party leader—functions frequently conjoined in Republicans at that level of state politics. Spiess was also a power in San Miguel County politics where he was relied upon by his state-level colleagues to keep that fractious county in some sort of union with the state organization. Holm O. Bursum, I, was also in frequent attendance at legislative sessions in his capacity as state chairman or national committeeman—activities he continued during an appointive term as U.S. Senator. He commanded a decisive influence in those counties not of a Republican majority but of sufficient convention votes to be important in the management of party affairs and nominations. The system was essentially the same as that made famous by the Taft forces in the national convention of 1952 or by the cabal nominating Harding.

Frank and Charles Springer, dominant figures for three decades, were influential in the local politics of the three important counties of Santa Fe, San Miguel, and Colfax. Their business and economic fortunes, however, were tied with the Maxwell Land Grant Company and the Rocky Mountain, St. Louis and Pacific Coal Company. The Maxwell Company became involved in one of the most famous community feuds and law suits in New Mexico's history, finally settled after some twenty years when Frank Springer made a successful presentation before the United States Supreme Court. Thereafter, Frank passed his political mantle to brother Charles and took up the life of the gentleman scholar, to become as good a paleontologist as he was a lawyer and flautist.[6]

The nuclear group for a time included the able, but later notorious, Albert Bacon Fall, one of the few who would press his personal demands to the point of intransigence. It is indicative of the composition of the Old Guard that only Fall represented no continuing community or corporate interest. Far more than his fellows he was political entrepreneur and a free agent.

THE SUBORDINATION OF GOVERNORS

To say that political leaders and subleaders of the Republican era had agreed tacitly or otherwise that no one man or group would achieve a clear dominance of party would perhaps be to go beyond the evidence, but that was the practical effect of the political organization of the time. Nominees at every level of the ticket were selected by a balancing process or, when necessary, by the concerted action of the party leadership. In 1918, for example, when the leadership disposed in convention of Governor W. E. Lindsey's attempt at renomination by selecting O. A. Larrazolo by a vote of 802 to 117, only nine of Lindsey's votes came from counties central to the Republican organization.[7] Two years later Larrazolo was in trouble with his home county organization in San Miguel and with the mining interests of the state. He was denied renomination.

As another illustration of the fate and role of governors, Merritt Mechem was a successful lawyer and a reluctant candidate who had stated his lack of desire " 'to join the melancholy list of ex-governors,' " but he finally yielded to the importunacy of his friends and agreed to make the race.[8] During Mechem's term, a U.S. Senate seat fell vacant, to which he appointed Holm Bursum over the opposition of Albert Fall. In explaining his appointment by Mechem, Bursum remarked:

> Ben Pankey was my first choice for governor and Mr. Pankey, as a truth-loving man, will tell everybody that this is the fact. Pankey

did not want to have his name voted on before the convention, I understand. I tried next to get W. D. Murray of Silver City to run. Judge Mechem was the third choice. We were endeavoring to get a candidate who would make a good race, a successful campaign.[9]

Merritt Mechem fulfilled his party obligations of consultation with party leaders on appointments and he conducted the type of administration of which they approved. He too, however, strained his party ties when it appeared that he was prepared to give somewhat more than perfunctory attention to securing passage of his party's platform— a statement in which numerous items paralleled those in the platforms of Larrazolo, and of Mechem's Democratic opponent Richard H. Hanna.

Mechem flatly refused to run for a second term, and Bursum later stated that Mechem found out his dislike for the job of governor two days after he sat in the executive chair: " 'I do not believe they could get Mechem to run again—not if they pulled him with a team of horses.' "[10]

Circumstances of the 1926 elections are equally revealing. The expenditure of money and effort for the campaign represented the culmination of a long period of party reorganization, but it was a little unusual in that it had become obvious that strong men in the image of Larrazolo could not be nominated and those like Bursum could not be elected. The party settled finally on Richard Dillon, " 'a clean-cut young fellow of average ability,' " acceptable to the various factions of the party.[11] A measure of the party's difficulty is the fact that at such a time and with the talents it contained it was constrained to turn to Dillon. But, their use of strong local organizations exposed members of the Old Guard to attack; and, identified as they were with economic conservatism, they were probably unable to advance with much hope of success a candidate too clearly cast in their own mold.

The role permitted governors is indicative of the nature of the order. When I suggested to a leading Republican of the era that the party did not always, or even usually, advance strong gubernatorial candidates, he bristled with anger momentarily; but then, upon reflection, said: "We neither needed nor wanted strong governors. We had the senate and we could control our own political organization."

So the Republican party could, and sometimes did, but this mode of operation resulted in anomalies, like that made apparent by an incident in the senate, in 1923, when a Democrat was governor. During an exchange on the floor of the senate there was an interruption for the reading of a message from Governor Hinkle concerning the Colorado River Compact—a matter of considerable importance. Then, with some sarcasm:

> Republican majority leader Phillips suggested it be referred to the senator from Quay County, and the senator from that county, Democratic Leader Zinn, retorted that if the carrying out of former Governor Mechem's message had been left in his hands a greater number of his recommendations would have been enacted into law.
>
> "The governor should be the dog of the administration and the legislature the tail," said Zinn. "The dog should wag the tail and not the tail, the dog, though this was attempted during the fifth legislature."
>
> "If the majority of the fifth legislature, the G.O.P., had put more of Governor Mechem's suggestions on the law books, especially those to safeguard the sanctity of the ballot," he continued, "the state would now be better off and the G.O.P. would be better off."[12]

In sum, it was apparent to the acute Mr. Zinn, who was later to demonstrate redoubtable political prowess, that the Republican party was obliged to nominate governors who would function in their sphere as party manager Ed Safford functioned in his. That is, governors were to execute that policy which was already formed, and they were to consult with the Old Guard when it was not. The legislature, similarly, was the recorder of policy, not its generator.

PARTY AND LEGISLATURE

V. O. Key's prescriptions for the reconstitution of the political capacities of the states were a part of the going order in New Mexico's politics of 1912-1931.[13] A major exception was a narrow but unresponsive legislative party-balance in which a system of multi-county legislative districts operated to Republican advantage, although each legislator represented an equitable share of the citizenry.[14] Remaining features characteristic of a vigorous two-party politics were present.

And a habit of tightly patterned party rather than split-ticket voting sometimes mitigated the usual consequences of a large plural-executive.

The parties were organized to govern, and they did. Each contained an institutionalized, long-continuing, and identifiable leadership. Each party had a policy attitude permitting it to be slightly separated from the other on the scale of liberal-conservative, and each confronted the other as a combatant in the legislature as well as before the electorate. And, (in that area of legislation where the issues do not come to the surface, where matters are important but technically abstruse, and in which narrower interests are difficult of reconciliation with broader public needs) the parties perhaps also passed another test proposed by Key: The party organization of the day gave some evidence that it had "a strength and unity of its own [sufficient to] limit tampering with the jury and permit some considered search for the general welfare in these more or less private disputes colored with a public interest."[15]

For nearly twenty years the legislature of New Mexico was the instrument of party as much as it was the arena of policy. After statehood, the minority's share of the legislative membership never varied much from its average of 35 per cent, so two-party legislative competition was never foreclosed. By virtue of party selection or approval, legislators served as *bona fide* members of their parties. Hence, they represented not merely their community or district, but they also served as party functionaries. It was for this role that the bulk of them had been selected or permitted to run, and their expertness or knowledge of legislation was a secondary consideration.

But the inexperienced legislators of the day were not turned loose to exercise their judgment in the manner suggested by either Burke or Rousseau. The lobby of organized interest groups has always been in attendance in New Mexico, no less than in other states, but, in large degree, the lobby was simply an extension of the Republican party. Many of its dominant and most able members were also party leaders. And, in addition to these, the state chairman and other party leaders were typically in attendance in their party capacities. It is notable, also, that the legislature was singularly free of the venality that cropped up from time to time in so many states. Whether or not the parties were conducting a stewardship of enlightened self-interest is a matter opening a wide area of judgment; but it is certain that the dominant interests of the day had no need to subvert a government that so accurately and efficiently reflected their attitudes and goals.

Apportionment, Selection, and Tenure of Legislators

The twenty or so counties of the late territorial era elected a twelve-member council or senate and a twenty-four-member house from districts of vast extent covering several counties.[16] By basing legislative districts on key counties of a sizeable and Republican vote, it was readily possible to dominate the legislature. Consequently, in the decade preceding statehood, the number of Republicans ranged from a comfortable nine to twelve in the council, and in the house the Democrats could muster only six members in their best year. The constitution of the new state doubled the size of the legislature by placing membership of the state senate at twenty-four and of the house at forty-nine. All members of the senate were elected at the same time for concurrent four-year terms, and house members served for two-year terms.

The gerrymander of the territorial period was tempered somewhat by the constitution, but much of its effectiveness remained. The twenty-four districts for the election of senators each elected one member, but they were so arranged that sixteen members were elected from counties within multiple-county districts. Article IV of the constitution provided, for example, in the case of San Miguel County.

The county of San Miguel, one senator.
The counties of San Miguel and Mora, one senator to be a resident of Mora County and to be elected by the electors of Mora and San Miguel counties.
The counties of Guadalupe and San Miguel, one senator.

In similar fashion, Colfax County could dominate the election of two senators; Rio Arriba, two; Socorro, three; and Bernalillo could elect two. The counties of Valencia, Santa Fe, Taos, and Doña Ana could elect one each. The arrangement consequently gave the key counties of the Republican heartland practical control over the election of sixteen, or two-thirds of the members of the senate.

The arrangement existed also in the house where four multi-county one-member districts based upon Rio Arriba, Santa Fe, San Miguel, and Socorro counties generally gave Republicans a membership bonus of the four members. The basic house apportionment, plus the four bonus members, gave eleven counties electoral control of twenty-six members of the house. Although the narrow majorities on the state tickets seesawed back and forth until 1930, Republicans lost control of the house only twice, in the elections of 1922 and 1924, and their supremacy in the senate was never in doubt until 1932.

The institution making the apportionment so useful in legislative management was the state convention. Legislators elected from one-county districts were nominated in the county conventions. Those from multi-county districts were nominated by district conventions held at the same place and time as state conventions. Those nominations were thus within the control of the state organization, so that it could determine who was to serve in the legislature just as it could determine who was to run as candidate for governor. According to Republican party leaders of the period, some legislative candidates were selected or drafted as capable and reliable politicians presumed to have a potential legislative capacity. A former officer and gubernatorial candidate of the Republican party states that the shoestring-district senators were usually "outstanding and intelligent men." Picked or induced to run after considerable discussion, political "leaders of the various counties in the district selected them to balance the tickets." Another former chairman has stated that legislative candidates were often "salaried men who could retain jobs and salary while working in the legislature. It was a question of getting good men and the state leaders would step in in those counties where the Democrats were strong." Of certain of the others, a long-time political operator in Taos commented that available Republican legislative candidates—like other candidates—were three deep. He made it clear that, although many felt called, only a few were chosen. State leaders kept hands off in one-county districts containing strong local organizations. In these, the dominant local members of the Old Guard were often expected to take care of the problem. Those picked for more than one or two terms were apt to be strong local leaders. The remainder were called upon to run when their local apprenticeship had been served and it seemed their turn had come.

Whatever the reasons, however, the brevity of tenure of New Mexico legislators of the six sessions of 1925-1935 is remarkable. Hyneman's study of legislative tenure and turnover in ten states for the same period found that 35 per cent of the members of those bodies were serving a first term—a degree of transiency he marked as ill-serving the health of those legislative systems.[17] In New Mexico only one man in five or six came to any session as an incumbent, and but very few others had served in any prior session. Table 35 compares the sessions of service of New Mexico legislators serving in the sessions of 1925-1935 with the averaged composites for the ten states.

Defeat at the general election was even less significant as a cause of

TABLE 35. SESSIONS OF PRIOR SERVICE OF NEW MEXICO LEGISLATORS
AND MEMBERS OF TEN OTHER LEGISLATURES, 1925-1935

Chamber and state	Percentage of members by sessions of service		
	First	*Second*	*Third or more*
SENATE			
Ten states[a]	20	19	60
New Mexico	35	33	33
HOUSE			
Ten states[a]	40	24	37
New Mexico	70	21	9

a. Data are derived from Hyneman, *op. cit.*, Table I.

legislative turnover in New Mexico than it was in the states of the Hyneman study. In those states, defeat in the general election caused the retirement of 16 per cent of all house members and of 7 per cent in Maine. As a cause for turnover of senators, general election defeat accounted for percentages ranging from zero in New York to 29 in Illinois, to strike an average of 15 per cent. It was 7 per cent in New Mexico for both houses.

A scoring of the "causes" of termination of service of New Mexico's legislators is set out in Table 36. When the data are compared with those of Hyneman's study it appears that a legislator of those ten states was about three times more likely to return than a member in New Mexico. It is unlikely that the conditions of service in New Mexico were so much more onerous that they could account for the difference. It is also unlikely that the state organization could not have

TABLE 36. TERMINATION AND CONTINUANCE OF SERVICE OF NEW MEXICO
LEGISLATORS, 1925-1935

Chamber and year	Defeated in general election		Not renominated by convention		Renominated and re-elected	
	Number	Percentage	Number	Percentage	Number	Percentage
HOUSE						
1925	1	...	39	...	9	18
1927	4	...	37	...	8	16
1929	1	...	39	...	9	18
1931	8	...	35	...	6	12
1933	2	...	32	...	15	21
1935	3	...	30	...	16	33
Totals	19	7	212	72	63	21
SENATE						
1925	1	...	20	...	3	13
1929	1	...	17	...	6	25
1933	3	...	15	...	6	25
Totals	5	7	52	72	15	21

exerted sufficient influence to secure the renomination of more members. The inference seems warranted that the party, particularly its county units, did not seek to arrange for a stable legislative membership.

This casual attitude about longevity of legislative service did not extend, however, to maintaining the strength of the legislative rosters. Key's inference that the type of political organization and competition engendered by the convention serves to provoke candidacies even in strongly one-party districts receives considerable support in New Mexico.[18]

In the elections of 1920-1930, Democrats allowed only five (2 per cent) of the 294 elections to the house of representatives to be lost by default. Republicans failed to put up candidates 6 per cent of the time in defaulting on 18 of the 294 contests. The corresponding ratio of seats uncontested by one or the other of the parties in the elections of 1946-1954, after installation of the primary system, was 22 per cent, nearly three times the rate of that in the 1920 decade. Table 37 sets out the incidence of uncontested house seats by party in the 1920's.

About half of the contests Republicans allowed to go by default were in the Eddy-Lea county district where voting odds were impossible. Most of the remaining defaults by both parties were quite

TABLE 37. UNCONTESTED RACES, HOUSE OF REPRESENTATIVES, 1920-1930

		Seats uncontested		
Year	Seats	By Republicans, number	By Democrats, number	By poth parties as percentage of total
1920	49	2	1	6
1922	49	4	0	8
1924	49	4	1	10
1926	49	2	1	6
1928	49	4	1	10
1930	49	2	1	6
Total	294	18	5	8

deliberate. In districts or counties seating two or more representatives, the party in the minority would nominate fewer candidates to the party list than there were seats to be filled. The voters might then so distribute their votes among, for example, three candidates for two seats that the one candidate of the party in the minority would get a larger vote than one of the two opposition candidates.[19]

Legislative Direction and Organization

Legislative control was so essential to Old Guard purposes that organization of house and senate could scarcely be left to chance.

The second state legislature (1915) was typical of many to follow. Of its composition a reporter commented:

Of the seventy-three members of the two houses . . . twenty-four are wholly or largely interested in the raising of [live] stock. Of these twenty-four, a large number are exclusively concerned with sheep. There are seventeen lawyers in the two houses, nine farmers and five doctors. The newspaper men number three, but one of these has had the good sense to combine farming with his newspaper activities. Merchants, railroad men, and real estate and insurance men are represented among the remaining members. There is but one banker, one capitalist, and one industrialist among the members of the two houses.[20]

That forty-nine of the seventy-three (67 per cent) were freshmen was also typical. Sixteen had served a previous term and only eight had served two or more previous terms.

But the new members, fresh from their ranches, law offices or locomotive cabs, did not serve in limbo or chaos. As the press reported, Charles Springer and Charles Spiess, "generalissimos of the Republican party" had preceded them upon the scene and leased a local residence.[21] It was observed:

Such an unselfish and unostentatious interest in the good of the people does these gentlemen great credit. Quietly and unobtrusively, year after year, they lay thus at the disposal of the legislature their valuable services, asking nothing but the satisfaction of knowing that they are assisting to boost the Common Geezer along the pathway of progress, to lighten his burdens. . . . To other altruistic souls [of the railway lobby in their private cars], who modestly remain in seclusion at Lamy, wishing to keep personality entirely in the background as they labor for greater blessings for the rank and file of our citizenship, still warmer and more grateful thanks are due.[22]

The arrangement was a feature of the order. Springer and Spiess functioned as party strategists and bill draftsmen, and could rally to their aid, if needed, other leading members of the party. It was they who were largely responsible for the technical work of translating pressures, information, and judgment into policy. Under ordinary circumstances the legislature was their instrument for such purposes.

Republican leaders assembled in Santa Fe would know in detail who was available for such positions as chief clerk and majority leader in each house, and the speakership, as well as potential chairmen for the more important committees. Of committees, there were sufficient so that in the senate every Republican member had an excellent chance of being chairman of one and vice chairman of another, and in the house about twenty committees were sufficient to provide most of the majority members with a chairmanship. Invariably, party leadership and governor (in those years when Republicans succeeded in winning the office) took part in the legislative caucus. Their collective judgment ordinarily determined the organization. There were occasions, however, when the choice for speaker or clerk was almost foreclosed in that the freedom of choice of the party leadership was narrowly limited. Thus, in 1915, San Miguel County's powerful Secundino Romero was opposing Nestor Montoya, a party chieftain from Bernalillo County, for the speakership. In the caucus attended by Springer and Spiess, U.S. Senator Thomas B. Catron, and Ralph Ely, state chairman, Montoya was prevailed upon to withdraw his candidacy to make the selection unanimous. Thereupon, Blas Sanchez of Mora County—sometimes said to be a fief of the political barony of Spiess's and Sec Romero's San Miguel County—was made chief clerk. The leadership could probably have denied the speakership and clerkship to Romero and Sanchez, but the move would have been disruptive. In the following legislature of 1917, W. H. H. Llewellyn of Doña Ana County and close political associate of U.S. Senator Fall was made speaker; and in 1919, Lorenzo Delgado, San Miguel, the political protege and associate of Secundino Romero, was made chief clerk.

In the closing days, or sometimes the last two or three weeks of each session, it was customary also to make a rather radical change in the committee arrangements of both houses. There were too many committees to be adequately staffed, in each case, with a good sprinkling of the more able members and, in addition, the bulk of the more important bills would have been assigned by presiding officers to those committees deemed most able to deal with them. Other factors contributed to an excessive accumulation of deferred items and so, to expedite matters, there would be appointed a "steering" committee.[23] With a few exceptions all bills remaining in the standing committees would be turned over to the steering committee which reported them for placement on legislative calendars. The committee in either house would typically be composed of five to a dozen, including a sprinkling of minority members. The arrangement obviously placed a great deal of power in the hands of those who served, so the men appointed to the steering committees generally were those already vested with organizational posts or status, and membership would often include several chairmen of the more important standing committees.

The Republican arrangement in the senate of 1925, when a Democrat served as governor, was a little more circumscribed than usual:

During the rest of the session [about ten days] all bills will be referred to this committee except those dealing with general appropriations, roads and reservoirs which will go to the finance committee. Other standing committees are not considered abolished but will continue "for such purposes as the senate may deem proper." All committees except the finance [committee] were asked to turn over all bills they have in their possession to the steering committee.[24]

The Democratic leadership of the house of 1925 appointed a steering committee composed of party leaders and whips and apparently hindered them with no restrictions.[25]

Arrangements like the steering committee, and the extreme rate of legislative turnover, doubtless served to augment the capacity of the Old Guard to determine the course and content of legislation. Few members served long enough to acquire the parliamentary skills and develop areas of knowledge that might have made them relatively independent of the leadership.[26] The committee structure resembled that of most other states, but, as McKean found in New Jersey, a pervasive control by party leaders, facilitated by the steering committee, prevented the standing committees from developing as independent centers of authority.[27]

Leiserson has observed that in these matters a broad relationship seems to be determinative of the internal arrangements of the legislature: If it be subject to one executive committee "acting on behalf of an electoral mandate to a majority party to determine legislative agenda and calendar," then the legislature is subordinate to party; but if the legislature divides itself into committees enjoying a substantial autonomy, then the party management is "reduced to informal methods of consultation and pressure."[28] The generalization is confirmed in New Mexico, as in Connecticut; for New Mexico's politics of the 1920's bears a strong resemblance to the more recent pattern in that state. Lockard found that party dominates in the internal arrangements and direction of the Connecticut legislature, where the leadership is composed normally of the governor, a few powerful outside leaders, and those ordinarily vested with formal authority. "Choices of these intra-legislative leaders, while formally made through election by the representatives and senators of the party in question, are in reality made by the state chairman and the governor."[29] Lockard also observed a "liberal-conservative" cleavage helpful to party leaders "in getting party unity," and evidence that the membership of Connecticut's general assembly "relinquished to the leadership the power to formulate substantive policy decisions."[30] In essence, this was the situation in New Mexico, where only the mechanics of it differed in a few details, and where the governor's was a relatively subordinate role.

Party Aims and Party Government

In the view of politicians of the more populous states, New Mexico's politics of the period would no doubt have seemed simple in the extreme. Her 1920 population of 360,000, approximating that of a good-sized city ward, was thinly scattered across an area of 122,000 square miles. Only 18 per cent of that population lived in the twelve urban areas, and the proportion had increased only 25 per cent at the end of the decade. Much of that portion of the population which was urbanized (small town is more descriptive) was clustered in four or five county areas in which mining had developed. Albuquerque was slowly developing as a trade and transportation center; and several other communities had progressed from country villages largely because they were divisional points on the transcontinental railways. The number of inhabitants and way of life of towns like Taos and Santa Fe were changing almost imperceptibly. Of the trades and professions only seven — law, dentistry, embalming, medicine, osteopathy, optometry, and pharmacy — were subject to a licensing requirement prior to 1917.

In this domain of the Old Guard, the organization and direction of government did not differ essentially from that of the states which Tocqueville saw in 1831. Chief among those services which it performed was the essential one, for a society so organized, of providing in law and politics, the equivalent of a market place; but one designed for social transactions—the broadly economic and political—rather than the commercial.[31] The institutional requirements for New Mexico's market place of political transactions were simple and needed but little more than the parties and the legislature already at hand. Aside from the traditional activities of government, little was attempted, for the needs of the economic interests recently arrived in the state were usually those of legal definition rather than administrative oversight and activity.

The Purposes of Power

The Old Guard's control of this environment was not fortuitous. It was deliberately sought in the state, as in the nation, as a means to a policy, in Schattschneider's words, "of giving business a free hand to exploit the economy with a minimum of governmental interference."[32] As an instrumentality of that objective the system of party management was economically quite efficient, for neither government nor party was a costly operation. Nor could they have been, unless they were to be deliberately used for exploitation of the populace, for a per capita income ranging from $250 to $300 was so low that the state in 1928 could yield less than $2.50 per person in federal income and profits taxes. The party was maintained in pursuit of the purposes of the Old Guard and although those objectives were largely limited to expressing the economic orientation of the day, it was to that degree a "programmatic" outlook.[33]

The workings and objectives of the system of legislative control were plainly visible, also, to all who cared to look. Walter observes of the late Governor Arthur Seligman's long career as an effective Democratic politician:

> It was his boast that he always voted the Democratic ticket straight, and yet his closest advisors in legislative matters were leading Republicans such as the late Charles A. Spiess, the late Charles Springer, Judge Edward R. Wright, Levi A. Hughes, Jan Van Houten, and other stalwart conservative Republicans.[34]

And the president of the Taxpayers' Association wrote in similar fashion of Charles Springer, archetype of the Old Guard and counsel-lobbyist for the railroad and mining companies of northeastern New Mexico:

> There used to be a lot of kicking by the opposition because Charles Springer . . . mixed so much in the making and drafting of laws. . . . Probably no one has ever been so continuously and bitterly assailed. His fad was roads. . . .
>
> He was probably overzealous in his planning and too big in his visions. Probably also he was unbending is his determination to use every admissible or acceptable method of gaining his objectives for road building. . . . Probably he was the best fitted, the most expert legislative drafter New Mexico has ever had and during those days, too, there were in and about the legislatures and governors, others who, whatever their policies or prejudices were clear-headed, competent lawyers.[35]

Some part of the operation of the system was plainly and directly linked to an ingrained attitude of mind reflective of the social characteristics of its members. One can only wonder whether a prisoner during the Larrazolo administration was to feel aggrieved or merely abashed by the result obtained when he asked for executive clemency — a matter in which governors of the days were normally exceedingly generous. On one of the occasions when rancher-politician, Lieutenant Governor Benjamin Pankey acted as governor in the absence of Larrazolo, he wrote as follows in connection with a prisoner of the state penitentiary:

> There is no disposition—on my part at least and I do not think on the part of Governor Larrazolo—to even consider a pardon for this man Jones. I have never pardoned a cattle thief yet, and I can assure you in this case that I will take no action as to the pardon of this man.[36]

Actions of the legislature were often clearly taken in response to the economic outlook of the leadership, even though the more narrowly partisan interests would have produced a different result. At least two of the bills of the 1915 legislature designed for the harassment of the Democratic governor succeeded in getting the majority in trouble with interests powerful within the Republican party. The machinery of control was brought into play in the senate and:

As a result of an agreement reached between the majority leaders and the influential Republican sheep-men, the house bill creating an all-Republican Sheep Sanitary Board was killed in the senate this morning. The vote on the passage of the bill was 8 to 14. . . . The pressure for the passage of the bill was removed yesterday. Nominations for members of the board to succeed the present members . . . will now be made by the governor.[37]

On the same day the house retreated from its position on a bill drawn by the banking association and accepted senate amendments "to restore to the governor the rights given him when the bill was drawn."

Centralization of the Administrative Mechanism

The lawyers, ranchers, and business men making up the Old Guard may have been entirely innocent of administrative theory, but they were given able instruction from time to time by the New Mexico Taxpayers' Association, an organization instrumental in devising a long series of enactments contributing to a rather unusual degree of state supervision over local government units.[38] The author of the legislation establishing the tax commission indicated to the governor that the "permanent" commission of "broad centralized powers" was designed to give an efficient control over local assessors. That objective was never fully gained, but by 1930, under the tutelage of the Association, the commission had fully established its capacity to determine the budgets and hence influence the programs of schools and other local government units. Similar instruments, the state board of finance and office of the comptroller, took some ten years to become fully operational, but, by the time the state board of finance had reached its majority as a result of successive statutory grants of authority, the three public positions on it were highly prized appointments. Its public members tended to be recruited from legal and banking circles, and few gained appointment solely because they were bona fide party men. Many were good partisans, of course, but governors generally found themselves constrained to appoint men acceptable in other areas as well.

For over twenty years, however, the technical work of assembling budget data and drafting appropriation bills was vested by custom and default in the Taxpayers' Association.

In 1922, the Association reported that for the preceding six years its director had "been accorded every opportunity to assist the governor and the legislature in ascertaining the needs of the state departments and institutions and in the preparation of the appropriation bills."[39] A similar statement was made after each session through that of 1933.[40] The role of the Taxpayers' Association was so thoroughly a part of the governmental fabric that an adequate history of it would provide a significant insight into the political-economic structure of early statehood.

From early territorial days until 1934, property taxes furnished nearly all the receipts of schools, local governments, and the state. Sharp increases in price levels incident to World War I were but slowly followed by relatively sticky state and local revenues. Revenue needs of local governments, particularly, produced sharply increased millage levies, but locally set assessment ratios were quite flexible with the result that corporate taxpayers complained increasingly (with some cause) of discrimination. Countermeasures by the more readily organizable interests illustrate the relationship of the association to the state's government and politics. The broadest strategy was formation of the Taxpayers' Association by railroads, mine operators, and a sizable number of prominent ranchers. Of a fundamentalist economic hue, the association was also sternly non-partisan, for most of its cattle-ranching members were Democrats and the sheepmen were Republicans. For some years, also, the association received more than a proportionate share of support (when measured by wealth and population) from interests and individuals prominent in southern and eastern counties.

The relationship between the association and the Old Guard was one of mutual and overlapping interests, but the association was able to maintain its identity and integrity in spite of its "natural" ally. An early and longtime president, Herbert Hagerman, from Little Texas had been forced from the territorial governorship by northern Republicans, but his board of directors generally included members of the Old Guard. Rupert Asplund, the association's executive director, was properly regarded as a budget expert and became an institution in his own right, for he died at his post after nearly forty years.

Existence of the Taxpayers' Association served, however, to permit Old Guard access to the points of effective decision (appropriations committees and governor's office) when the opposition held the governorship.

A less diffuse approach in a related aspect of the tax question was taken by mining interests closely associated with the Old Guard, (an approach quite naturally and ably furthered by the Taxpayers' Association, and quite indicative, also, of the Old Guard style). In the face of proposed new mine-tax laws, mine operators strongly countered with a demand for 100-per-cent ratios of assessed value of all property to true or market value. To the degree this was successful, discrimination was foreclosed. An Old Guard statute created a study commission which employed Robert Murray Haig as its counsel. Reputable authority has it that: "The published Hearings and Report of this commission together constitute one of the better state tax studies in the United States."[41] These gambits were costly for a time to the mining companies, but they settled the issues to their satisfaction; for the next step was a valuation survey firmly committing the state to the proposition that production rather than reserves was the measure of a mining company's holdings.

In view of the statutes written by or with the approval of the association providing standards and procedures for the preparation of budgets by the governor and state agencies, it is intriguing to read an association statement on the going practice:

the director of the Association has acted as the governor's budget clerk and secretary of the committee of the legislature. . . . The state has no budget machinery though we have excellent laws on the subject of budgets. *It is probably an ideal arrangement to have an association representing the taxpayers given an opportunity to assist.*[42] (Italics added.)

To have established a functioning budget office with the means to develop budgets and exercise policy or program controls would have resulted in some slight cost, but it is unlikely that this was the deterring factor. There is small doubt that if an executive agency had been performing this function there would have been less need to grant the association unlimited access to administrative offices and the committees and floors of the legislature. After he had assembled the budget requests and acquired thereby much essential information about agency operations, the association director then usually found himself requested to write, or help the committee to write, the appropriation bill. Only twice in a twenty-year period did the association indicate by substantial criticism of the legislature that the system failed to achieve its major goals.

The system of financial management also provided the Old Guard and institutions related to it a significant measure of control over local government; and, in consequence, an additional bargaining power over local political organizations.

The Civic Obligation

There was more involved in the politics of the Old Guard than a simple brokerage of interests dedicated to economic exploitation or development. A sense of stewardship or obligation to community was also in evidence, for the men who developed the community lived in it as well, and they were not indifferent to the amenities, costly though they were.[43] In the main, members of the Old Guard possessed a political style and orientation closer to those of a Marcus Hanna than to a Platt or Harding. The government of the day was by no means a closed or a static system. Some of the accommodations made came grudgingly; others occurred with a speed and skill that make them appear to have come about inevitably.

The concept of prior and beneficial appropriation of water as the legal doctrine governing water rights was accepted almost as a matter of course from the Spanish and Mexican practice, and by 1907 the territory had established the administrative and adjudicatory agency still called the office of the state engineer. The engineer's early became one of the most complex but efficiently organized offices in the state, endowed with secure financing, and buttressed by a long series of statutes and judicial constructions. Here was a function governed in the awareness of a particularly explosive mixture of economic interests and seen as too involved for run-of-mine politics. It required a measure of thoughtful attention.

Two of the carefully devised statutes written by Charles Springer provided the means of cooperation with the new Federal Aid Highway Act and established a highway commission and department with language incorporated into later statutes and constitutional provisions. Their author then served for over ten years on the commission he created; directing an agency that was subject to his administrative control as well as to his legislative direction. Succeeding statutes defined and established the principal highways of the state, so in each period the "plan" of the department was found in the statutes. The highways to which Charles Springer was dedicated were of benefit to ranchers and isolated communities, but his scrupulous and economic administration served, and cost, other interests as well.

And there has long existed in Santa Fe an institution which is as remarkable a monument to the civic enterprise of some of the Old Guard as it is to their political acuity. This is the Museum of New Mexico — founded, as a practical matter, by two historians, P. A. F. Walter and R. E. Twitchell, archeologist Edgar L. Hewett, and paleontologist Frank Springer. That they were also shrewd and knowledgeable men in the affairs of politics was more than coincidental. They succeeded, with the help of Charles Springer and Charles Spiess, in drafting and enacting a statute, creating the institution, which enabled it to remain almost fully insulated from the streams of politics and pressure in which the ordinary institutions of government must make their way. Not until 1959, after a full decade of legislative experimentation with modernized systems of fiscal and administrative control, was a statute passed bringing the museum fully into the purview of legislative and administrative oversight.

SEVEN

One-Party Government, and the Advent
of the Primary

THE groups and Democratic leaders who so swiftly brought order
to the emergency session of 1934 after Governor Seligman's death
were to divide into sharply different factions, but their conduct of
government from 1934 through 1942 was that of a party group possessed of an authority sufficient to match its voting majorities, and
the two-party politics of the preceding thirty years changed dramatically to a one-party mode. For a brief period governors, as well
as party chairmen, were figures of considerable authority. Brokerage
of interests occurred at this new point of effective access—the office
of the governor—and the Democratic governor, as party leader,
controlled the legislature as he had never been able to do during the
hegemony of the Republican Old Guard.

Gubernatorial nominations of Clyde Tingley (1934, 1936) and that
of John Miles in 1938 were by conventions of a party which had
captured a marginal control of those counties once the basis of Republican strength, but an imposing majority in the remainder of the
state. Internal stresses of the party and the attractions of office brought
to the surface the struggle for control, and as a result of that factional struggle the direct primary law was enacted in time to become
effective in 1940.

The legislature came to a brief but sharp division as a result of
the struggle between Governor Tingley and Party Chairman Miles,
but that division merely reflected the degree to which the legislature
of the day was not yet an autonomous institution. Legislative freedom from external party control was limited in the northern counties
by a spirited two-party competition that was to differentiate rather
sharply the conduct of north county legislators from those of the
southern and border counties. Legislative turnover was about as high
as during the period of Republican dominance, but the southern

counties were beginning to show the pattern of legislators' renomination and re-election that was to underlie the party and legislative system of 1950-1964. A part of the factional conflict of the period was also the classic one of city versus state. The clash between Tingley and Miles was to determine, however briefly, whether the state party organization and its county components or the city-commercial-business group would dominate party and state affairs. Democratic politicians of the day achieved a measure of autonomy—a relatively high degree of freedom from group domination—by their means of self-financing from employee contributions and by the size and stability of the party's electoral margins.

PARTY LEADERSHIP AND THE NEW BASES OF PARTY STRENGTH

When Governor Clyde Tingley addressed the joint session of the 1937 legislature in his second term, only three Republican members —the senator and two representatives of Taos County—represented the minority, and even they were but the current winners of the endless factional disputes of that county.

Tingley's 58 per cent of the 1936 vote set a record not broken until 1964. Democratic gains over the lows of 1928 were 13 percentage points in the governor's race and 22 in the presidential, but the rise to power which transformed the Democratic party of New Mexico into the vehicle and broker of the dominant and emerging interests of the time had not occurred in one dramatic movement. The 1930 and 1932 elections were contributors to existing trends, and they brought to Democratic support the sizeable Progressive group associated with Senator Bronson Cutting. The Cutting men were ostensibly Republicans again in 1934, but the majority were avowed New Dealers by 1936 with the result that the Hispanic counties were marginally Democratic for the remainder of the New Deal period.

Victory of the Democratic executive and legislative candidates was complete and every area of the state had contributed to it, but it was in the counties growing as trade and mining areas that the sharpest and most significant electoral shift had come. Those counties had been the least involved in the traditional politics of the previous decades, and it was their shift which contributed most to the long period of Democratic dominance. Enlistment under the New Deal banner of new voters augmented the standing ranks of active voters with a strong party commitment. Firm electoral majorities, and changes in internal party control gave New Mexico's Democratic governors a brief period of control over government and politics that was different in kind, and perhaps greater for that reason, than that which had been exercised by the Old Guard.

There is but little doubt that the New Deal's avowed intention to improve the lot of the common man operated to vest in New Mexico's party men a degree of political independence from locally organized interests greater than had been previously enjoyed. About a quarter of the electorate of 1936 had apparently not been voting in 1928. Some had probably been so uncommitted to local interests that the active and intense politics of the earlier period had not essentially involved them. The New Deal did, however, involve them — directly and dramatically. Work-relief and related programs were urgent, tangible, and direct. Moreover, they were on a scale that at times involved nearly a fifth of the state's population.

In essence, two entities of government operated in every area of the state. The traditional offices of state government operated as before. They were expanded somewhat so that they touched more people directly and in a manner which made them more visible, more involved in voter consciousness. At the same time, an overlapping pattern of federal work-relief and related agencies based on local and state units or areas of government grew rapidly. Legally and financially distinct though the state and federal agencies were, they were also, politically and operationally, so closely related that they were staffed and directed from the same source—the active members of the Democratic party of New Mexico. News accounts and rosters of state agencies and federal relief agencies clearly indicate that personnel of the two were of the same group and completely interchangeable. The National Youth Administration director of one year was likely to be the congressional candidate of the next; the area Works Projects Administration supervisor was apt next to be his county's candidate for county assessor. As one of them phrased it to me: "The WPA was useful in making Democrats and we had county and precinct chairmen in it as bosses and straw bosses. The whole relief apparatus was used by Tingley." Others indicated that Tingley, as governor and as mayor of Albuquerque, had excellent access to Washington officialdom.

There occurred both a shift and a reconstruction of political power. It cannot be said without qualification that there had been a shift of the "locus" of political power, for such a figure leads to the conception that all of the elements of power were neatly concentrated at a given point or in the hands of a readily identifiable, and small, group of men. That was not the case. It was a large group which shared, and came to quarrel over, the political power they helped to establish and generate. Of these, there were, of course, some who had the ability and means to shape or influence significant economic and social forces and decisions. The economic involvement and orientation of these was analagous to that of the Republican Old Guard, but the Democrats of this type tended to a more intermittent political involvement which was one step removed from active party direction. There were others who were directly involved in political operations and management but who were, in turn, a step or two removed from the significant arenas of economic influence. What had been one group in the Republican era became two under the Democratic leadership. The politics which, in Weber's distinction, had been avocational for Republican Old Guard leadership, became vocational for many of the group which followed. Thus, where the Republican leader had tended to be simultaneously the spokesman for political as well as group or economic interests, events in the Democratic era divided the two functions so that a man was party leader, organizer, or candidate in the one set of political relations; or spokesman, contributor, or policy advocate in the other. Those whose orientation was to policies usually remained in the background; those whose proclivities were in the field of party operations usually emerged as candidates and managers of candidates.

For the most part, Clyde Tingley, John Miles, Will Keleher, Dennis Chavez, J. O. Seth, A. T. Hannett, Carl Hatch, James McGhee, *et al.*, were visible enough to the public but they were so as politicians, or advisers to politicians, rather than as men associated with specific and conspicuous economic organizations or interests, although they were not foreigners to either. Their trades were law or politics, or both.

In the palmy days when Miles and Tingley were able briefly to function as a chairman-governor team, they made successful use of other groups which have not ordinarily achieved in New Mexico the force sometimes accorded them in other states. Party leaders were able, for example, to find a use for, as well as foster, the state's "Young Democrats." In recent years both parties have tended to be a bit chary of such organizations, for they tend to be heedless and headstrong when caution seems warranted and noisy at those intervals when policy is still critically unresolved. The Young Democrats of 1930 to 1940, however, were ably led by men associated with the regular organization at the local levels and with the administration and legislature in Santa Fe. One, J. R. Wrinkle, a Silver City attorney, served as secretary to Governor Tingley and as an officer of the group, which he and his associates made function as an electoral rather than as a policy organization, so that the Young Democrats were kept comfortably close to the role and activity suggested for the organization by officers of the National Democratic Committee.

Legislative measures of interest to Tingley and Miles and their major elements of group support were often drafted by such attorneys as Will Keleher and J. O. Seth—both served for years as advisers and draftsmen for governors—but Tingley added a touch reflecting the New Deal orientation of the time by calling upon the services of Joe Dailey, an Albuquerque attorney who was spokesman and agent for labor organizations. Labor groups had never before (and it is unlikely that they have since) had so effective and direct address to governor and to the legislature. Dailey had been one of the Albuquerque men long associated with Tingley's local organization. A good part of his effectiveness as a labor spokesman came from the role Tingley assigned him of representing the administration as one of its legislative "beaters" or legmen on the floor of house and senate. By Tingley's second term, Dailey was free to represent labor, as well as the governor and the party, on the floor of the legislature.[1] The orientation and policies of the New Deal would have obtained for New Mexico's Democratic party a good deal of support from labor groups under any circumstances, but Dailey's role with legislature and governor confirmed and improved that support. It was evidence, too, of official and political recognition of the new political power of the mining counties of Colfax, McKinley, and Grant.

Labor had its heyday in Tingley's administration, but the administration of Governor Miles represented the apogee of the political and legislative authority of the organizations of school teachers and administrators. During the 1941 session some twenty laws—a tenth of the total product—represented legislative goals of the New Mexico Education Association. Only two or three of the session's total of twenty-three education laws were measures the association opposed in some degree; and these, it is safe to say, could have been killed by veto had the association wished to press. A former and longtime speaker of the house served in 1941 as chairman of the education committee, and the current speaker not only made the appropriate referrals to that committee, but acted as liaison man between committee and the governor's office on behalf of the association. Miles gave his support to measures designed to lessen local political interference in the schools—a transaction making good political sense to one with a governor's perspective. Reduction of autonomous areas of patronage and strength under the control of local and district schools and boards was in the interest of both the governor and the New Mexico Education Association, and in turn the governor benefited from the support of a numerous and relatively independent group with a statewide organization.

THE RECASTING OF POLICY

Adjustments of policy and party organization cementing Democratic control of the state came in a rush after 1933. Only a year or two was required to make needed changes, and thereafter the course of party and legislature was so well set that momentum engendered by the impulse of forces associated with the New Deal was long sufficient to keep the party moving with but minor new additions of social or political energy.

Governor Seligman's death in 1933 did not result immediately in a new formulation of policy, but it did permit a drastic change in legislative organization and direction, enabling forces which were to operate in the administration of Governor Clyde Tingley to make the needed adjustments.

The special session of 1934 was preceded by months of work by agricultural, oil, railroad, and educational interests. The Taxpayers' Association led or responded to a score of local associations anxious to recast the tax system of the state, and the accession to the governorship of Lieutenant Governor Hockenhull then opened the doors of executive offices to all who sought to participate in the changes. The 1934-1938 center of effective governmental authority shifted from the northern and Hispanic counties to those groups associated with the politics of Bernalillo, and the eastern and southern counties. But Hockenhull neither led nor restrained the forces seeking to achieve a new balance—he merely permitted his administration to become their instrument; for he was not a Rooseveltian type who in a hundred days could dramatically change the course of government.

The eighteen-day special session of 1934 enacted thirty-five statutes, of which the principal ones established employment agencies pursuant to acts of Congress, revised portions of the irrigation and water codes, and, most important, set up the emergency school tax act, but it was the regular session of 1935—Tingley's first—which established a record as a legislative mill to join together the complementary activities of political and non-governmental groups. In its operations it was but a continuance of the special session of the preceding April (the special and regular sessions together took but sixty-four days, for the regular session's forty-eight days of the sixty allowed set a record for brevity). A score of the more important bills had been prepared or outlined in advance of the session by administration attorneys or by the groups presenting the bills. Some of the measures were designed to give local effect to New Deal measures recently enacted by Congress, and these were recognized as closing the links of a political chain to bind New Mexico to Washington and the New Deal. Other measures were of local import and origin, but they had the effect of organizing several agencies of the state government. Together the sessions were sufficient to set the course of government and administration for nearly twenty years, for relatively few of the statutes that came after tended to be of such broad significance, while many were but variations on the changes rung in 1935.[2]

The groups and their spokesmen called or permitted to assist in devising the 1935 legislative program were given a more formal role for the 1937 session. The Taxpayers' Association noted that Governor Tingley had indicated his intent to have a legislative program ready "to lay before the solons on the opening day. To that end he will name a committee in the next few days to aid him. Other committees will be called in representing labor, farmers, business men and other groups for suggestions."[3] It was later reported that nine committees were appointed by Tingley in the fields of public affairs, labor, agriculture, land and livestock, education, etc.[4] The rosters of the committees were bipartisan, composed of well-known people, and provided an accurate index to the personalities and groups which had been so effective in the prior session.

There was a substantial difference in the product of the two legislative sessions, however. The 1935 session produced only 151 law chapters; the 1937 session 233, for a 54-per-cent increase, but the laws of 1937 contained only two or three measures of significance, and, for the most part, produced relatively minor accommodations for this group or that. An examination of the law chapter titles indicates that representatives of few groups or municipalities left Santa Fe without some legislative token of the esteem and favor of the administration. Tingley, for a time, had entertained some notions about repeating his feat of the previous session in limiting its duration, but several legislative leaders balked, and he agreed to the suggestion of a committee calling upon him that he would support a full session.[5]

The legislature that, under the Republican Old Guard, was often the instrument for registering decisions taken by party leaders with but nominal reference to the governor's office, became, under Tingley and Miles, a mart the governor controlled. Tingley, it was said, "kept the senate and house well in hand at all times, and the magic words 'this is an administration measure' were sufficient to bring a unanimous, or nearly unanimous, roll call in every case."[6] Not unexpectedly, however, in view of the experience of other states, internal cohesion of the Democratic legislative party during the Tingley and Miles administrations was somewhat lower than it had been in earlier sessions when the party balance was closer.[7]

INSTRUMENTS OF GUBERNATORIAL AND PARTY CONTROL

Tingley's base of operations was the city of Albuquerque, just then beginning its remarkable period of growth, and of which he was several times mayor before and after his governorship. His orientation to his city and to the needs and prevailing attitudes of people of the counties of the central and southern part of the state was obvious, and it is clear that Hispanic political leaders of the north knew and resented his leaning. (One of the Hispanic legislative leaders of the day told me in retrospect: "Tingley and I didn't get along. He insulted me by insulting my people when he said none of mine were competent for white collar work in the FERA offices.") Tingley's manner was to act, and speak, with a brusque forthrightness that became legendary; and he is the principal of numerous salty anecdotes, but, in spite of the yarns and legend, Tingley was considerably more than the boodler that some would see in him.

More than Miles, Tingley developed policy orientations to which he gave expression, but Tingley's interest was in economic policies and things—the latter often being those in which he tended to involve his personality, to say nothing of his name. He created the Carrie Tingley Hospital for crippled children and then proceeded to stretch nearly every control and financial statute of the state to build, finance, and equip it. He did far more than he needed to do to build and finance the state fair (with its Tingley Coliseum), but he saw to it that it was to stay in Albuquerque. Major federal work relief projects tended to gravitate to Albuquerque or the counties to the south, and Albuquerque's Tingley Park and Zoo, bordered by Tingley Drive, greatly benefited from federal funds. Aside from these expressions of personality, there is no doubt that in Tingley economic groups could more readily find a reponse than could social or other relatively subtle interests.

John Miles much better fits the notion that a politician lends himself to persons and forces without engendering thereby any firm personal involvement. That is, political commitments are to be honored, but geographic, social, or personal attachments are to weigh but little if other considerations seem paramount in the effort to organize and direct political groups. As much as any man in his party, Miles became the symbol of the professional politician. A Quay County dry-farmer, Miles became a precinct chairman in 1912. He lost a nomination for county commissioner in 1916 and was elected assessor in 1920, to serve two terms while serving as county chairman. Appointed tax commission secretary for the 1925-1926 term by Governor Hannett, he then served as state Democratic secretary from 1926 into the mid-1930's, and was appointed tax commissioner by Governor Seligman for the two terms of 1931-1935. He became state chairman in 1935, and held the post while serving as chief of the field division of the U.S. Internal Revenue Service. He was nominated and elected governor in 1938 and, after his two terms as governor, he served an appointive term as public service commissioner, two elective terms as land commissioner, and one as congressman. Nominated in 1950 for governor, he was the second Democrat (Senator Dennis Chavez was the first) to lose a statewide election in the period 1930-1950. In the fractious politics of the early 1960's, Miles was one of the few likely to be greeted at a party meeting by a spontaneous ovation.

Tingley and Miles were both quick to use whatever means were at hand to develop to the utmost instruments of legislative control and to develop party self-financing to a degree that probably curtailed the ability of broadly organized or typically uninvolved groups to act as restraints on the conduct of government. Opinions of other political leaders of the time vary on the question whether Tingley or Miles was the more effective as leader-commander of party and legislature, but both men are conceded to have been much more effective than either of their two successors—Governors John J. Dempsey and Thomas J. Mabry. It appears that Miles was closest to the sociologist's conception of control; the flamboyant Tingley to the popular: Miles' low pressure operations and intimate knowledge of personalities and party operations gave him much more authority over the party than appeared on the surface, and when two important showdowns came Miles was able to thwart the gubernatorial wills of Tingley and Dempsey.

Party and Policy: "The Governor's Men"

An Hispanic legislative leader who bridged the Seligman and Tingley administrations impressed upon me that Tingley "ran the legislature with an iron hand and only when he saw a few votes being organized against one of his bills would he call us in." Another Hispanic legislator who began a long series of terms under Tingley thought that "Tingley, like most governors, had a firm grasp on the legislature at all times." An astute lawyer and participant of six sessions recalled that Tingley and Dempsey were relatively loose on the reins, while "Miles was absolute." This member had no recollection of any attempted intervention by Tingley in the selection in 1937 of the senate floor leader; another stated that Tingley probably opposed Thaxton's selection but was induced to accede to it by the intervention of leading Republicans to whom Tingley was obligated, and by Judge Fred Wilson, who had served as leader in the previous session. But whatever the situation was concerning the senate leader, J. Q. Thaxton, it probably was not of too much importance to Tingley, for Lieutenant Governor Hiram Dow, his good friend and political colleague from the Little Texas county of Chaves, was serving as president of the senate. A skillful politician in his own right and highly effective as parliamentarian and party spokesman, Dow kept his floor leader directly under his control. Few senate presidents have attained the authority over the chamber that Dow exercised.

One of the more independent of the era's series of floor leaders of the senate recalls that:

> Under Miles' administration when Gail Carter, General Charleton and Johnny Michael hit the senate floor you might as well go home. They were the governor's agents. Miles was in absolute control of the legislature and the words "administration measure" were all that was necessary to pass a bill.[8]

This same member, in comparing the several administrations, said of the Tingley legislatures that Joe Dailey, John Simms, Sr., and Will Keleher were often around, but he was puzzled because they "didn't exercise more effort and influence on the floor." The phenomenon puzzling the senator probably means that the governor was quite sure that his legislative coterie would act responsibly and effectively as his agents.

Seniority had little weight in the senate or the house, and important chairmanships and committee assignments were apt to go, in the house particularly, to those individuals who met with the favor of state chairman and governor.[9] For example, Joseph M. Montoya (U.S. Senate, 1964-), the majority leader of the house in one session, had just attained the age of 23 and had served in only one previous session. The member who served longest as speaker, Alvan White, was regarded as the governor's man and completely dependable, regardless of who the governor was. For five consecutive sessions the position of chief clerk of the senate was filled by the same person. But individuals such as these were merely part of a broad array of disciplined political talents available to Democratic organizations of the time. In the legislature they served as Miles served in the party, although as agents rather than as principals.

Legislative organization was worked out in the interest of the party as well as of the governor, and the party chairman and other leading members were on hand for the sessions. Tingley, it is said, did not have an entirely free hand. Miles, Tingley and party leaders would get together until they could agree, but, in Tingley's legislature, "leading senators had to be consulted also on their offices." Miles was apparently in firmer control, for, as one of the most influential members of Miles' legislatures has described, somewhat as follows, his impressions: "When legislative factions were choosing up candidates they would send delegations to Miles, who would say, in effect, that he would be quite well satisfied if their man got the legislative leadership position or positions. However, at the same time, he would have his men working for the list of his own choosing, so that the caucus would inevitably pick Miles' choices."

Floor leaders and other elected legislative officers were given considerable voice in the selection of committee members; and the speaker, acting as a gubernatorial agent, could then effectively control legislation by making bill referrals to the appropriate committees. The Republican device of the steering committee promptly fell into disuse, for Democratic governors of the period learned to use their administrative officers as legislative agents to act in concert with the elective house and senate leaders. Administrative officials and floor leaders would get their instructions in the daily "calendar sessions" in the governor's office, relay with marked calendars the orders of the day to a few legislators and to the governor's beaters, and the calendar would usually be dispatched without a hitch.

Jobs and Legislative Control

Republican leaders and lobbyists of the earlier era of New Mexico politics had been wont to assemble legislators—who were then and into the 1940's paid $5.00 per day—around the "Dutch-style lunch" and the whiskey barrel maintained first by Springer and Spiess and later by the railroad lobbyists. Democratic leaders of the following era employed a more effective and direct means of guiding and forming legislative opinion and providing the bones and sinews of organization. Their method involved the placing of increasingly large numbers of legislators on the public payroll; and no legislator, under Miles at least, could be appointed to a job, or obtain one for a constituent, without the endorsement of his county chairman. In the words of a senator of a realist or non-reformist tendency: "Jobs for legislators were damned influential. Dickason's bill [which became effective in 1945 to outlaw the practice] was a very good one." The reformist senator who introduced and finally secured passage of the measure, Albuquerque's Don Dickason, told me simply: "Tingley had quite a few legislators on the payroll, but not so many as Dempsey and Miles." On the floor, however, Dickason stated for the *Journal* of the senate:

> I want to see this bill enacted, and I feel certain that it will meet some opposition if the amendments now on the bill are stricken. I don't think we could do anything better in this legislature than to take a step forward in making the legislature an independent body standing on its own feet, instead of a bunch of rubber stamps subservient to the will of the Governor when he chooses to make it such.[10]

During the height of the controversy over Dickason's bill, political observer and columnist Will Harrison, then of *The New Mexican's* editorial staff, observed:

> A good many house members in the past have sought election merely to get a job with the state. . . . At one time or another during the past two years eighteen members of the legislature of 1941 have been in state pay.[11]

With a few exceptions—the men who were strong enough at home to deal with the governor on their own terms—the members of the legislature who accepted state employment were counted among the stalwart supporters of gubernatorial programs.[12] Since these were often effective members in key positions, the legislative leverage available to the governors of the time was considerable. The member who told me: "Governors of those days didn't have to negotiate with us," was substantially correct.

The Loaves and Fishes of Party Finance

Victualing the armies of politics does not require the long baggage trains of conventional warfare, but the logistics of the supply of money is nearly as important a concern as marshalling the party's voters. Republican operators of the earlier era of New Mexico's politics relied heavily on the contributions of their wealthier members, friendly ranchers, and corporations. Democratic campaigners of the lean days of the depression learned to forage on the countryside, and for the levy of troops substituted cash levies against payrolls and contractors, to acquire thereby a significant measure of independence from extra-party centers of control.

In the early 1930's, when depression had all but dried up the wellsprings of contributions, Democratic party managers turned to a regular 2-per-cent assessment upon the salaries and wages of all employees and officers except the teaching staffs of the state's colleges. Although sporadic efforts to establish a contributory system had been made earlier, Ed Safford, Republican state chairman, charged that the Seligman administration began the 2-per-cent levy system in April, 1931, and supplemented it with an additional 1 per cent in November, 1932.[13] A Democratic party leader of the day, who later became one of the state's judiciary, was also of the opinion that Seligman institutionalized the system "which became as well managed as a business, and he [Seligman] also started the shakedown of contractors for contributions." In a campaign of the late 1940's, according to a former manager of the state highway contractors' association, the contractors contributed $35,000 to the Democratic ticket and $22,000 to the Republican organization. During the construction slowdown of the war years, this source of funds had been much less fruitful. Not until the large bond issues under Tingley, however, did the state's highway contractors become a lucrative and reasonably steady source of contributions. (Bonds authorized by Tingley's legislatures totalled $13,000,000 and by Miles' $10,000,000. Measured against the scale of the state's operations these were large sums.)

The system promptly drew a Democratic factional attack in the form of HB 340 of the 1933 session, banning employees' payroll contributions to party funds. Rep. Willis Ford (Dem.), Chaves County, the bill's sponsor, alleged that the party had not only indulged in a "high-jacking" of contractors, but said employees were fired if they failed to pay. As a newspaper account had it:

the house, acting in the role of a Democratic state convention, officially approved the system when it defeated the bill 33 to 12. Reps. Greaser, Gary and Hinkle advocated the measure.

Meanwhile Ford attempted to put the "Kingfish," otherwise state Democratic Chairman W. J. Barker, "on the spot" as the big shot in administering the "racket." Ford exhibited cancelled checks to prove alleged hi-jacking of contractors and the working of the two per cent assessment.

. . . . .

Ford pleaded guilty to inventing the assessment system in 1923 when on the highway board, said it was then voluntary and declared it had developed "into a racket of the worst kind."[14]

Highway department maintenance crews were under the patronage of county chairmen, and several of the more enterprising of the local party functionaries acquired equipment which they then leased or rented to the department.[15] Not all of the patronage could be dispensed by the governor and his men, however, for accidents of law and governmental organization often served to establish pockets of local autonomy. The schools as well as county or city courthouses and a few independent governmental entities could be under the control of local and dissident factions:

[Filo] Sedillo has told friends that he has been stripped of state patronage for the Valencia County loyal. However, he doesn't particularly need it. The Valencia County Democratic chairman rarely has trouble landing stalwarts on the Middle Rio Grande Conservancy payroll or in the Valencia schools.[16]

Party funds made available by the payroll assessment were calculated by one observer to approximate $40,000 per year—a prize that made party control worth the effort.[17] In one account, the use of the state-level funds was at the "discretion of" the state chairman and his advisers, but: "It is not unheard of in state politics for the governor to take over the collection and expenditure of party funds."[18]

The Book of St. Matthew relates that they "that had eaten" of the five loaves and two fishes "were about five thousand men, beside women and children." They that ate of New Mexico's patronage loaves and fishes numbered as many, and again not counting women and children. The January, 1940 roster of officers and employees of the previous year numbered 6,484, of whom all but college teachers and the professional personnel employed in offices subject to the restraints of the Hatch Act were exposed to the levy upon their pay.[19]

Warp and Weft of Party and Administration

Prior to the New Deal years, New Mexico's Republicans had often used statewide conclaves of active party members to review and resolve issues, to review possible candidacies, and to exchange the gossip so necessary to politics. The Republican pattern was to assemble groups of two hundred or so when problems of consensus or candidacies were in need of attention, but the groups assembled for determining legislative or administrative action, or making the hard decisions concerning slates and funds, were much smaller and involved only the Old Guard's "inner" or "inner-inner" circles. Under Miles' direction as chairman and as governor, the Democratic meetings were not large, for they usually were limited to three to five men from each county. The meetings were generally called every three or four months for sessions of one or two days and were conducted by the state chairman.

As might be expected, the gatherings were typically concerned with party personnel and personalities, organization, patronage, financing, and party tactics. During Miles' administration particularly (but the degree of difference was not great), they also served to bring administrative policies and considerations directly into the purview of meetings initiated for other concerns. During the period 1935-1940, one could normally find on the roster of state officers and employees from a third to half of the county chairmen and a considerably larger number of precinct chairmen and other party operatives whose activities or connections assured them of state employment. The duplication of names set forth in the official *New Mexico Blue Book,* 1941-1942, as officers or employees of the state, and the names set out as state and county party officers provides an index of the degree to which government and party were one. As a result, the majority of the membership of the quarterly meetings was already at hand in Santa Fe, employed in positions ranging from janitor to commissioner of revenue.

It was Miles' practice to delegate considerably more authority and discretion in the administrative realm than he did in the political. Whenever he was in the capitol, his office was apt to be open for phenomenally long hours, but even so "they were standing in the halls." His style of operation assured, as he probably desired, that Miles would serve as his own state chairman. But those to whom he had delegated extensive administrative authority tended as well to be his political operatives. Those men, whose names were still familiar in the 1960's to many New Mexicans, were the dominant personalities at the *juntas* of political-administrative chieftains. J. O. Gallegos, J. O. Garcia, Gail Carter, J. R. Wrinkle, S. T. Jernigan, Earl Stull, Sr., John B. McManus, Ben Luchini, Tom Summers, Russell C. Charlton, Harold B. Sellers, A. L. Atherton, Murray Hintz, and A. M. Fernandez were among the more prominent. Each had a position of sufficient importance to require its listing in the *Blue Book*. Several were good administrators as well as accomplished politicians. Taken together, they were a formidable crew, and it is scarcely to be wondered at that they could make and execute political decisions.

REGIONAL AND FACTIONAL ROOTS OF THE PRIMARY

The sometimes inelegant posture of New Mexico's Democratic party of the Tingley-Miles era of 1935-1943 was due, in part, to its ancient need to stand on two stools. As they had for the preceding twenty years, the factions and segments of the party still distributed themselves into two elements based, in turn, on the two geographic and cultural areas which had long shown characteristic attitudes about the possible adoption of the primary.

In the legislature, the virtual disappearance, for a time, of the Republican minority permitted a distribution of the majority members into a division corresponding to the electoral factions of the Democratic party.

Tingley enjoyed a nearly unqualified support from members from the six counties of Little Texas, and a high but less marked loyalty from most of the counties of the periphery of the state. Miles drew his key legislative support from a group of nineteen members of whom only six (from the counties of Bernalillo, Colfax, and McKinley) came from counties other than the ten in which a majority of the citizenry were Spanish American. In a set of thirty-two roll calls on measures endorsed by Miles, this subgroup turned in an average level of support of 90 per cent. Comparable results are evident in

Table 38 showing relative support of all members from the Little
Texas and Hispanic counties for bills identified with the two administrations.

TABLE 38. LEGISLATIVE FACTIONS: LOYALTY TO TINGLEY AND MILES

Area of legislative representation	*Per cent of Democratic House members voting in support of party or governor*	
	Tingley, 1935 (46 roll calls)	*Miles, 1939 (32 roll calls)*
The 9 Little Texas members	87.0	61.8
The 10 Hispanic counties:		
Hispanic members	72.0	82.3
"Anglo" members	89.1	81.8
All members	77.2	82.1

The Tingley factional support came primarily from the areas
which were the least likely to support a nearly even and highly competitive two-party politics; the Miles legislative strength came from
Hispanic counties which had been central to the old Republican
hegemony. Consequently, Miles tended to draw his legislative strength
from members coming from counties in which the Democratic candidates ran about even with Republicans—an unexpected result in
view of the experiences of several states, in which legislators from
marginal or atypical districts tend to be relatively independent of
party voting.[20] County organizations in these competitive counties
were closely aligned with Miles, and provided most of his impressive
strength in the state organization and party conventions. County
chairmen in these relatively poor areas could, in turn, call their bills
of political credit due for payment in generous allocations of state
jobs—a matter essential to their local authority. With these awards
at his disposal, the capacity of the county chairman to influence the
local party and its nominations was great. Legislators, no less than
other candidates, were dependent upon support of their county chairmen for nominations, as well as for jobs for themselves, family
members, or friends. These webs of mutual obligations assured that

legislators from these highly competitive counties could normally be relied upon by the governor to vote as the whips suggested. In the circumstances, party discipline was doubtless enhanced by the need to maintain considerable unity against the still great strength of Republican organizations in the Hispanic north.

The differing legislative factions giving support to one or the other of the two governors show characteristic differences in their reliance upon community as opposed to party ties. The members returned for two or more sessions were typically nominated by the unofficial direct primary which had been operating in the southern and eastern counties for some years. Members from the northern and Hispanic counties often sought to serve a term or two in the legislature after filling the maximum two consecutive terms in a county office. After the legislative interval they were then free to run again for the more lucrative local offices. In the four sessions of 1935-1941, the proportion of experienced legislators returned per session was only slightly higher than in the previous decade, for about 80 per cent of the members of each session's house and senate were serving a first or second term. In portent of the future, however, the remaining 20 per cent consisted of forty-eight individuals, of whom only seven (14 per cent) came from the ten Hispanic counties, while thirty-seven (77 per cent) came from Little Texas and a few other border counties. The primary and other institutional changes described in the following chapters served incidentally to augment and confirm the legislative and other political powers of the peripheral counties, but the legal statements were neither precedent nor causative.

Although the direct primary had been a political issue in New Mexico since the constitutional convention, few Republican leaders (and fewer still of the Hispanic leaders of either party) wanted any part of it.[21] Democratic partisans, however, were deeply split on the matter. Generally, those active in party affairs and management in the northern counties opposed; those in the eastern and southern counties favored the primary.

Curry records that the "voluntary primary, each candidate for a nomination to be assessed a small amount to pay expenses of the primary election" was first used in Chaves County in 1890, and that voters of Eddy County soon followed suit.[22] By the early 1900's, the unofficial primary was a standard device in several of the border counties, where it was almost invariably used only by the Democratic party, while Republicans remained with the convention. The local Democratic party organization was responsible for setting up the necessary arrangements in each county or multi-county district and for establishing the rules to govern them. "We used [in Chaves County] certified copies of registration lists for voting."[23] A convention would be held later, but convention delegates were pledged to ratify the choice of the voters in the primary.

The voluntary primary began to be used by Grant County Democrats in the 1920's, and by 1934 Governor Hockenhull reported, in urging adoption of an official direct primary, that:

> About one-third of the counties of our state are now attempting to hold direct primaries with no law whatever to guide them, and the remaining two-thirds will soon be calling political caucuses with no law in force to guide them.[24]

The primary system as used in the border counties did not run counter to any substantial need to offer a ticket that was balanced *vis-a-vis* Hispanic and Anglo candidates. In the northern counties, however, balancing the ticket had early become an essential function of party leadership, and Hispanic political leaders, particularly, were quick to state their opposition to the primary on grounds that it would impair their ability to secure nominations for their followers.

The issue became very much alive in the 1937 legislature, when several state senators from Albuquerque and the southern areas pressed for a bill. Tingley refused then to endorse the primary measures, seeking instead proposal and passage of a constitutional amendment removing the limitation on the number of consecutive terms state officers could serve. This was defeated in the special election of the same year when it received only 38 per cent of the large vote cast. U.S. Senator Dennis Chavez and Congressman John J. Dempsey strongly opposed Tingley's "self-perpetuation" amendment, and while State Chairman John Miles made no statements on the issue, he, too, worked to defeat it. Miles' opposition led to a break in his, by then, tenuous relations with the governor, and, although Tingley made no overt move to depose Miles, he denied Miles any further control of party finances and blocked wherever possible his control of the organization.

Tingley's next gambit was to call a special session for consideration of a direct primary law—a move bringing strong and immediate opposition from members of the northern counties, but a powerful and prevailing support from the southern counties and most of the press.[25] The bill passed with margins too narrow to qualify it as an emergency measure which could govern the 1938 nominations. Miles easily dominated the convention, to receive the nomination; but the election, in turn, reflected the issues that had been called up and clearly showed the shape of the regional forces at work. Miles' vote in the Little Texas counties dropped nearly 10 percentage points below Tingley's share of the 1936 vote, and 12 points in Bernalillo County, but he bested by a point or two Tingley's mark in the Hispanic counties.

EIGHT

Electoral and Legislative Systems, and the Conduct of Government, 1940-1965

COINCIDENTAL with the declining but still great electoral popularity of the New Deal, the war in Europe, and the beginnings of a rapid growth and shift in her population, New Mexico first used, in 1940, the direct closed primary and a permanent registration statute. (The "closed" primary enables only the duly enrolled members of a party to vote in it in making the party's nominations. The registration act served a dual purpose by providing a publicly maintained list of each party's members eligible for candidacy or for primary election voting and a roster of citizens eligible to vote, whether as party members or not, at the general elections.) Of the connection of the two laws, the press observed: "The primary code, without the registration act, would have been far less effective than it may now be."[1] The primary, its advocates held, was essential to the internal democracy of the newly preponderant Democratic party; the registration law was designed, in part, to discourage the formation of disciplined factions free to move, as Senator Bronson Cutting had demonstrated, with decisive effect from party to party.

Significant changes ensued in the state's politics after 1940. The frequency of interparty competition for legislative seats declined sharply and immediately upon installation of the primary. A reduction of party activity in the recruitment of legislative candidates not only opened the field to candidates more rooted in community than in party, but it quickly posed the questions of whether and by what means the legislature might be organized by and around the governorship, and whether and when it might so order itself that it could function in relative independence of gubernatorial leadership or authority. Certain other possible effects were more remote in time and more contingent upon other factors: A long-term decrease in the proportion of active to potential voters was sharpened for a time, and the electorate was apparently less and less bound by party ties (but both were tendencies by no means peculiar to New Mexico). As the party balance shifted to the Democratic side of the scale, increasingly diverse regional and group differences became more critically sensitive as elements underlying the sometimes close electoral margins. A series of legislative apportionments and other alterations in the legal specifications of constituencies, and increasingly important changes in the methods of electing legislators gained momentum after 1949. Meanwhile, the parties became less instrumental in framing policy and more strictly confined to electoral activities (although the efficiency of the parties as electoral organizations showed no increase), and the legislatures of 1945-1965 came to demonstrate quite clearly an increased measure of independence—a capacity for self-direction Young has termed "legislative autonomy."[2] Legislative independence from party and governor was, in part, a somewhat sporadic outgrowth of changes in the electoral systems and of a series of redefinitions of legislative constituency; but was also, patently, a resultant of adjustment to the frequent presence of a governor of the opposition party, even though divided government in the earlier era of legislative dominance had produced no such effect.

These tendencies and changes were all, by and large, complementary and congruent, but they converged upon a paradox. Political organization and electoral activity at the local level became a realm clearly separate from statewide organizational and factional activity, and members arriving for service in the newly autonomous legislature came increasingly as independent spokesmen-delegates of their local constituencies. Yet, many of the new crop of legislators were able and ambitious young men, and the political entrepreneurs among them who would try the fit of the governor's chair or a congressional seat promptly converted the legislature into a proving ground and policy arena. Perhaps in spite of themselves, some fostered and some acceded to the claims of party, and they twice enacted a pre-primary convention law providing a measure of party control at the state level many would have been loathe to accept at home. Out of the whole complex of legislative and executive activity grew a cumulative and accelerating series of changes in governmental activity and organization.

NOMINATING SYSTEMS: INSTITUTIONAL LIMITS AND EFFECTS

New Mexico's experience strongly confirms the proposition that inter-party competition for legislative seats can diminish as a result of the direct primary.[3] It also appears that the primary accelerated a long-term trend of increasing longevity of legislative service, but, in this case, the connection is somewhat less clear. A tangle of influences obscure the primary's influences upon the fortunes of Spanish-American candidates. Some limited effects can be traced in the case of candidates for state office, but Hispanic legislative candidacies have also been clearly affected by reapportionment, changes in ballot arrangements, and in the definitions of constituencies.

Legislative Nominations

Republican conventions of 1938 put up candidates for 96 per cent of the seats of the house of representatives. Two years later, in the first official and statewide primaries, the party had candidates for only 69 per cent of the seats, for the number uncontested by the party rose from two in 1938 to fifteen of the forty-nine in 1940. The sharp differences in the two elections were extreme but not unrepresentative, for the percentages of seats uncontested by one or the other of the two parties during the ten campaigns immediately preceding and the ten beginning with the first primary are: 1920-1938, 9 per cent, 1940-1958, 23 per cent. Of the uncontested seats, nearly all resulted from Republican failure to contest. Table 39 extends the comparison by relating it to changing differences, in strongly Democratic counties, in the apparent odds against Republican success.

A prefatory warning is in order, for Table 39 presents some puzzles. The spread between gubernatorial and legislative votes was greater in the 1950's than in the 1940's. Coattail effects mentioned in Chapter IV were not generally uniform except in the closer legislative races tending to occur in counties producing tight gubernatorial majorities. There was a reduction by one-half, during the 1950's, of counties casting more than 55 per cent of their ballots for the Democratic candidate for governor in the 1940's (some had once been Republican or nearly so, and were reverting to old allegiances). Hence, if all their legislative places had been contested, marginally Democratic counties could possibly have yielded a few more Republican seats than

TABLE 39. ELECTORAL STRENGTH, NOMINATING SYSTEM, AND
            UNCONTESTED SEATS

Elections	House seats in counties casting a vote of 55 percent or more for Democratic candidates for governor		Percentage of all seats uncontested by Republicans
	Number of counties	Percentage of total seats	
CONVENTION ERA			
1920-1930	10	27	6
1932-1938	10	22	10
PRIMARY ERA			
1940-1948	12	33	24
1950-1960	6	15	20

the three or four they did at times. The percentage of uncontested
seats in the later decade declined but little, however, even though
only 15 per cent of all the seats were now in territory out-and-out
Democratic by this measure.[4] By this arithmetic, legislative chances
should have been at least as good during the era of Eisenhower and
Mechem as they were during the bleak years, for Republicans, of
Miles and Roosevelt. (It is difficult to make such claims with undiluted
confidence in view of the complexities of background and change in
the voting habits of the population as described in Chapters II through
IV. However, there is some evidence, and some appealing conjectural
reason, to support the notion that the poor circumstances of the
minority party resulted in part from its failure to exploit its various
opportunities. Why it has not done so is another matter, and a portion of the burden of the current discussion.)

Nevertheless, the data of Table 39 seem to reflect effects of institutional or electoral machinery of the eras covered. During the 1920's
the Democratic share of the vote of the several counties ranged from
25 to 85 per cent, yet both parties strove to field candidates and
maintain an active organization in each county. The Republican and
Democratic organizations described in Chapters V and VI used their
paid and unpaid officials like Ed Safford and Arthur Seligman to

foster candidates, enlist factional support, and act with local groups and conventions as agents of their state parties. During the 1920's, the Democratic party failed to put up candidates for only 2 per cent of the house seats available; Republican lapses in 6 per cent of the nominations (an average of three seats per session) occurred only in the extremely adverse areas or where opportunities were present to attempt "best two out of three" contests. (The state's party-column ballot was not greatly conducive to success of the strategem, but, if Republicans in a district electing two or three members fielded one strong candidate rather than two or three of a more modest appeal, it sometimes happened that he could attract enough switching votes from each of his opponents to win with a result such as: Democrat One, 43 per cent; the Republican, 30 per cent; and Democrat Two, 27 per cent.) Control of the legislature as a party instrument was a prime objective of both parties. Nor did the schism in 1934 of the Republican organization entirely disrupt the pattern, for by 1938 the party again had its men before the conventions, and the list of candidates was virtually complete in spite of the drubbing the party was taking during the first two Roosevelt administrations.

Upon the installation of the primary, the activities of the Republican party and its factions came to a radically different result.

With conventions held subsequent to the primaries, the formal party leadership at the state level tended to hold off action until the gubernatorial nomination had been made. State Republican leaders and those in many of the counties and judicial districts were slow to find legal and economic means of filing candidates for each legislative nomination. After the first primary, each of a series of four gubernatorial nominations was contested by two or more candidates, and the energies of the supportive factions of the candidates were directed to obtaining a favorable primary vote rather than to encouraging legislative candidacies. The duty of all was performed by none. Seats in the marginal and Democratic counties more often went by default; and, except for the 1946 campaign when the party's old pro, Ed Safford, was seeking the nomination, the party's history during the 1940's shows little of a calculated policy to foster legislative nominations. And perhaps for most of the decade all was done that could be done, for the shifting pattern of gubernatorial nominations reflected the still deep division in the party. Conservative nominee

Tondre was followed by liberals Miera and Gunderson; "Old Guarder" Safford was followed by liberal Lujan, and he by conservative Mechem.

The party's successes in legislative elections in 1952, activity engendered by the pre-primary endorsement conventions of 1952 and 1954, and the state chairman's policy of encouraging local nominations in the 1954 campaign brought that campaign's uncontested legislative seats down to the same 16 per cent that the Safford campaign of 1946 had produced.[5] But ordinarily, in the primary era, the prime impulse sustaining the enlistment of candidacies in the more difficult areas was that of periodically improved individual prospects of victory rather than fulfillment of a party-imposed duty to take advantage of every useful variation in the odds.

The arguments of the preceding paragraphs cannot be demonstrated with impressive precision, but Table 40 provides them with

TABLE 40. THE PRIMARY, AND HOUSE SEATS CONTESTED AND
WON BY REPUBLICANS

Year and nominating system	Republican candidates		Number of seats won by Republicans	Republican seats as a percentage:	
	Number	As a percentage of 49 seats		Of total	Of seats contested
CONVENTION					
1932	47	96	8	16	17
1934	41	84	12	24	29
1936	42	86	2	4	5
1938	47	96	7	14	15
TOTAL	177 (of 196)	90	29	15	16
PRIMARY					
1940	34	69	9	18	26
1942	31	63	16	33	52
1944	38	78	19	39	50
1946	43	87	19	39	44
1948	41	84	13	24	32
Total	187 (of 245)	76	76	31	41

some support. Democratic voting margins in the period 1932-1938, preceding the primary, were broader than in 1940-1948, when Republican effort slacked off. In the later period Republican candidates contested fewer seats, even though they won twice as many as they had in the preceding four elections. It is apparent that, had more candidates been entered in the more favorable period, the rate of failure would have increased, but the gap between the number of seats won and the number available might well have been somewhat smaller.

The 1960 campaign provides another intimation of the relation between Republican party effort and legislative candidacies. The campaign began in the late spring of 1959, when the party's executive committee authorized the employment of a research and campaign assistant to the state chairman and directed that efforts be made to conduct an intensive campaign.[6]

The executive committee was dubious that it would again be able to enlist Edwin Mechem as its gubernatorial candidate, and it sought to make the nomination as attractive as possible. The first strategem was that of watching and publicizing every move of the Democratic administration. The second was that of encouraging local party activities. To these ends, the state chairman directed the research assistant to prepare a campaign analysis, which turned out to be an analysis of secular voting patterns and a set of suggestions for taking advantage in various areas of favorable trends and diverting the unfavorable.[7] The resulting document was given a limited circulation and the remaining copies promptly placed under appropriate safeguard. Then, in a series of party meetings, it was determined that every effort would be directed to securing legislative candidacies and preparing platform and campaign materials well in advance of primary filing day. The next development was a little disconcerting to the high command, for not only Mechem but another strong candidate, Paul W. Robinson of Albuquerque, filed for the gubernatorial nomination. Both, however, had been fully aware of the party's activities in exploiting publicity opportunities and both approved of the effort to commit local partisans to legislative candidacy. Neither man attempted to interfere, and, although some adherents of each watched the proceedings with considerable suspicion (a few did so with real alarm) the efforts of the executive committee and state chairman generally met with approval. (One county chairman was extremely reluctant to put legislative candidates in the field in his heavily Democratic county. "It will just stir up the opposition," was his objection. No Republican legislative candidates put in an appearance in that county, although the state campaign staff made considerable effort to enlist them. As for the stirring up of the electorate, it was daily becoming more obvious to party chieftains that either a Kennedy or Johnson nomination, but for different reasons, would bring out a very large vote in the eastern counties. It was a gloomy day for New Mexico Republicans when they learned that *both* Kennedy and Johnson were nominated.)

To enlist candidates did not prove to be difficult, although it entailed a great deal of activity. The meetings involved were numerous and exhausting, but they and the unexpected surge of publicity were sufficient to excite local interest. Prospective candidates in adverse areas were always assured that this call to party duty was likely to be a painful one, and probably not successful for the individuals concerned. And it was stressed that filings were encouraged in the anticipation that local candidacies would generally improve the chances for success of the state ticket's candidates. The primary system presented a few hazards, however, of the sort that some of the old-timers had been fearful about. A few feelings were bruised in efforts to discourage the poorer of the prospective candidacies excited by all the noise and activity, and one or two outrageous candidates resisted every effort to induce them to withdraw—a matter a convention might have handled summarily.

As Chapter IV indicates, the vote was a heavy one, measurably influenced by the presidential candidates and issues. The counties were sent further along their long-term routes and many of the sixty legislative candidacies suffered accordingly. Several of the more heavily Democratic counties increased their vote to the Republican legislative candidates, but not to winning margins; in some areas, as in the north, their percentage of the vote was below the long-term norms. It was a losing but, within its objectives, a successful campaign. The candidates for governor and lieutenant governor were elected and several of the rejuvenated local organizations displayed a commendable capacity and ingenuity. Whether, over the long pull, such tactics would redress some local party balances has to remain conjectural until they are tried. However, the experiences of the 1960 campaign appear to warrant Key's observation that an increase "in the effort devoted to the development and maintenance of a statewide integrated party system might offset institutional depressants of party life that operate when such effort remains more or less constant."[8]

The Primary and the Political Cultures

The uses and results of the primary have clearly differed in the several cultural sectors of the state—differences reflecting important features of its politics.

A foregoing chapter noted that there has evolved "a notable longevity of service of legislative members from Little Texas"—counties in which "the uncontested legislative primary and general election is most frequent." The relationship, it was suggested, was a matter indicative of "centralized structures of local political authority in a one-party environment." Prior to the 1960's about 90 per cent of the seats contested at neither primary nor general election were in a sprinkling of border counties and in Little Texas—areas of heavily predominant Democratic registration and a normally broad margin of Democratic votes at the general election. In these, not only have fewer candidates from the minority been disposed to challenge the 60-40 odds, but the incumbent legislator has been challenged much less frequently at the primary than has elsewhere been the rule. In sum, these are the counties which might disclose the highest internal concentration of political authority, just as they have developed a most significant and disproportionate weight in legislative matters, and a potential capacity to dominate statewide nominations.

Six Little Texas counties plus six similar counties of the border regions (Grant, Hidalgo, Luna, Otero, Quay, and Union) provide the data on the relationship of incumbency and intraparty competition outlined in Table 41. Legislators of Little Texas and the border counties, it is clear, are opposed less frequently, stay in office longer, and are less frequently defeated than others in the state. Not reflected in the table is the result that their limited number is normally quite fully compensated for by the skills and leadership their experience and legislative positions give them. Hispanic legislators are apt to be subject to a rather continuous and critical scrutiny of their electors; the border and Little Texas counties, perhaps quite accidentally and unwittingly, confer a broader freedom. A substantial degree of freedom of the latter legislators from the parochial restraints which seem to be inherent in the politics of more competitive districts, and

TABLE 41. INCUMBENCY AND PRIMARY COMPETITION OF LEGISLATIVE
CANDIDATES IN TWELVE STRONGLY DEMOCRATIC COUNTIES,
1956-1960

Area and number of nominations	Percentage		Percentage of incumbents	
	Incumbents in primary	Total nominations contested	Opposed	Defeated
Little Texas and border counties (69)	62	46	41	9
Rest of state (129)	40	60	71	21

their close personal identification with the values and dominant groups of their communities appear to require them to act as delegate spokesmen in matters of clearly defined local interest, but permit them to act as "politicos" free to represent a broader interest in all other matters.[9] Perhaps in consequence, these legislators became increasingly visible and successful after 1950 as potential candidates for statewide and congressional office.

The situation has been quite different in the Hispanic counties. There, as this chapter will describe below, political leaders and organizations have been more able and more prone than those elsewhere in the state to monitor and dominate the recruitment and endorsement of legislative candidacies. And these counties and politicians resisted enactment of the primary as warmly as Little Texas voters endorsed it. As Chapter II may have made clear, Hispanic leaders perceived their political involvement as a matter directly and vitally related to other interests. From their point of view, they have been more successful in limiting and controlling the effects of the primary upon legislative candidacies than they have upon those offices for which they must compete with other groups in the state.

Although the operation of the convention system from statehood to 1940 seldom obtained for Hispanic candidates the 50 per cent of the available nominations often demanded on grounds that Spanish Americans comprised that percentage or more of the population, it

did allocate to them slightly over a third of the state-ticket nominations—a consideration which no doubt impelled much of the Hispanic
opposition to the primary and subsequent efforts to restore statewide
conventions. (Conversely, the opposition of the great majority of
Hispanic politicians to woman's suffrage was probably based simply
upon a cultural preference. In that case, residents of Sandoval County
were prompt to petition the legislature to refrain from adopting the
suffrage amendment, pleading that " 'the government be continued
in this pleasant condition.' "[10] Ordinarily, however, Hispanic reactions
to proposed innovations in government or political forms and procedures appear to stem, as with other groups, from judgments of
anticipated advantage or disadvantage.) In the 1940's, Hispanic
aspirants for statewide office received 32 per cent of the available
nominations—a level nearly as high as that in the convention era—
but only 18 per cent were accorded them in the next decade. Some
part of the declining ratio of Hispanic candidates must be attributed
to the declining proportion (37 per cent in 1950, 28 per cent in 1960)
of Hispanic citizens in the whole population, but the remaining portion of the drop is probably traceable to the operation of the primary.

Under ordinary circumstances during the convention era, the
leaders of both parties, whether Anglo or Hispanic, quite clearly saw
the necessity of offering state tickets balanced to attract the Hispanic
voter. They were not only successful in the effort to apportion a sizeable number of nominations to Hispanic candidates, but it appears
that party leaders must consciously have attempted either to match
particular candidacies or to allocate certain positions to Hispanic
candidates.

In the thirteen state conventions of each party from 1911 through
1938, the Democrats allotted fifty-one nominations to candidates of
Hispanic surname, and the Republicans, fifty-nine. Conceivably, fifty-
one matched or Hispanic versus Hispanic candidacies could have
resulted, and a total of thirty-five matches did occur. Considering
that the typical convention made nominations for twelve positions
and that the various conventions of each party nominated Hispanic
candidates in numbers ranging from two to six, the matchings that
occurred were far more numerous than would be assumed to have
occurred by chance. Just short of 63 per cent of the fifty-nine Republican Hispanic nominations went to candidates for congress, secretary

of state, auditor, and corporation commissioner; 75 per cent of the
fifty-one Democratic Hispanic nominations were for the same offices;
and most of the occurrences of matching in the convention era are
found in those nominations. The likelihood of Hispanic nominations
to certain offices diminished with the primary, and where 69 per cent
of those nominations in the convention era resulted in matched opponents, only 36 per cent did so in the first eleven primaries.

Although matching of opponents by ethnicity probably made a
difference in the series of tight elections of the convention era, the
matter could not have affected the rate of Hispanic office holding in
the primary years, for Republicans were winning so few elections.
Hispanic office holding declined simply because it became increasingly
difficult for Spanish Americans to win Democratic nominations. The
primary's effects upon Hispanic legislative candidates are less clear,
however, for their number and fortunes appear to have varied in
accord with other factors.

The change, in the 1930's, in the Hispanic counties from Republican to Democratic majorities was paralleled by the reduction in the
ratio of Hispanic legislative membership graphed in Figure 16. The

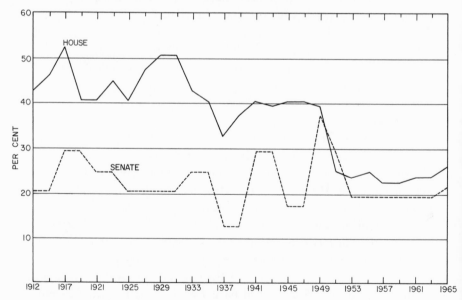

FIGURE 16. New Mexico legislators of Hispanic surname as a percentage
of House and Senate membership.

reduction may have reflected the somewhat different internal composition of the two parties, for, at the time, the Republican party in
the northern and valley areas enlisted a greater proportion of Hispanic members than did the Democratic. Then, in the 1940's, the
state's population and local proportions of the total began to change
so rapidly that some counties once Hispanic became so Anglo that
competition in their primaries tended to result in a smaller percentage
of Hispanic nominations.

Other significant changes in the relative size of the Hispanic legislative membership coincide, as Figure 16 indicates, with the reapportionments of the 1950's, which shifted legislative weight to Little
Texas and the urbanizing counties. There is no indication in the
electoral data that Hispanic legislative representation suffers as a
result of the primary in those counties in which the Spanish-American
citizenry numbers 40 per cent or more of the population. It is likely,
however, in the absence of other institutional factors, that the primary
severely limits Hispanic chances in those counties where their relative
number is smaller. Consequently, we turn next to the influences of
the districting base and ballot form in various apportionment formulas.

Legislative Turnover and Apportionment

The state's initially extraordinary rate of legislative turnover was
described in Chapter VI in the light of the ten-state survey Hyneman
made for the period inclusive of the six sessions of 1925-1935. Where
60 per cent of the senators of Hyneman's ten states had served in
at least two previous sessions, only 33 per cent had in New Mexico.
And the ratio of house members serving a third or subsequent session
was only a fourth as great as in those ten states, for 37 per cent of
those legislators were so serving, while only 9 per cent in New Mexico
could count at least two prior terms. But the amateur status of New
Mexico's legislators has so steadily declined, as Figure 17 indicates,
and brevity of legislative tenure has so diminished since the days
of the Republican Old Guard, that they are now merely typical rather
than astonishing.

For twenty-five years after statehood, the parties continued the
pattern established in the territorial era of nominating and returning
but a small percentage of experienced legislators. A long-term decrease
in the proportion of freshman house members became a little steeper

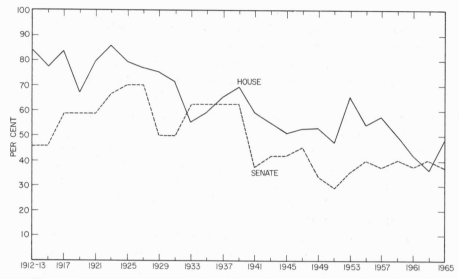

FIGURE 17. Legislators without prior experience, 1912-1965.

after 1939—the last legislature whose members had normally received nominations by convention—but, with that date, sharply increased percentages of returning senators reflect profound changes in the role and mode of party in their selection and recruitment. Not all constituencies developed quickly a capacity to return incumbent legislators, but, in the six sessions of 1951-1961 (considered successively), members of one to three previous terms accounted for 44 per cent of the membership, and those who had served four or more prior terms, for 9 per cent. No legislature convened in the longer period 1941-1963 consisted of more than 55 per cent of first-term members. Save for increases in freshman membership due to Republican control of the house in 1953 and increments in the size of the house, the pattern of increasing legislative longevity was about as consistent as such things are apt to be. The following summary, an abstract of the data represented by Figure 17, provides a measure of the change:

	Percentage of legislators without prior experience	
	Senate	*House*
Convention era (1912-1939)	59	74
Direct primary era (1941-1963)	39	52

At this point, if the reader will bear with it, a digression charting some apportionment and related changes may aid him greatly in plotting the drift of this and the following chapter.

Chapter VI described the Republican Old Guard's system of party wardship of a legislature in which few members were renominated in convention for continued legislative service; and it described the underlying apportionment based on countywide and multi-county house and senate districts each accorded one to three members, and so drawn that the more populous Republican counties were in two or three senatorial districts. An equitable arrangement initially, in that it gave each voter surprisingly equal shares in the legislative enterprise,[11] it was also (Democrats justly complained), an adroit gerrymander which enabled Republicans to spread thin electoral margins over a decisive number of counties (of which most were Hispanic). The New Deal era proved the Republican advantage to be readily erodable by electoral currents, but a more difficult problem ensued with the rapid post-war shift and growth of population. Bernalillo County (Albuquerque) was given three, and Little Texas counties three of the six additional house seats created in 1951; but, for their part of the exchange, the small counties (with the aid of Little Texas) insisted that each county should have one senator regardless of the enormous disparities in population to be represented. The next apportionment, effective in 1957, increased house membership to sixty-six and improved the position of a number of growing counties, but Bernalillo County was again accorded an increase of only three members (from six to nine), about half of what most of the customary formulas indicated were due it. As in other states in such cases, the matter was taken to the courts with the result (but not until the years closing this chronicle) that the issue came to a reasonably equitable solution. Table 42 provides an outline and chronology, by session and unit affected, of the several apportionments of 1900 through 1966.

Until 1957, the various apportionment and ballot formulas provided for unsegmented lists of each party's candidates for the whole number of positions accorded a representational unit. Consequently, each of Bernalillo County's three Democratic candidates ran, in effect, against each other as well as against all the nominees of the Republican list, for voters at the general election could choose any combination of the six (later twelve) candidates. Early in the county's

TABLE 42. LEGISLATIVE DISTRICTING AND APPORTIONMENT

Senate *and* *Territorial Council*	*House of Representatives* *(Two-year terms)*

Late Territorial

12 members elected at-large for 2-year terms by single or multi-county districts.

1912-1951

24 members. 13 members elected from single-county districts and 2 from counties later divided; 9 members from districts finally composed of 2 to 5 counties (5 counties electing a member separately also shared in 1 to 2 multi-county districts). Co-terminous 4-year terms.

1953-1965

32 members. Each county (except Los Alamos in 1953) elected 1 senator. 4-year and 6-year terms initially, then half elected each two years.

1967

42 members. (Apportioned by U.S., 3-judge, District Court.) 30 members from 11 counties electing 1 to 10 members (26 of the 30 by single-member districts); 11 members from 20 counties elected at-large from 8 districts of 2 to 3 counties; 1 member from Los Alamos and northern precincts of Santa Fe County. 4 and 6-year terms, then half to be elected each two years.

Late Territorial

24 members elected at-large by single or multi-county districts.

1912-1949

49 members. 26 one-county districts of 1 to 3 members at-large; 4 multi-county districts of one member each.

1951-1955

55 members. 23 counties with 1 to 6 members at-large elected 44; 8 multi-county districts elected 11.

1957-1963

66 members. Each county elected 1 to 9 at-large. If 2 or more members, by numbered ballot position or place.

1965

77 members. (Apportioned by state district court.) Each county allotted 1 to 18 members; if more than 1, by single-member districts based on precincts.

1967

70 members. (Apportioned by 1965 legislature in conformance to judicial standards.) 59 members from single-member districts of 14 counties electing 2 to 18 members; 6 members from county-wide, one-member districts; 5 members from 12 counties elected at-large from single-member districts of 2 to 3 counties.

history, when its population was small and its voters more likely to be aware of legislative and other minor political personalities, delegations were sometimes split between the parties; later, the whole of a party's list was quite likely to share a common party fate determined largely by the success of the presidential and gubernatorial nominees. In addition, in the 1940's and 1950's, when the conjunction of the primary with the list device was conducive to long arrays of primary candidates attracted by the prospect of nomination by a small plurality of votes, the primary list sometimes led to the chagrin of party chieftains, for a few rather extraordinary candidates won nominations. Urban party leaders and legislators countered the problem in the 1957 apportionment with the requirement that candidates in counties electing two or more house members would be nominated and elected at-large from a whole county but for a specific position or place numbered as such on the ballot (the same position-numbering device which came to be used, after 1958, for the nomination and election of congressmen).

These and similar details of the mechanisms of politics are of more than picayune importance, however, for they serve to determine what persons and what groups have access to office. Position numbering permitted candidates to choose (and exposed them to) specific opponents, and, in the counties sometimes casting a close party vote, it also occasionally gave an outstanding candidate of the minority party a fighting chance (as had the list system) to upset the odds. Position numbering did nothing, however, to counter the disadvantage inherent in the at-large system for minority group, ethnic, or other less-than-modish candidates.

The new arrangements will probably change and stabilize somewhat the legislative party mix, for they will permit easier entry to Republicans as well as to men representative of minority groupings. But, if viewed from the perspectives of 1910, the new districting may appear to localize and emphasize, if not clarify, features of the old and familiar group and regional tendencies. Spanish-American counties once normally sent convention-chosen legislative delegations deliberately balanced to recognize Anglo and commercial interests— a useful habit that has been losing its force. Little Texas, on the other hand, has normally sent men unequivocally representative of dominant local values, and, in the main, they probably will continue to do so. Now, however, in either region and in others, specific and

localized groups and values may be more able than they have been
to jostle their way to recognition and to an official place in the scheme
of things. Legislative values may be somewhat less a faithful reflection of the broader culture's predominant values and orientations. For,
even though the apportionment scheme is designed to redress the
balance in recognition of the needs of the urban voter, the legislature
is apt to be less clearly confined to the Main Street and Chamber of
Commerce attitudes of its recent urban delegations.

The new system may achieve more or less accidentally and automatically what a thoughtful and courageous set of party leaders
would do deliberately: produce a balanced ticket. For example, when
running at-large in 1962 for numbered positions in Bernalillo County,
the only two Republican candidates there to win house seats defeated
the only two candidates of Hispanic surname who had survived the
Democratic primary. (Personal differences abounded, but the two
Republicans and the seven Democrats the county sent up to the 1963
house were a homogeneous group. With one or two exceptions, it is
quite likely that they accurately and unself-consciously reflected
middle-class values.) Two years later, the competition in the county
was for eighteen seats representing as many precinct-based districts,
and each voter could cast only one vote to nominate or elect. Of the
Hispanic primary candidates in 1964, eight won in competing for
eleven Democratic nominations, and each of four Republican entrants
won. In November, four of the eight Hispanic Democrats defeated
the four Republican Spanish Americans, and, of the remaining four,
two defeated Anglo Republicans. The final score: Eight Republicans
(all Anglo and all reasonably representative of the business and professional communities), and ten Democrats of whom six were Spanish
Americans. Effects of the change were evident elsewhere. San Juan
County returned the Democratic majority leader, his Navajo running
mate, and two Republicans. McKinley also elected a Navajo (a representative of a group sometimes in competition with his county's urban
Hispanic citizens!). The effects recounted in the house of representatives are likely to occur in some measure in the reapportioned senate,
some of whose members are to be chosen, as in 1966, by the electors
of geographically small and relatively homogeneous constituencies
which depart in many respects from the mode of the broader community.

ELECTORATE AND INTRAPARTY POLITICS

One more thread should be untangled before we turn to an accounting of the executive-legislative politics of 1945-1965. In its broader characteristics, New Mexico's recent levels of electoral participation have approximated those of the nation, with a third to a half of the states falling below its rate of turnout in presidential elections. In spite of the antipathy of Hispanic leaders to women's suffrage, the state's level of voting in the 1920's, during the convention period of a tight two-party balance, was five to ten percentage points higher than in the nation, and it varied but little from presidential to off-year elections. (The national increase in voting during the 1930's was about double that in New Mexico, which began the period from the higher level of participation.) Since 1940, a variety of circumstances, perhaps such as those besetting the nation, contributed to an increasingly variable pattern of voting in the general elections.[12] Although ratios of actual to potential voters are in cadence with national elections, voting in the primaries, as might be expected, has exhibited domestically induced differences at various times and places in the state. Table 43 provides an outline of the range and mean of percentages

TABLE 43. VOTER TURNOUT IN ELECTIONS AND PRIMARIES, 1920-1964

Years	*Percentage of potential electorate voting for governor*			
	General elections		*Primary elections*	
	Mean	*Range*	*Mean*	*Range*
1920-28	58	54-60	. . .	. . .
1930-38	62	56-67	. . .	. . .
1940-48	48	36-65	27	16-45
1950-60	52	43-61	28	21-33
1962-64	56	50-62	25	20-30

of voter turnout in the general and primary elections for governor. Post-1940 turnout in New Mexico's general elections is well below that of 1920-1938.

The Vote in the Primary

The rate of primary participation of New Mexico's electorate is slightly below that of the sampling of fifteen states examined by Key.[13] In these states primary voting by 25 to 35 per cent of the electorate set the modal rate of participation. The novelty of the first primary in 1940 attracted 45 per cent of New Mexico's electorate, but in only two of the ensuing thirteen primaries did the rate slightly exceed 30 per cent. And, as might be expected of the dominant party, the rate of participation in the Democratic primary is well above that in the Republican. Party differences in primary participation are a measure of the leading party's degree of dominance, but a more direct approach is that provided by the registration data of Table 44, which also indicates that the attractions of partisan affiliation have reduced by about half the initially high percentage of voters of independent or minor party registration. The independent voters have apparently moved into both major parties, with Republican gains in Bernalillo County and Little Texas offsetting Democratic gains in the Hispanic counties.

Over the course of the thirteen primary elections of 1940-1964, the Democratic primary usually attracted about four times as many voters as the Republican, but this difference was, in part, as Table 44 suggests, a reflection of the registered strength of the two parties. Republicans have been accustomed to send about 27 per cent of their currently registered strength to the primary; Democrats to cast 39 per cent of their registered vote. Hence, since there were consistently two

TABLE 44. NET SHIFTS IN PARTY REGISTRATION, 1941 TO 1964.

Area or county	Registration in percentages					
	1941			1964		
	D	Others	R	D	Others	R
Hispanic counties	80.2	7.7	12.1	80.4	2.2	17.4
Little Texas counties	60.1	10.3	29.6	66.0	5.3	28.7
Bernalillo County	63.7	16.7	19.6	60.8	6.9	32.3
State	64.8	11.3	23.9	68.1	4.9	27.0

Sources: 1941: *New Mexico Blue Book, 1941-42.* 1964: Compiled from *Albuquerque Journal*, October 27, 1964.

and a half times more Democrats than Republicans, much of the
disparity in the size of the primary vote of the two parties is traceable
simply to the relative sizes of the parties—a conclusion that reveals
little of how the 2.5 to 1 registration ratios got that way in the first
place.

Statewide Democratic majorities in the five gubernatorial elections
preceding 1940 (and they were strongly New Deal years) ranged from
52 to 58 per cent for a mean of 54—figures comfortably exceeded by
subsequent Democratic registration. Electoral majorities were somewhat more erratic thereafter, but always, until 1964, well below the
party's level of registration in every area of the state. It would appear
that those pressures to community conformity which have been ad-
duced as long-term factors increasing party imbalance may well show
up in the very short run. It may be presumed that the registration
statute provided for a type of forced entry into the Democratic primary, for it was enacted when the effects of depression were still
highly evident in New Mexico, and when considerable economic and
political pressure was being exerted upon the voters of many communities. Hence, the administratively logical, and universally approved,
device of permanent registration may be accounted one of the "institutional depressants" of the minority party. The major factor, however, is doubtless the tendency of voters and potential candidates to
give their attention to the primary of the party most likely to dominate
the general election.

By measures derived from primary voting, New Mexico has long
been a predominantly Democratic state in spite of its two-party general
election vote for president and governor. In the thirteen primaries of
1940-1964, Republican gubernatorial candidates attracted a total
primary vote, on the average, of 23 per cent of the nominee's general
election vote; Democratic candidates received a total vote in the primary averaging 82 per cent of their party's general election vote in
the series. Key puts the relation thus:

as the decision of the nominating primary comes to be more certainly the final decision, the reality of the politics of the state comes
to consist more largely in intraparty battles of factions and personalities within the stronger party. This transfer of politics to the
primary in its most complete development results in the formation
of factions, more or less transitory, themselves organized and func-

tioning somewhat after the manner of political parties in the usual sense of the word.[14]

The relative emphasis accorded in New Mexico to the primaries of the two parties may be surmised from the data of Table 45. All Republican candidates received a total statewide primary vote of less than 40 per cent of the nominee's subsequent general election vote, but in setting a range from 43 to 123 per cent, the Democratic primary on three

TABLE 45. PARTY DIFFERENTIALS IN PRIMARY VOTING, 1940-1964

Total primary vote as percentage of candidate's general election vote	*Gubernatorial candidates*			
	Republicans		*Democrats*	
	Number	*Percentage*	*Number*	*Percentage*
0-19	4	31	0	0
20-39	9	69	0	0
40-59	0	0	3	23
60-79	0	0	2	15
80-99	0	0	5	39
100 plus	0	0	3	23

occasions attracted more voters than the candidate did in the general election.

If New Mexico were to be fitted into a group of states Key has ranked by relative general election strength of gubernatorial candidates and proportionate total party vote in nominating primaries, the addition would produce a marked distortion in an otherwise orderly progression.[15] Key uses the mean Democratic percentage of the general election vote as the base against which to measure the differing rates of primary participation in the primary of the dominant party of twenty-one states. The states of the group range from Vermont, with a mean Democratic share of the general election vote of 30 per cent, to Nevada with 53 per cent. Vermont's Democratic primary vote as a percentage of the Republican primary vote is 6.3; at the other extreme, Nevada's is 150. New Mexico, with a 1940-1960 Democratic general election average of 51.5 per cent, would precede Colorado, the first in a group of five states "leaning Democratic," yet its ratio of Democratic to Republican primary vote (expressed as a percentage) is 409, far above that of the other states of the group. The ratios of Democratic to Republican primary voting making up the New Mexico average range from 228 to 694 for the 1940-1960 primaries, to average 330 in presidential and 504 in non-presidential years.

In pursuing the implications of similar data from states with a competitive two-party politics, Key examines the proposition that in statewide direct primaries "a disproportionate part of the vote would be cast by residents of areas strongly attached to a party."[16] In those areas, the citizenry would tend to be concerned with the dominant party's nominations for local office and that party's primary turnout would be relatively heavy, while the far outnumbered opposition would cast a lesser vote than their capabilities. Hence, one-party areas would also make a disproportionate contribution to the total vote in statewide nominations of the dominant party. By this measure also, New Mexico's regional and cultural areas carry to an extreme the relationships exhibited in a broader context by the states of Key's study.[17] Table 46

TABLE 46. PARTICIPATION IN PRIMARIES IN RELATION TO PARTY STRENGTH

Area and election	*Percentage of registration Republican*	*Index of primary balance*[a]	*Primary vote as percentage of area general election vote*		*Index of primary distortion*[b]
			Dem. (1)	*Rep.* (2)	(1) — (2)
1958					
6 Little Texas counties	...	2,088	128	10	118
Remainder of state	...	671	100	18	82
Bernalillo County	...	405	94	15	79
Los Alamos County	...	405	76	22	54
10 Hispanic counties	...	364	93	25	68
State		577	102	18	84
1960					
6 Little Texas counties	14	953	94	12	82
Remainder of state	27	365	88	24	64
10 Hispanic counties	31	249	79	34	45
Los Alamos County	32	224	86	30	56
Bernalillo County	33	204	68	27	41
State		319	82	25	57

a. Total Democratic gubernatorial primary vote as a percentage of the total Republican gubernatorial primary vote.
b. The difference between column 1 and column 2.

ranks the familiar regional groupings of New Mexico counties by an "index of primary balance" and sets out their differentials of party primary vote for the pairs of primaries and general elections of 1958 and 1960. (Similar relationships held in previous sets of elections.) Inspection of the index of primary balance reveals that Democratic participation in the 1958 gubernatorial primary in Little Texas was 2088 per cent (in other words, nearly 21 times larger) of that in the area's Republican primary, but in 1960, relatively more Republicans turned out and the Little Texas Democratic primary vote in that year was only about nine and a half times the size of that of the GOP. Similarly, in Bernalillo County, the number voting in the Democratic primary was 405 per cent of the number voting in the Republican; but in 1960 (a year in which Republicans boasted a spirited primary fight of their own), only two Democrats turned out for each Republican, so the index figure in Bernalillo County for that year was only 204. The first item in the next column, for example, indicates that in Little Texas the contestants for the Democratic nomination attracted a vote that was 128 per cent of the vote the nominee later received in the general election; the Republican primary attracted only 10 per cent as great a vote as that party's nominee received in the general election. In every area of the state the Democratic primary attracted far more attention than did the Republican.

Primary Factionalism and the Party Strategy

Characteristics of regional electoral turnout indicated in Table 46 could be translated into a nearly unshakable control of nominations by the Little Texas and border counties if they were but subjected to a discipline like that underlying the dominance of the Boston Irish in Massachusetts' politics, but factionalism and an ancient tendency to an extreme degree of county localism have largely served to deny to that area the full influence it might otherwise exert in the primaries. Although the northern and Hispanic counties no longer possess the bulk of the state's population, the adage of New Mexico's Democratic politicians that "the North selects and the South elects" can still hold true.

The fourteen gubernatorial primaries of 1940-1966 drew a total of 40 candidates and only on two or three occasions were the Little Texas and border counties able to support one nominee solidly. Southern and Little Texas candidates for the lesser state offices can fairly readily

avoid factional alignments and get a vote there sufficient to overcome
the candidates from or favored by the North. But gubernatorial candidates are often forced to identify with factional groupings, and, in
so doing, automatically forfeit or split a fairly large portion of the
heavy primary vote of Little Texas. Occasionally, thereafter, many of
these voters have demonstrated a great facility for voting for the opposition when their party's nominee displeases. The resulting, and painful, awareness of the rebellious qualities of Little Texas and similar
voters has done much to foster trials of the pre-primary endorsing
convention.[18] (With a generous measure of help from big Bernalillo
County in a hard two-man primary likely to yield a large turnout, a
factional candidate from Little Texas can defeat either a neighbor or a
candidate from the North, and go on, then, with an excellent prospect
of winning the general election. In a three-man race, a substantial
faction of Bernalillo County is apt to be found allied with the North
in a winning primary combination—the contingency which has several
times caused decisive numbers of voters of Little Texas and the border
counties to defect to the Republicans in the general elections. It is a
relationship which the convention can take into account.) Republicans
have derived some profit and a wry pleasure from the Democratic convention strategem, for in order (among other motives) to give southern electors an even break in determining nominations, and so reduce
the likelihood of their post-primary ire; Democratic leaders from every
camp and region have reluctantly joined to enact the pre-primary
convention laws. But the irascibly independent voters of Little Texas,
profoundly convinced of the virtue of primaries, continue to dislike
the convention, seeming to see it as another self-serving device of
politicians.

In the ten straight primaries of 1940-1962, the Democratic primary
drew an average of three contestants for each of the dozen or so nominations made for each election. Of 126 Democratic nominees of the
ten primaries, 122 were elected, so the general election served largely
to ratify the choices of Democratic primary voters. At all levels of the
ticket there has been just enough of the heady feeling that the primary
is a lottery any man might win to encourage filings that many party
leaders and some beleaguered but distinguished candidates have pri-
vately disparaged (a good many of the state's judges have profoundly
disliked the primary). Although the minority party has consistently
been strong enough to prevent the Democratic primary from becoming

the Donnybrook it sometimes resembles in neighboring Texas and Oklahoma, the majority's factionalism is held by many leading Democrats to have contributed to losses of the governorship and to several tight congressional elections. It is the party leaders of this persuasion who have twice led the successful campaigns to diminish the role of the primary by the use of the pre-primary endorsing convention.

Twenty-seven of the 126 Democratic nominations available in the ten primaries not held in conjunction with an endorsing convention went to the 21 per cent of the candidates who had no party opposition. Thirty-two, or 25 per cent, were sought by two candidates each, and sixty-seven nominations, or 53 per cent were sought by three or more candidates each. Rarely could the official party organization be held accountable for the quality of the nominees.

The statistics resulting from the three pre-primary endorsing conventions of 1952, 1954, and 1964 are radically different from those of the ten straight primaries, and may lend some weight to the arguments of the pre-primary or convention proponents. Table 47 compares the effects of the two nominating methods on the fortunes of incumbent and non-incumbent candidates by the incidence of competition. In the three pre-primaries, the mean number of candidates per nomination dropped from the primaries' three to one and one-half, few incumbents were opposed, and, in the case of opposed nominations, the convention-favored candidates were likely to achieve a heavy primary majority. (The latter relation did not hold in 1966 in a contest illustrating the capacity of the voters to use the subsequent primary to nominate the convention's second choice. In that case, T. E. Lusk, former senate majority leader and a resident of Eddy County in Little Texas, was given a ballot position for the gubernatorial nomination by the convention in which U.S. Senator Joseph M. Montoya and numerous delegates from the Hispanic and mining counties gave the first endorsement to former governor John Burroughs of the Little Texas counties of Roosevelt and Chaves. In the ensuing primary, Lusk enjoyed the support of much of the press, an impressive segment of the state's legislative leadership—for fifteen years a potent grass roots force in New Mexico—and most of the party's elders. Otherwise, the relationships apparent in the results of the first three pre-primary endorsements would be sharpened by inclusion of the 1966 data.) Under

TABLE 47. EFFECTS OF DEMOCRATIC PRE-PRIMARY CONVENTION
ENDORSEMENTS OF 1952, 1954, AND 1964

Nominating system	Contests involving incumbents		Contests involving no incumbents		Totals	
	Number	Percentage	Number	Percentage	Number	Percentage
TEN PRIMARIES						
Candidates:						
Opposed	45	66.2	53	91.4	98	77.8
Unopposed	23	33.8	5	8.6	28	22.2
Totals	68	100.0	58	100.0	126	100.0
THREE PRE-PRIMARIES						
Candidates:						
Opposed	3	12.5	14	77.8	17	40.5
Unopposed	21	87.5	4	22.2	25	59.5
Totals	24	100.0	18	100.0	42	100.0

either system, nominations in which no incumbents were involved
were very apt to be contested. Two-thirds of the incumbent candidates
in the ten straight primaries drew opponents, but, in the case of the
three pre-primaries of Table 47, only three of twenty-four incumbents
(12.5 per cent) had to face challengers from their own party. The
incidence of competition for nominations to positions not sought by
incumbents dropped much less sharply—from 91 per cent to 78 per
cent.

LEGLISLATIVE AUTONOMY

If there were to be applied to New Mexico a scale showing the objective weight and importance in politics of legislature, party, and governor, it would provide quite different readings at different times. In
the three decades beginning with 1900, party would outweigh the other
two; the 1930's would draw a mixed result, but with the accruals of
advantage going clearly to the governorship; the twenty-five years
after 1940 would be shown to have all but relegated party to the status

of an electoral instrument. And, in the latter period, the scale would show the powers of setting policy orientations and decision-making to rest in an uneasy balance between governor and legislature.

In 1949, after an interval when he was not, the Democratic state chairman was of some weight in arranging the organization of the senate, but not since then has the state organization been able to determine the organization of either chamber. Legislative independence from direction by the official state party organization is virtually complete; and the state chairman of either party, once a commanding figure in legislative circles, is now a lonely one brought in or tolerated only on those formal and ceremonial occasions when his presence can be readily explained. The bonds of party do not sit lightly by any means, but it is not the state chairman who adjusts them, for U.S. senators, the governor, and, to a surprising extent, the legislature have assumed the leadership of party. (U.S. senators can be of great influence on critical legislative matters but the senators, too, have usually entered this arena's struggles with caution amounting almost to diffidence. After 1950, Senators Dennis Chavez and Clinton P. Anderson each commanded a factional following in the party and the state just as they have among legislators, but neither ever attempted to duplicate the feat of Senator Bronson Cutting in establishing a legislative group whose objectives and tactics he could determine. Senator Joseph M. Montoya is impelled to seek the leadership of the Chavez following and there is every indication that the old factional division will continue, and with about the same scale and type of influence upon the legislature.)

The legislature, in the four sessions of 1935-1941, had been an instrument for registering decisions taken or negotiated in the office of the governor. By 1945, it had come to a situation in which competent and strong-willed legislators, elected largely by their own efforts, could consciously strive for and achieve a measure of independence from the governor's office and from party direction. From Governor John Dempsey's first legislative session in 1943, house and senate leadership could usually be determined without effective interference from party and governor, and the more able and enterprising of the members were able to act as legislative entrepreneurs rather than as agents. Increasingly, during the sessions of 1943-1949, the legislature became the cockpit of Democratic factions corresponding to those of the party at large, and from 1951 to 1965 the legislature four times operated with a governor representing the opposition party. The Democratic majority, in the periods of divided control, was adroit enough to develop legislative programs identifiable with their party. Campaign statements, platforms particularly, have then laid stress upon legislative accomplishments.

In his first term, Governor Dempsey attempted to determine the committee arrangements of the two houses. His will narrowly prevailed in the house, but in the senate, then in its second session, a bloc promptly formed to overturn the leadership of the previous session. The maneuver placed in key positions men who were strong in their electoral districts and competent in their legislative positions. From that moment, the governor had to negotiate for every legislative item he desired, and some were denied him by sharply adverse votes. Thereafter, on several matters, the governor was "advised" to drop his measures without attempting to force them to a vote. The situation was without precedent, for when the senators of the Republican Old Guard era were indisposed to favor a governor's wishes it was with the advice and consent of the party's leadership.

After the 1943 revolt of the senators, the newly elected majority leader was asked if "his election meant he would be obligated to support and sponsor administration measures in the senate." He is reported to have said:

I haven't discussed any matters with any representatives of the administration. I was asked if I would take the place and I said I would accept without any strings attached. I am free to vote on any bills as I see fit and sponsor any bills of my choice. But as floor leader . . . I expect to see that the administration program receives prompt attention and action by the senate. My hands are in no way tied and I am not committed on any measure.[19]

Governor Dempsey declared he would keep hands off the organization of the legislature of his second term in 1945, but if he did not, his influence was apparently quite limited.

Like its predecessor, the legislature of 1945 proceeded at times almost in indifference to the governor's office. The new senate met, and without much consultation organized itself much as it had in the previous session and around most of the same personalities. In the house, for some years a bastion of gubernatorial control, an experienced but independent young lawyer defeated the speaker of the previous term. The majority leader, who had served previous terms as leader and chief clerk, this time gained his office as a result of a vigorous pre-session campaign, thereby setting a precedent in the internal organization and direction of the legislature.

The changing roles of party floor leaders of house and senate are indicative of differences arising in the relationship of governor and party leaders to the legislature after adoption of the primary. Previously, the Democratic floor leader had generally been chosen by or on behalf of the governor. He was deemed to be the administration's agent and spokesman on the floor, where, as in a good many states, his activity was restricted to legislation endorsed by the governor or included in the administration's program. Of the 1939 session of the house it has been said:

> At this time the floor leader handled only administrative matters. So when he arose on or worked a measure he did so as the administration's spokesman. Otherwise, in the 1939 session, when bills came up the floor leader was just another member.[20]

During and after the session of 1945 the floor leader of each house tended to become not only a power in his own right, but one who served also as the parliamentary instrument of the speaker or the majority in charge of dispatching and managing the business of the house concerned. In the senate, particularly, the majority leader became an officer of significant authority.

Events in the 1946 campaigns and in the ensuing administrations of 1947-1950 compelled rather than permitted the legislature to act to an unprecedented degree as a policy-making entity. There had previously come to prominence Victor Salazar, an able young administrator-politician, who, in 1946, was placed in charge of the Bureau of Revenue—long a key position for party management and patronage distribution. He served effectively as a legislative agent, and so extensive did his reputed powers and influence become that the press dubbed Commissioner Salazar the "second-floor governor." Salazar became more, it appears, than simply the governor's legislative agent. It is clear that, by the 1949 session, members were often in doubt as to whether Salazar was representing solely the governor in legislative affairs, or whether he was representing his own or other interests not related to those of the governor and administration. A number of members of that session are apparently convinced that Salazar was often approached directly by those interested in legislation and that some of the resulting legislative measures or arrangements were without the governor's knowledge or involvement, but on this matter opinions differ.

One of the key Republican members of the 1947 session offered the judgment that Vearle Payne, speaker of the previous session, and Murray Morgan "were the obvious choices for speaker and leader, and Mabry probably had little effective choice." Morgan, this member indicated, "may have been somewhat more the governor's choice since it seemed to fall to his lot to push some of the governor's stuff." As to Salazar, I was told:

> Victor worked the legislature for Governor Mabry. He seemed [in the house] to concentrate, for the most part, on about a half dozen or so individuals. He was a smart and vigorous administrator and politician, and Mabry tended to turn over much of the detail of dealing with legislators to Victor.

In noting that legislative leaders suffered a sense of frustration, one stated that he was elected to his position because "they had no one else." This individual, who attained an exemplary reputation as officer of both house and senate, explained to me:

> I was a mechanical man. There was no program. Messages contained little. Nothing was spelled out. After thirty days I still had no contact with Victor or administration men. I got hold of Gene Allison about the lack of messages and information from Mabry, but after this there were only two conferences with Mabry although a good many with Victor.

Salazar wielded an obvious influence in the house, but, in 1949 particularly, his authority there was tempered on many issues by an easily triggered combination of Republicans and a bloc of "conservative, Young-Turk Democrats." (The numerically strong Republican house minorities of the sessions of 1947 and 1949 were involved in fifty-one and nineteen party-versus-party votes, respectively. Their 1947 index of cohesion was 42; that of 1949 was 32, very close to a fifty-fifty split.[21] Hispanic members and a few Republicans seldom voting with the Young-Turk Democrats tended to be aligned with Salazar, deepening the split of both parties.) The leading Young Turk, Speaker John F. Simms, Jr., could best Salazar on the floor of the house if he had to, and he enjoyed sufficient legislative authority to command the ear of the governor if necessary, so it was in the senate that Salazar found his realm. The point should not be taken to mean, however, that Salazar and Simms were always or even usually in opposition. Each had his own commitments and responsibilities, not the least of which were those to the administration. But each was a competent legislative politician and could deal with, or without, the other as the occasion required. Simms had defeated (by secret ballot in caucus) the governor's choice for speaker, but he was thereafter conscientious in keeping the governor informed and providing impetus to administration bills. Both men, in short, were legislative entrepreneurs typical of many who followed. Of Salazar's role in the senate, my notes (derived from interviews with an adroit member) boil down to:

> Mabry tried to control. He was not neglecting his duty and he was certainly not indifferent to it. He did, however, work through Victor Salazar a great deal. His [Mabry's] election was the result of a combination built by Salazar, Johnson, and Tingley and acquiesced in by the Chavez organization.[22]

Meanwhile, where a governor had formerly been able, in lieu of pay and billet for his legislative troops, to control by holding out offers of employment with the state, other means had been developed to enable legislators to live on their $5.00 (later, $10.00) *per diem.* One device used was payment of room rent of the more needy legislators out of party coffers, and several received small allowances which one member describes as "walking-around money." One difficulty with the allowance was that the party was sometimes outbid by other groups, as in the bill to split Eddy County, which produced some of the most notorious legislative spending and lobbying the state has seen.

Then, since the ordinary routine of legislation had to go on, the 1943-1949 leadership of the house resorted to a variant of the device of the steering committee which had fallen into disuse after the days of Republican dominance. The new committee did not supersede the work or authority of the standing committees, as was the case with steering committees of the Republican era, for it served principally to coordinate committee work, convey information, and establish the daily calendars after consultation with the governor's office. The steering committee of this era was creature and instrument of the house, however, not of the governor or party.

Party Government and the Legislative Majority

In the eight sessions of 1951-1965, the legislature came to a mode of operations flexible enough to achieve without strain the accommodations essential to changes in party control of the governorship. The relationship of legislature to governor during the period when Republican Edwin Mechem four times held the governorship is easily summarized: If the governor was of the party of the legislative majority, then he was the chief spokesman for the party and the one chiefly responsible for identifying party policy with the product of the legislature. When the governor was not of its party, then the legislative majority insisted upon the right and capacity to enact and interpret its own version of the party's policy, and to do so with but little deference to the formal party organization outside of the legislature.

This is not to say that New Mexico's house became completely akin to the highly structured and leadership-centered institution that is the U.S. House of Representatives. Nor did the senate become a "citadel" in which an aloof club of guardians conserved the traditions and institutions of the polity.[23] Yet, the sum of the era's changes took the state's legislature a step or two in that direction, so that it became, in its place in the state's politics, more like the federal model. In its internal organization, in its relationship to party, and in its manner of adjusting its relationship to the governor of either party, the legislature also demonstrated both the mood and the ability to achieve a degree of autonomy sufficient to make it a significantly different institution from that which it was in several previous eras.

The changes previously described in the manner of legislators' recruitment—the direct primary, districting, and ballot arrangements —doubtless made a difference in their conduct. Democratic legislators, particularly, became more likely to have sought their posts initially, and to have been renominated and re-elected, without the assent or assistance of the state party organization; and some tended to become influential in their own right in their local party organizations *after* they served successfully in the legislature. Judah and Goldberg found that Democratic legislative candidates of metropolitan Bernalillo County were "largely self-starting."[24] Republican candidates, they found, were recruited by their party, "thus when a candidate was decided upon and he agreed to run, a mutual obligation between himself and his party was recognized."[25] Organized labor's Political Education Committee, and other civic-political action groups like the Grass Roots Democrats and the G. I. Forum directly intervened in enlistment of candidacies, but their activity merely served to accentuate the lack of comparable party efforts to find acceptable candidates.[26] As Judah and Goldberg put the matter:

> The Democratic leadership, then, took no formal and little informal part in recruiting candidates for the state legislature, and its efforts to shape a ticket out of the material that presented itself were scarcely rigorous. Neither were they particularly effective.[27]

In a representative northern county, however, recruitment of legislators is an example of the traditional pattern still frequent, if not prevalent, in other northern and competitive Hispanic counties. Judah found there that the "primary had simply removed nomination from the county convention, where organization leaders submitted their ticket to the convention delegates, to the primary, where the same leaders submit their decision to the voters."[28] Non-political groups have little influence in legislative recruitment, for the "leaders of the party organization select candidates," and the self-starting candidate is quite unlikely to be successful.[29]

The candidates from a Little Texas county were found to be young men of higher than the average of their communities in educational and economic attainment.[30] As in Bernalillo County, party activity in legislative recruitment was limited and of small effect, but candidates were much fewer than in Bernalillo County.[31] Those who decided to run did so for reasons "varied and personal," and not for those of partisan attachment, although politics had "a fascination."[32] These attributes probably made them more representative of their fellow legislators after 1950 than were the members from the northern counties. The impression that emerges is that Little Texas and border county legislators have had a strong sense of identification with their communities and counties, so that most maintained strong relationships with certain of the social and economic groupings of their areas.[33]

Yet, it must be said that party (and identification with it) remained a pervasive influence.[34] Legislators of the two decades who attained successive terms have typically, I am confident, identified their legislative membership, the more authoritative committee positions, and many an item of legislation with their party. So, in addition to their function of representing their communities, they have seen themselves as key elements of the party-in-the-legislature. Simultaneously party men and free agents, they have regarded themselves as the party's representatives and guardians. To a great degree, in their estimation, their collective legislative membership *is* the party, and they have deemed themselves largely responsible for interpreting and transforming their version of the party's policy into the official policy of the state. I base these and related observations largely upon impressions derived from an eight-year association (1951-1959) with the New Mexico legislature as director of its council service. They should be read as confined to those members who attain two or more terms of service and an official legislative position comparable to committee chairman, leader, speaker, or authority within the party caucus. But, given the rate of legislative turnover described above, these positions (even if some highly motivated holders thereof boast what may seem but a modicum of legislative service) denote the accession of the legislators concerned to key points in the system. And the actions of lobbyists and administration officials approaching or monitoring the legislature attest their belief or perception that legislators in official positions have been, in fact, at the linkages of the legislative network.[35]

Legislators and Governor

After 1950, past and current members of the legislature provided all of the successful new congressional and gubernatorial candidates and most of the losing hopefuls who aspired to nomination. Few party conferences held for the discussion of organization and programs were called without a large, and sometimes authoritative, representation from the legislature. Nor have legislators graciously brooked overt interference from the governor, whether he has been of their party or of the opposition, although a Democratic governor and his men could sometimes "turn the lions loose in the halls" with decisive effect—that is, to call upon friends, customers, clients, employers, and hometown associates of legislators to apply directly as much pressure as could be generated.

The relationship between governor and legislature came to be one perhaps best described as one of mutual accommodation of two essentially independent entities. Each derived authority from a different source of support. Legislators have often achieved an electoral and community support of their own; governors have sought factional support within a statewide party organization which normally eschews interference in local affairs.[36]

Legislators seeking a position as an officer of the house have typically engaged in spirited and independent campaigns in which a good part of the bargaining was done with the coinage of seats and chairmanships of the more authoritative committees. If possible, the governor's office or the governor-elect was usually solicited for any support available from that quarter, with the result that Democratic governors of the decade were consulted, but as little more than as *primus inter pares.* Governor Simms, in 1955, was influential in determining who was to serve as chief clerk in each house, but the men chosen as senate leader, house speaker, and house leader were sufficiently strong on their own so that it apparently seemed unwise to the governor to do more than gracefully accept their selection. The speaker of the 1959 session engaged in a long campaign for the post that was marked by a good deal of discussion through local informal caucuses which, in all probability, determined the ultimate allocation of some of the choice committee prizes; but he was then deposed, in 1961, by a rival who used the same techniques to achieve the speakership. Both disclaimed the making of any specific commitments. This is perhaps the case, but the mere fact of campaigning, of soliciting support, for such an important position creates a web of obligations which must be paid in some reasonable and responsible manner if the individuals concerned wish to retain support in the future.[37]

In the 1961 house contest, the battle was joined, just as it had been in other periods of a Republican governor (1951, 1953, and 1957), in virtually complete independence from the Democratic state organization. Nor were U.S. congressmen and senators of much weight in those contests. The house officerships were gained in hard and independent campaigns; those of the senate were several times determined by deliberation among the elders of that body, but, in 1961 and 1965, there were head-on contests between pairs of senators who campaigned, in the manner made familiar by members of the house, for the majority leadership. In the 1961 case, the recently defeated governor and other party leaders were virtually ignored as potential allies and sources of strength in an interesting contest between Fabian Chavez of Santa Fe County and R. C. Morgan, a senior legislator from Roosevelt County in Little Texas. Chavez was one of six Spanish-American members of the thirty-two—a ratio so historic that it was the source of a firm tenet that an Hispanic member could not be elected to the leadership—and, in the preceding term, he had had the chamber's least desirable seat behind a post (a back-of-the-hand reward for his brashness). He won the leadership by prowess and hard campaigning. In 1965, an alliance between the governor and a coterie of influential committee chairmen of the preceding several sessions was barely successful in turning back a strong group of maverick senators.

Legislative Caucus

The Democratic majority has shown a strong bent to create its own role, to establish itself as a continuing entity, and to insist that it create policy as well as endorse it. This inclination goes far to create a mood placing considerable emphasis on the legislature as a major institution for dealing with the emergent and ancient conflicts dividing and re-dividing various segments of the state. But, to the extent that such divisions and conflicts exist, and to the degree that the legislature is independent of outside forces such as party and governor, it must settle conflicts on its own, although its internal divisions reflect those setting apart the communities or groups represented. In consequence, the caucus and policy committees came to be used to a degree which would astonish legislators of many of the states.[38] The house sometimes uses a policy committee to guide and inform its caucus; in the senate the caucus relies primarily upon advice of standing and interim committees, although the policy committee has occasionally been used.

Calvin Horn, the speaker of the house of the 1951 session, had campaigned vigorously for John Miles, his losing gubernatorial candidate, and campaigned no less strenuously for the speakership. This achieved, he sought the means of developing a legislative policy cor-

responding to the reformist and "good government" platform he was
so instrumental in fostering for the losing campaign of the previous
year. The party created a legislative committee; the house and senate
majorities created a policy committee. Then, in a gesture indicative
of its evolving mode of operations, the senate balked at the prospect
of subordination to the formal party. The press reported:

> The legislative policy committee scheduled to meet for the second
> time last night, instead will meet this afternoon with everyone ex-
> cluded "who are not members of the legislature."
> [Chairman Wall denied] that state Democratic Chairman Ray
> Rogers was invited to last night's meeting, although Rogers was
> on hand when the committee decided not to go on with its work.
> "Rogers was not invited . . . nor were any other non-members
> of the legislature," Wall said.[39]

Thereafter the policy committee became two, for it was the inclination of each house to insist on the identity of its own group.

A custom evolved for the majority party in each house to call several caucuses per session for the discussion of a considerable range
of issues. Issue and the bills or proposed bills dealing with them, the
identification of legislation with the party platform, implications of
attitudes of the press and voters back home, the obligations of the
party to its backers, and similar matters were covered generally and
sometimes in detail. It has usually been the goal of the caucus to
come to a consensus or at least such agreement as can be acted upon,
although matters so treated were not dealt with firmly and members
were free, as a rule, to vote their own preferences. But members
could know, in such cases, how the majority of their colleagues were
apt to stand. And in both houses, but in the senate particularly, frequent ad hoc caucuses have been called for the disposition of particular issues. When it has appeared that some unforeseen contingency
could not be dealt with easily from the floor, or when a previous
caucus agreement threatened to fail, then a word from the floor leader
to president or speaker has been sufficient to recess the body so that
party members could attempt to settle the issue at hand.

Although house and senate leaders as well as outside party leaders
have attempted to bring them into use, joint caucuses of party members of both houses have been relatively rare, and even more rarely

were they successful for much more than ceremonial purposes. Influential members have developed their own means of access to members and committees of the other house, and there has been a reasonably high degree of communication and cooperation between the elective leaders of the two houses in spite of sometimes strained intercameral relations. On the occasions when a Democrat served as governor, the daily sessions in the governor's office of speaker, leaders, and whips were ordinarily sufficient to keep the two houses in an orderly relationship, and caucuses were less frequent.

That the matter of joint or coordinated action on matters suitable for identification with the party, as well as caucus action generally, is of particular concern when the governor is of the other party is illustrated in the 1957 session. Early in that session, various members of the house and senate met with the state chairman and a national committeeman to establish a liaison committee composed of six members from each house "in order to effect a definite program for the Democratic members of both chambers."[40] The senate later agreed to the proposal, but with the reservation that liaison committee members would merely work out details of policy programs which would then be held in abeyance "until approved by the majority of the caucus of the individual houses."

Some of the caucus discussion follows:

Senator Lusk [majority leader] explained that ordinarily when you have a governor of the same party as that of the majority of the legislature, that you looked to him for organization and advancement of the Democratic party, but at this time, since the situation is different there is no one who has any leadership over the members of the houses. He further explained that he felt that this liaison committee might be the answer for a strong Democratic program and that he was willing to give it a try. He added that it hadn't worked out in the past, but with joint application of following the Democratic party platform that it might result in a positive program to the best interest of the party and to the people of the state.

Senator Fabian Chavez, Jr. commented that from the choice the House had made on the liaison committee it appeared to be too one-sided, as there were too many from the East Side [Little Texas] on the committee.

Senator Lusk said that it would leave lots of gaps from an economical, racial and sectional standpoint, and that he thought the Senate members should take these three factors into consideration when they made their choice.

. . . . .

Senator Gordon E. Melody, in explaining further the purposes behind the liaison committee, said that if a piece of legislation was brought before this committee of twelve, and that if a majority of the twelve favored such a program that they could take it back to their respective caucuses and sell it to their members, however if no agreement could be reached in the liaison committee, then it would only stand to reason that that particular measure would probably be a dead issue since it would be hard to gain the support of both houses. In other words, he explained, on a group vote in the committee we would be warned enough if it were brought to the floor of the house, not to obligate or identify the Democratic Party with that particular bill. He admitted that he felt that the individual caucuses would be better equipped to work out their own problems since they were smaller in number. He felt that the individual caucuses should have the right to say what type of legislation they were going to support, however, it would behove [sic] the members of the separate houses to try and judge how the wind would blow in the other chamber—and this would be the purpose of the liaison committee.[41]

Gubernatorial leadership in the manner indicated by Senator Lusk was heavily emphasized in the following session, when it was once used to whip an extremely reluctant senate majority into line on the confirmation of highway commission appointments. The incident contributed to a long train of events illustrative of the ironies of politics. To obtain confirmation of his appointments, the governor was constrained, as one of his predecessors described the technique, to "turn the lions loose in the halls." The dramatic struggle attracted the attention of the press and the opposition. Then, in the following eighteen months, as commission activities attracted the scrutiny of the Bureau of Public Roads and congressional committees, Republicans were successful in exploiting the issue by recalling the governor's clear intent to force confirmation of his appointments. The governor was defeated. Six years later he won convention endorsement, only to be badly

defeated in the primary by the majority leader of the 1959 session—
a man acutely aware of the old issue. Of this factor (among several
others), one political reporter observed: "Undoubtedly Burroughs'
record in his first two years as governor hurt him. . . . There were
repeated reports that the voters had forgotten, but apparently this
was not true."[42]

Oversight and Innovation

No one has recently thought to call the state's legislature dormant.
It has not only attracted the services of aspirants for higher office, but
it has kept them busy enough to expose and test their intellectual,
political, and moral reactions to stress, opportunity, and responsibility.
Each session after 1945 has been spiced with a sprinkling of members
who have so consciously sought for the means to improve legislative
mechanics and organization that the fact, as well as the results, of
their search is doubtless a source of gratification to their former teachers of civics and government. Much of the change wrought in the
legislature, and elsewhere in the apparatus of state government during
the 1950's and 1960's, is largely and directly traceable to a succession
of young members but a few years removed from college and law
school courses which apparently gave them a strong predilection for
experimentation.

Innovations in governmental organization have stemmed primarily,
however, from a different source than have impulses to change in the
substance of policies and programs. Legislators who moved to seek
sometimes radical changes or improvements in governmental mechanics and processes were usually the young men representative of
the urbanism emerging nearly everywhere in the nation's South and
Southwest. Although, from individual to individual, theirs was not
a stance or a set of objectives which necessarily warrant the label
conservative, they acted, nevertheless, to maintain most of the governmental policies they found operating when they arrived in the
legislature. Some of the opposition to this group of organizational
innovators but program conservators was a group of legislators drawn
largely from the northern counties and other areas enjoying relatively
small shares of the fruits of a burgeoning economy. It is these counties
which, in elections of 1960-1966, provided the largest increments of
support to Democratic presidential and gubernatorial candidacies,
and it is their legislators who have endeavored to favor smaller com-

munities in the distribution of school funds, worked for labor and
equal opportunities legislation, and sought generally to alter the allocation of governmental costs and benefits. These diverging elements
sometimes joined, but we shall consider here only the legislature's
predilection for organizational change.

Doubtless, it is more than coincidence that the legislative article,
amended only once between ratification and 1940, became the most
amended part of the constitution. The article was amended six times
in the 1940's, with most of those changes coming late in the decade.
From 1951 to 1961 it was changed eight times, and nine other proposed amendments of the article failed of ratification.[43] And, that the
legislature's intentions may have been as honorable as its workload
was heavy is supported by the fact that, although it three times sought
to change its pay scale, it also thrice sought in the decade to gain
approval for annual sessions—a matter finally yielded by the voters
in 1964. However, it was in its formal and informal committee structure
—matters perhaps essential to legislative influence upon governments
of the type we discuss here—that the legislature best demonstrated
its desire to cope with its internal problems. For, as Leiserson has
put the matter, "An autonomous, potent legislature finds it politically
wise and expedient to delegate its duties of investigation, [and]
policy-determination . . . to powerful committees."[44]

The senate did its business for years through twenty or so committees, and the house ordinarily had twenty to twenty-five; but, in each
body, the lesser committees tended to be moribund until in the closing
days of a session. When they then came to life, it was virtually impossible to so schedule their meetings that the members, who served
on from four to six committees, could apportion their time without
conflicts. The result was that the inferior committees often met without
a quorum and without a sufficient number of able or experienced
members. A familiar evil, it is one often complained of in textbooks
of state government.

With the session of 1955, the senate began to conduct its legislative
business through seven standing committees directed to post a calendar of meetings so scheduled that each might sit for two or three
days a week throughout a session. Members served on no more than
two standing committees, the majority leader served on only one,
but with ex-officio membership on all. An eighth committee, known
as the "committee's committee" and comprised of officers and party

officers of the senate and two or three other members, was endowed with authority to allocate committee seats, designate committee chairmen, do all the purchasing, write the feed bill, handle employment, and otherwise attend to necessary housekeeping functions. The committee's committee promptly became an agency of authority which needed to bow only to a clear vote of the majority caucus. Pre-session conferences sponsored by the legislative council served to bring the membership together in ample time for the election of officers of senate and caucus and the designation of the committee's committee. Thereupon, the committee has set about its task of establishing rosters of committees and selecting employees so that the body has been fully ready to function upon its convening.

The house of representatives adopted a similar mode of organization in 1957, when it began to employ only twelve standing committees, designated "substantive," authorized to consider legislation. Although the rules were silent on the matter, it was the practice to restrict each member to service on two of the substantive committees, for each of which there was posted a schedule of meeting dates. Four other "procedural" committees were the usual committee on committees, enrolling and engrossing, printing and supplies, and rules and order of business. None of these enjoyed the power or status of the senate's committee's committee, for the speakers increasingly put into effective commission this aspect of the formal authority of the house. It is the speaker, the rule stated, who "shall designate the chairman when the committee is appointed." Speakers vested little authority in the rules committee; while the committee on committees was expected to carry out the wishes of the speaker in assigning members to substantive committees. The committee has been active, helpful, and effective, but members negotiating for an assignment could, and occasionally did, appeal to the speaker, who thereby kept visible his own strands of authority and communication.

The new committee arrangements were accepted and institution-alized by the membership with surprising speed and equanimity, but they did not bar quick adjustments to other considerations. In the 1961 session, for example, the matter of financing the public schools emerged, after developments of several years, as an issue engaging the attention of several committees as well as several groups extraneous to the legislature. The house majority and leader were not disposed to permit the department of education or the Republican governor to determine the matter; it was apparent that adjustments would be required across a range of sometimes long-standing funding formulas, statutes, and budgetary expectancies; and it was equally clear that the legislature could not unravel the issues *en camera* or through any of its standing committees. The organizational expedient was a house "policy committee"—the equivalent of an ad hoc caucus committee —whose seven members included the caucus chairman and members of the several standing committees developing the legislation. The policy committee went through a dozen sessions and pre-empted a large proportion of the available staff talent in devising a complex but professedly temporary plan for coping with the emergency. But, it was a program diverging in important respects from that favored by most members of the senate and the governor (whose veto would have been decisive). Then, in the senate, where frequent caucuses dispensed with the need of a policy committee, the leadership and the chairmen of two powerful committees brought the membership around to a policy which the house could accept.

Where the legislatures of the earlier decades of statehood were seldom involved in the detailed review of governmental policies, organization, and programs—functions then so much in the province of the Republican Old Guard that it was even called upon by some Democratic governors to advise and consent—those meeting after 1943 were apt to include a number of members with a penchant for the review of policy. They found no legislative instruments at hand for the purpose. The experienced staff of the Taxpayers' Association and the newly formed staffs of groups like education associations were available, but some members sought freedom from these as well as from party and governor. Attempts late in the 1940's to develop mechanisms for the review of policy and administration either failed of passage or were aborted by legislative failure to understand that what they sought would require them to commission suitable administrative agencies.

Successful devices for legislative oversight were established in 1951, when a reform-minded group stemming from the Young Turks of the previous session dominated the house, and when many of the majority were looking for instruments which might enable them to cope with the first Republican governor of their experience. Republican members were equally anxious to develop legislation which might be identified with the governor. Three items emerged that year as related reforms and drew comments indicative of the stresses involved in achieving them, for they represented items from the programs of the Democratic Policy Committee and the defeated candidate for governor, but were enacted as a result of a bi-partisan agreement. Each of the new agencies resulting—a legislative council and council service, a board of educational finance for the review of budgets and appropriations of colleges and universities, and a governmental reorganization ("Little Hoover") commission—were either quickly accepted and augmented by the legislature, or were followed by similar agencies.

Although the new legislative council, choosing to refrain from policy recommendations, refused to offer more than bill-drafting or research assistance, it quickly established interim committees of legislators for the review of reasonably specific problems, and the legislature then continued the practice. In the matter of the board of educational finance, one objective was to reduce the harrassment of legislators by importunate college administrators, but another was to obtain "de-watered" appraisals of budgets. (Legislators continued to be harrassed by university officials and, in their turn, legislators learned to badger the educational finance board and staff, but they did achieve the competent program budgets and analyses they sought.) The numerous recommendations of the reorganization committee, as has been the case in other states, met with faint enthusiasm, but a permanent legislative finance interim committee succeeded to much of the mandate of the earlier group and produced, sometimes at the rate of a faltering step or two at a time, much broader results. The departmental structure of government has been little touched but most state agencies have been made acutely aware of financial, budgeting, and personnel procedures which tie them closer to the governor's office and, simultaneously, render them more readily subject to legislative review. The auditor has been taken off the statewide ballot and made a legislative official, the state's three correctional institutions have been placed under one board, and seven state hospitals and eleemosynary institutions have been placed under the control of another. The annual sessions so long sought by legislative leaders were finally granted by the voters in 1964, but a related proposal to restore the highway department to executive and legislative control was rejected. (Voters have been remarkably relaxed about yielding to the legislature's numerous proposals for constitutional change, but the more controversial items are often appraised and rejected a time or two before they are passed. Suggestions of the constitutional revision commission established by the 1963 legislature will also probably hang fire for a time.)

Without adding appreciably to this already overlong accounting, what other point might be made to sum these aspects of political and legislative change in New Mexico? The most simple and direct, I think, is to note that the direction and the sum of the changes in legislative activity and organization in the state indicate a remarkable achievement if they are viewed in the perspective of the recommendations of the 1966 American Assembly—a small annual convocation of leading scholars, participants, and observers convened ad hoc for the consideration of carefully described public problems.[45] The legislature failed to reapportion itself in an equitable and lawful manner. (If there is a law of politics, it must be this: Legislators cannot and will not vote to deny office to their colleagues, or representation to their communities.) It has not pressed as hard as it might have to remove constitutional clutter inhibiting the management of debt and public funds, and it has, a few times, so developed legislation that it would provoke a referendum. Otherwise the record is good. Legislative longevity increases, annual sessions are required, work progresses on the constitution, private and special legislation is not only prohibited, but seldom attempted under any guise. The legislature is ably staffed and well equipped. In its new building after 1966, it will have ample office space, and it utilizes but a few and strong standing committees. The legislature is characterized by a continuous awareness of the nature and requirements of party competition, and it is more blessed than it knows by the lively scrutiny of the press as well as, sometimes, by its approbation. The latter, most observers would agree, is a very rare thing in the United States.

NINE

Patterns of Political & Governmental
Change

Sᴇᴛᴛɪɴɢs of economic sails and sociological rudders are at differing angles in the state's communities, with the result that impulses and party winds common to all impel them in diverging directions. And the electorate, or a part of it, may select its legislative representation by votes and out of motives quite different from those guiding its response to candidates for president or governor. In one community the legislator can be elected as an unknown name found in the Democratic or Republican column, but in the other he may be elected in a primary in which group and community, not partisan, considerations are paramount. In still another, the legislative candidate may be well known to a large number of voters only to be elected or rejected as a partisan by voters placing a high value on party. From these diverse sources have come assortments of humanity which somehow, miraculously, contrive each session to organize into a group, but one divisible, when necessary, into legislative majority and minority.

From a governor's point of view the legislature must often be a little like Alice's croquet mallet—a most absurdly animate and demanding instrument with its own objectives in the game. They are representatives of their towns and parties, but legislators also come to represent each other. Issues productive of legislative discord and division are settled if necessary, avoided if possible; and so, from many a legislator's point of view, party and governor, and the issues they bring can be capriciously disruptive of fraternal harmony.

In what follows I sum these and related matters, review their sequence, and attempt to tie them together. I then reward myself for my labors by speculating a bit on the capacity of this complex little political system to produce a few new increments of social justice.

If, at that point, a reader should suspect me of a restrained but genuine optimism, he would be quite correct.

STABLE GROUPS AND FLEXIBLE POLITICS

To recite, as in previous chapters, sequences of political events is perhaps to evoke a spurious implication of cause and effect. Yet, the interactions of individuals have produced group results falling into marked, and uniform, patterns of change in the state's politics.

When measured by voting responses at presidential and gubernatorial elections, the state has reacted much as has the nation to successive contests of half a century; but, the net secular change in party balance is slight. Conversely, if one gauges change by the periodic statewide results, it is to gain the impression that from time to time various issues have stirred the electorate with dramatic results —results which then tend, apparently, to erode away. But if the electoral results are assessed in reference to groups and communities, then the extent and incidence of change assume quite different aspects.

Some areas in the nation have clung steadfastly to ancient party loyalties; others long ago set out on a course of change sufficient to produce broad shifts in the local party balance. When the party vote is used as the indicator of change in New Mexico, the state's more significant groups and areas are seen to have taken the second alternative—marked regional shifts in party allegiance have occurred and give no immediate evidence of abating (although they someday must).

A majority of the Hispanic counties have moved from Republican to Democratic adherence. In voting for president and governor, the counties of Little Texas have come nearly to a two-party balance from a once extreme Democratic attachment. Mining counties of a strong trade-union tradition are apt to be increasingly Democratic at all levels of the ticket. Urbanized areas of rapid growth present a more confusing picture of a highly variable, two-party vote quite sensitive to issues. When the counties are further judged by the test of trends in voting majorities, their shift from one party to the other has generally been in directions consistent with underlying economic factors. Counties of increasing Republican vote percentages are ordinarily those of the higher rates of increase in per capita income—a concomitant of increasing urbanization. The voting of New Mexico's urban areas places them in company with others of an increasing Republican vote in a broad band from Richmond and Miami to Phoenix. Counties of an increasing or stable Democratic vote are usually those holding less advantageous positions on the economic scale.

When judged by statistical measures discounting the effect of secular change on variability of the party majorities, the counties also display characteristics indicative of differing degrees of restraint by party ties and party organization. More frequently than not, the more important of the counties displaying a steep rate of secular change from one party to the other manifest also a proclivity to cast a highly variable party vote from election to election. Such counties are typically: (1) those which have moved most sharply from extreme positions of one-party dominance; (2) still least characterized by a two-party politics; and (3) most urbanized and of most rapidly changing populations.

And, when the two measures—degree of secular change, and party-vote variability—are used as if simultaneously to appraise political characteristics of the counties, the following conclusions emerge: factors underlying the capacity of several areas to cast a highly variable party vote appear to be related not only to the extent of secular shifts in party attachment, but to stem from social, cultural, and economic characteristics. For example, the degree to which the party vote may vary is quite congruent with the capacity of several areas to respond to abstract, non-party issues such as constitutional amendments. In short, areas of the most flexible party vote are also quite likely: to have steep gradients of political change; to respond most heavily to abstract issues; to produce frequent split tickets; to cast proportionately larger shares of the state's total vote in years of presidential elections; to have, except in Los Alamos County, a weak minority party; to exceed the state's averages in per capita income and level of education; and, to be characterized by increasing urbanization.

Impulses stemming from political events of fifty years have caused about half of the counties to shift their normal party margins significantly, and seven or eight have reversed them. Response to Progressivism and third-party movements was greatest in the Democratic one-party areas which, in 1928, produced the most violent reactions to the Smith campaign. Although the vote cast in 1928 for and against

Smith represented a significant departure from the norms of every area, the counties have continued to move, with hardly an exception, in the directions to which they were so measurably jolted in that campaign. As a result, the vote of 1960 was usually but a slight distance from the norms established by the secular drift of the counties. So, in view of the extent and direction of movement of the presidential vote from the Smith to the Kennedy campaigns, it is clear that significant segments of the electorate have switched their party allegiance. Meanwhile, again to ring the changes, the state's communities have come to fall into place upon a gradient determined by personal income, degree of urbanization, and relative rates of growth. Those communities lower on the gradient increasingly cast a stable Democratic vote; those higher cast a variable, issue-dominated, and increasingly Republican vote. As a result, although the economic and social gaps between the citizenry of towns like Los Alamos, Hobbs, Taos, and Albuquerque may not be growing wider, they do appear to be producing a marked political separation.

Underlying these shifts are doubtless the accumulated effects of a long series of issues. However, those groups and areas making the most significant changes in party allegiance have clung steadfastly to other habits of political behavior. Their political style, as distinguished from their party vote, has so far changed but little in fifty years, although more critical changes of behavior may be in the offing.

The political styles of communities of the Rio Grande and upper Rio Pecos watersheds are still palpably different from those of the border counties and Little Texas. Durable factions of the Hispanic counties compete through primary slates and recognizable followings. An equally intense partisan conflict is carried through every election and every level of government. In most cases, their off-year vote is proportionately the largest in the state. Few tickets are split and changes in party membership occur slowly, but increments or losses in party strength are apt to persist. The Hispanic voter is by no means indifferent to the issues of politics; his party environment simply requires a particular mode of response. In his counties, the parties transform individual responses into partisan group responses, with the result that, although change is somewhat muted and less immediately measurable, it is apt to produce persisting group and individual alignments with the parties.

No county still heavily Hispanic approaches the capacity of Los Alamos or of counties like Curry, in Little Texas, to make radical election-by-election shifts in voter turnout or party majorities when state and national elections are at issue. On the other hand, the politics of Little Texas (and of several other counties somewhat similar in background) is essentially non-partisan at the municipal level—an arena of politics involving but a small portion of the electorate. Relatively few local issues and institutions in Little Texas are overtly political. Moreover, all political structures appear to have a quite real but narrow base involving the activities of relatively few citizens. Nor, my impression is, do other structures of community power in Little Texas seem to involve many participants; so, for many purposes, such communities may either sustain a high and narrow level of consensus or somehow conduct a politics which systematically deters many persons from participation. Yet, these increasingly prosperous, increasingly middle-class, Protestant communities are probably coming to an internal division similar to that found in many rapidly growing Southern towns and cities.

Responses of Little Texas to the Progressive era were the measure of a surge of liberalist sentiment. A protest vote there now is a conservative vote, frequently called up in reaction to state as well as to federal policies, and the old liberal protest element may be firmly embedded in the Democratic ranks. The evidence is reasonably persuasive that reactions to policies have contributed to a series of somewhat irregular steps in a slow realignment of Little Texas voters. Recent elections suggest those steps may be cumulating to a critical point conducive to a more rapid change. If "external" matters continue to produce a movement of the one-party areas to a two-party state and national politics, the community cleavages revealed may well be such that a long-submerged liberal element can contest for control of local Democratic party units, and so expose local politics to a broader range of statewide influences. If that result cannot be anticipated with great confidence, there is more assurance that a significant political division grows in the old Democratic strongholds.

Meanwhile, the politics of New Mexico is more accurately described by reference to characteristics of participation, degree and direction of change, and by its roots in different community structures than it is by reference to periodic electoral majorities.

ACCOMMODATION AND CHANGE IN THE ELECTORAL SYSTEM

New Mexico's experience conveniently serves the purposes of inquiry
into effects and characteristics of the convention and primary nominating systems. Nominations of 1911 through 1938 were made in
conventions; those after 1940 have been made in closed party primaries, sometimes coupled with pre-primary endorsing conventions.

The two eras present those contrasts which might be expected.
Some important differences between the convention and primary eras
appear to stem from broad shifts in electoral strength and attitudes;
others are more clearly traceable to the nominating systems. Neither
nominating method has apparently prevented or brought to fruition
those processes of change long underlying the politics of the state,
but, in all probability, some of the changes have been deterred or
accelerated by one or the other of the two systems. Although New
Mexico's experience generally confirms expectations, some deviations occur.

The Convention Era

From the turn of the century until 1930, so tight a party balance
prevailed that both parties were constrained to conduct strenuous
campaigns and, depending upon the situation, to be alert to encourage
or placate factional leadership. Multi-factionalism seldom appeared
at Republican state conventions in a form in which it could not be
readily controlled, nor apparently did it ever appear with much frequency at the county level. But the even division of party strength
fostered the appearance and notable success of a bi-partisan factional
group which frequently held an effective balance of electoral strength
in the state and in several counties. Local coalitions with one or the
other of the party groups were an effective factional tactic. Items
periodically appearing in Progressive programs emphasized the conservatism of the major parties and probably contributed to ideological
and programmatic rigidity of the majority Republican party. Both
parties were slow to adjust policies during the era of the Progressive
faction, when to do so would have meant yielding control of party
and legislative machinery to the cross-party faction.

The era demonstrates, however, that the convention system served,
under the conditions prevailing, to foster the statewide parties as
organizations based upon and controlling through local organizations.

Each party's organizational efforts reached into nearly every community in the state. Although it was a system inviting the formation of a bipartisan factional group, it forced insurgents to campaign at local and organizational levels as well as the ideological. Nor did a tight Republican organization prevent the liberal wing from gaining control, when, at last, insurgents concentrated their efforts on local organizations. In short, the factional system assumed a form consistent with the party system of an era of close competition. To have an effective influence upon either party's nominations, the faction had to be capable of making an overt and decisive shift from one party to the other. To balance or offset the faction, the parties had to be sensitive to local sentiments. Movements of the faction slowly contributed, however, to diminution of Republican strength in the northern counties. In those Republican strongholds the main components of the faction consisted of Hispanic voters—a group which, in 1936, made a significant shift to the Democratic party.

Existence of the convention system did not serve to check development of the two great and durable Democratic factions which became highly visible and contentious as soon as Republican opposition could be discounted. The two factions comprised groups characteristic of New Mexico's political geography. One based its strength on those counties still marginally Republican and still largely Hispanic. The other faction was based upon Bernalillo County and the again rapidly growing communities of Little Texas and the border counties—areas which became significant after 1950 in the electoral base of the Republican party.

The politics and legislative system of the convention era had provided a mechanism for maintaining the conservative governmental program of the Republican Old Guard, but it responded efficiently in coming to a quick resolution of the financial crisis of 1934 and 1935. It was not immune, however, to a type of deadlock which may be inherent in the system. The legislatures of 1929-1933 came to an impasse in which little policy could be made, for, by this time, the bi-partisan faction which neither party could control commanded a sufficient number of militant legislative adherents to block passage of party and gubernatorial programs—a deadlock broken finally by a cross-party conservative alliance.

Nor did the convention system hold stable the position of governors. The Republican governor tended to serve as an agent of the

Old Guard wing of the party, and the party itself retained the capacity to determine legislative policy. Democratic governors of the era, however, became focal points of party and factional strength. It was they who were legislative overseers, and, characteristically, each developed a strong legislative faction instrumental in enacting the gubernatorial and party programs. The membership of each governor's legislative faction was based upon the geographic area essential to his electoral margin. In those regimes legislative access could be obtained only through the governor's office. Democratic governors of the late convention era attained some measure of independence from dominant economic interests by their practice of relying on employee contributions. This, plus their control of the legislature, vested for a time a broad gubernatorial capacity to act as arbiters rather than representatives of interests. In this situation, however, the party itself became more clearly an interest group.

The convention did not bar the parties from developing characteristic styles of leadership. Perhaps because they were relics of an earlier day and a simpler society, leaders of the Old Guard were clearly identifiable as party financiers, spokesmen, and strategists. Their hand was visible in every facet of legislative operations. Old Guard interest in politics was avocational and supported by income derived from other pursuits. Those who emerged as Democratic leaders and party lieutenants were of two groups. Those with a policy-making orientation and capacity tended to be somewhat less visible to the public, to be based primarily on Albuquerque and the southern counties, to be active in law and their private businesses, but they were not as closely identified as were the Old Guard Republicans with dominant corporate and ranching interests. The other component of the Democratic leadership for years found its chief vocation and source of income as candidates and officeholders.

Some Attributes of the Primary

Key suggests that transfer of popular choice to the majority party primary "has brought a basic change in the role and structure of the inner party leadership within the majority party."[1] In New Mexico a pronounced change occurred in both parties at the state level, but the effects induced in local political organizations are neither so marked nor consistent.

Preceding accounts of Spanish-American politics stress that Hispanic counties retain a locally competitive two-party system, but one in which factions of the majority party divide into a continuing group dominating local politics, and into one or two other somewhat more ephemeral factions activated by the state and congressional primaries. But the primary in the Hispanic counties has not otherwise produced much change in the organization of political power in the majority party. The minority party in these communities also remains as a strong competitor. Key notes as puzzling, the fact that in small communities "the forces set in motion by the primary do not draw practically all voters into the primary of one or the other of the parties at least for local purposes."[2] In the Hispanic communities the party divisions that have sometimes existed for generations are often considerably altered, but they have not yet been appreciably abated by the primary. The durability of the parties indicates that they are deeply woven into the structures and habits of Spanish-American communities.

Nor has the primary produced an unequivocal effect in those communities long and heavily dominated by one party. Here prevail most clearly what Epstein terms "nonparty characteristics of state politics."[3] Chances are that the primary in several of New Mexico's heavily Democratic Little Texas and border counties serves as a seldom-needed safety valve for homogeneous communities in which there is typically present a strong and centralized structure of community power with a marked "apolitical" bias. The legally adopted primary of 1940 merely continued a long-standing practice of conducting informal direct primaries in the one-party counties, and seems to have produced a strengthened inclination to continue in the legislature those incumbents who appear to be reasonably representative of their communities. In those communities the principal change has come in the appearance of small groups of political operators associated with factions called into being by gubernatorial primary candidacies. Unlike the case in the Hispanic counties, these factions frequently eschew involvement in county and municipal politics. Whether their candidates are successful or not usually produces no significant change in the control or membership of the locally dominant organizations of the party, or the politics, of the old one-party, Democratic communities. A strong Democratic primary fight is frequently followed, however, by a heavier Republican general election vote—another matter which may be contributing to voter realignment.

Although many local units of the minority party were suddenly more quiescent and less visible, the direct primary produced no marked change in basic community patterns of political behavior and alignment. But, when the parties rather than communities are the objects of examination, effects of the primary are somewhat clearer.

Processes of time and death doubtless contributed to a weakening of the Republican party. Yet a significant decline in the party's organizational effectiveness is indicated by the sharp increase, immediately after installation of the primary, in the number of uncontested legislative seats. And, after 1940, the party was never able to direct its legislative members as a party entity. Those serving thereafter in the legislature served subject to a broad range of influences, of which the state party organization was but a minor one. The primary doubtless tends also to weaken the minority party at the electoral level, for its primary consistently attracts a relatively small portion of party adherents and but few contested nominations.

The degree to which the primary has hastened or retarded secular change of voter alignments is conjectural, although, as noted, it probably inhibited the minority's organizational activity in those areas in which it was most outnumbered. Yet, those secular shifts in party strength which had begun before the New Deal persist. Many voters have made their way to new party attachments despite a low level of party activity.

A more significant change in state party organization, and in the party's role in government accompanied the direct primary. The state organizations are now largely separated from the local, and usually make only the feeblest of efforts to align themselves with active local factions. Hence, the effective points of political activity are apt to be in local governmental units and communities, and these find a major agency of expression in the legislature rather than in the majority, statewide party. The organized party is largely that aggregation of county groupings and individuals available for capture or alliance by the successful gubernatorial nominee. The majority party is not organized in a manner to permit it to determine legislative membership. As a result two parties exist: the electoral and the legislative. The governor's problem now is to control them both.

THE LEGISLATIVE SYSTEM—DEPENDENT VARIABLE

Beneath universal similarities of organization and constitutionally prescribed functions, the state legislatures display a remarkable diversity. There has been discerned "a pattern in this variety, however, the outline of which derives from the degree of two-party competition in the various states."[4] Another view—in which the legislature is regarded as a group-centered system generating its own objectives, organization, and customary patterns of activity—stresses a fundamental tension between the internally regulated legislative system, and the external political, governmental, and social systems.[5]

To concede the utility of the latter view of the legislature as a system generative of its own approach and direction is not to deny that the legislature is nevertheless an element within a larger entity. The latter view does make obvious, however, the changing capacities of the larger entity to impress its will or leadership upon the legislature.

New Mexico's history makes clear the duality and tension involved in the relationships of the legislature to the party. It makes apparent, also, that the relationships of the two to each other are mutually and measurably affected by a broader range of events impinging upon the whole political system. At one stage (1900-1927), the legislature was the instrument of party, and those impulses which it generated internally as a social group and system were so confined and subordinated as to be relatively insignificant. At still another interval (1934-1941), the legislature assumed the second of its classic roles when it became clearly and directly responsible to gubernatorial leadership—again, a period when it was able to assert relatively few of the characteristics of an internally controlled group. Then, when the primary, the emergence of party factions, and the decline of minority party strength all contributed to a relaxation of external controls by the governor and state party, the legislature assumed more fully those attributes emphasizing its character as a self-contained, internally directed entity.

Patterns of Legislative Party Voting

The changing tendency of members to register party-versus-party votes is described in Figure 18 for those periods when the minority party commanded no less than 16 per cent of the membership of the

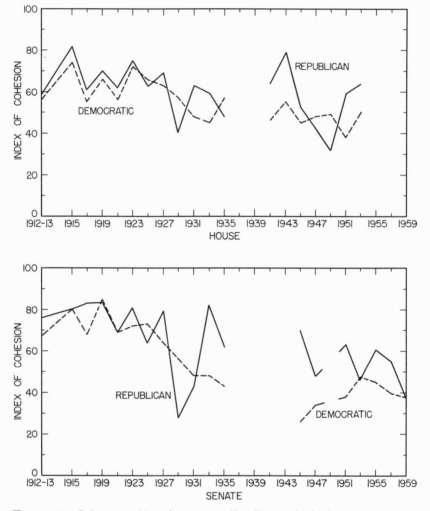

FIGURE 18. Cohesion of legislators in roll calls in which the majority voting of one party's members opposed a majority of the other.

house involved. The measure used here, the Rice index of cohesion, is introduced and explained at page 167 above. The party votes not graphed in Figure 18 are those in periods in which the minority party commanded less than 16 per cent of the seats—periods in which Republican members were in too small a minority to permit evaluating their votes with any degree of confidence.

The 1912-1927 level of party voting in each chamber was an extension of a pattern which had existed throughout the decade closing the territorial period. More frequently than is lately the case, issues were party conflicts in which a majority of one party voted in opposition to a majority of the other party. Hence, for nearly twenty years the legislature displayed a significant capacity to make responses determined by party direction. On matters setting the parties apart, members of either house seldom defied the party whips. Those points on the scale of Figure 18 representing subsequent sessions reveal a sharp decline in party cohesion in 1929 and 1931, and an erratic but generally low level of cohesion thereafter.

Figure 18 is apt to convey a misleading impression, however, of the frequency and degree of overt legislative party combat, and the system of legislative control underlying the data of the chart. The bare indices of party cohesion understate the degree of party control exercised before 1929. When the significant issues were joined, the Old Guard legislative management got its way, and, in those matters, the members who defected were few. Conversely, there was a broad range of legislation upon which the Old Guard exercised merely a technical oversight. Then, as now, the parties were indifferent to numerous items of importance to various groups and individuals. Consequently, the powerful steering committees were probably willing to accept many bills extraneous to party interests as items incidentally useful in preserving legislative harmony and individual acquiesence. Legislation of that order was usually screened, even in the days of party control, only for its contextual validity and draftsmanship, and governors have usually been disposed to sign it. This feature of legislative activity has changed but little since statehood. But if this permissive realm of group activity were removed from the record compiled by the Republican Old Guard and by several Democratic governors, there would remain a battery of roll calls marking a hard core of party or gubernatorial control in those periods.

Tables 48 and 49 summarize the incidence of roll calls resulting in uananimous votes and those evoking non-party and party opposition. Inspection of the various columns suggests that members have most frequently opposed legislation (i.e., voted against the majority determining the issue) because of various non-party considerations. The number of roll calls involving opposition by a "non-partisan" minority of the total membership is (except in the senate of 1912-

TABLE 48. PARTY AND ROLL CALL VOTING, HOUSE OF REPRESENTATIVES, 1912-1963[a]

			Roll calls		
Legislature			"Non-party"		Percentage
Number and years	Percentage of membership Democratic	Percentage unanimous	As percentage of total	With percentage of "no" votes	with parties opposed
1-8 (1912-27)	41	45	37	11	18
9-10 (1929-31)	41	47	41	13	13
11-15 (1933-41)	85	51	39	19	(18)[b]
16-19 (1943-49)	66	46	40	16	15
20-26 (1951-63)	79	61	35	16	(8)[b]

[a]Derived from Appendix, Table A-3.

[b]In these intervals, party-versus-party votes were not calculated for sessions in which the minority held less than 16 per cent of the seats. The figures in parentheses represent totals and percentages derived from the sessions represented in Figure 18. If all roll calls were used as a base, then the two parenthetical figures of the last column would be 11 and 4 respectively.

TABLE 49. PARTY AND ROLL-CALL VOTING, SENATE, 1912-1963[a]

			Roll calls		
Legislature			"Non-party"		Percentage
Number and years	Percentage of membership Democratic	Percentage unanimous	As percentage of total	With percentage of "no" votes	with parties opposed
1-8 (1912-27)	37	62	22	14	16
9-10 (1929-31)	29	50	38	17	13
11-16 (1933-43)	88	55	39	23	(15)[b]
17-19 (1945-49)	76	71	26	21	(4)[b]
20-24 (1951-59)	74	59	31	21	10
25-26 (1961-63)	86	68	32	23	..

[a]Derived from Appendix, Table A-4.

[b]In these intervals party-versus-party votes were not calculated for sessions in which the minority held less than 16 per cent of the seats. The figures in parentheses represent totals and percentages derived from the sessions represented in Figure 18. If all roll calls were used as a base, then the two parenthetical figures of the last column would be 5 and 3 respectively.

1927) consistently two or three times as great as those which divided the membership on party lines.

In Jewell's review of legislative party voting, the several states concerned are ranked by the percentage of non-unanimous roll calls in which the parties were opposed.[6] Their range is quite great. At the levels of party combat and cohesion attained early in its history, New Mexico would place perhaps halfway up in the list; after 1931, it would place nearly at the bottom. The extent of party voting in various eras (when unanimous votes are excluded from the roll calls) is summarized in the following tabulation:

Sessions	Party-versus-party roll calls as percentage of all non-unanimous roll calls	
	House	*Senate*
1912-1927	31	43
1929-1931	24	26
1933-1935	27	28
1941-1949	29	...
1945-1947	...	15
1951, 53, 57, 63	20	...
1951-1959	...	24

Party voting has declined significantly in both houses, but in neither has it been involved in much more than a fifth to a third of the roll calls involving dissenting votes. The level of party combat sustained in the legislatures of 1911-1927 has never again been approached.

The period of most strenuous partisan conflict in the legislature occurred, it will be recalled, when the more important and controversial legislation had usually been proposed, written, and ratified by the extra-legislative party as represented by its Old Guard leadership. Its obvious source made it an open invitation to combat, the legislative party was strong enough and cohesive enough to pass its legislation, and the minority was agile enough to contest it and to gain such capital as it could from its opposition. Later, during the 1935-1943 period of dominance by Democratic Governors Tingley and Miles, the Republican members were too few to act as an opposition. The number of "no" votes in both houses increased during the period, but only to such approximate levels as would have resulted in other sessions had the party "no" and the non-party "no" votes been added together.

In the closing three or four sessions of the 1940's the parties were in opposition only about as frequently and about as strenuously as was needed to preserve their reputations and identities as Republicans and Democrats. The significant divisions occurred in the house between two biparty factions of which one was oriented to cooperation with a senate faction corresponding to a liberal group of the non-legislative party. In the senate of 1945-1949, Republican members comprised a relaxed and agreeable minority seldom disposed to vote on party lines, and 71 per cent of the roll calls of the club-like body were unanimous. In the more fractious house of the day, only 46 per cent of the roll calls were without dissent.

The shift to service under a governorship held by a Republican on three of the five occasions of 1951 through 1959, made but small difference in voting behavior as measured by Tables 48 and 49. The senate, now somewhat less relaxed and amiable, dropped its percentage of unanimous votes to 59, but the house increased its fraction to 61 per cent. In the main, the legislature was continuing trends long in existence. Only 10 per cent of the senate's roll calls involved party-versus-party divisions, and, in the few house sessions in which a reading is feasible, about 8 per cent were party-versus-party votes and the percentage of individual "no" votes was not much changed from the preceding period.

Legislative System versus Party

To be considered here is a set of tables and graphs which, in essence, permit a reading of legislative votes as indicators of the characteristics of an internally controlled system. The cohesion levels of both parties in party-versus-party votes graphed in Figure 18 above, and the levels of Democratic party cohesion graphed in Figure 19 are summarized by various time periods in Tables 50 and 51. The measures of Figure 19 are restricted to the Democratic legislative party, for it consistently had a sufficient number of members (ranging from a strong minority to one-party majority strength) to permit graphing a complete series of its votes.

As a preliminary, we might note in Figure 18 and Tables 50 and 51 that, except for the 1929-1931 interval of the Progressive-Old Guard Republican split, Republican legislators have usually shown a higher level of cohesion than have the Democratic. The shift in party legislative control did little to change the pattern. Democrats, whether as majority or minority, have always had difficulty in bridging the gap between the northern-Hispanic, and southern-conservative

TABLE 50. PARTY COHESION IN THE HOUSE

| | *Indices of cohesion* | | | |
| | *Democratic* | | *Party versus party* | |
Legislature: number and session years	*All roll calls*	*All roll calls not unanimous*	*Democratic*	*Republican*
1-8 (1912-27)	83	69	63	68
9-10 (1929-31)	79	62	51	57
11-15 (1933-41)	80	60	48	58
16-19 (1943-49)	81	65	50	56
20-26 (1951-63)	87	66	42	57

Source: Derived from Appendix, Tables A-3 and A-5.

TABLE 51. PARTY COHESION IN THE SENATE

| | *Indices of cohesion* | | | |
| | *Democratic* | | *Party versus party* | |
Legislature: number and session years	*All roll calls*	*All roll calls not unanimous*	*Democratic*	*Republican*
1-8 (1912-27)	88	68	72	77
9-10 (1929-31)	81	62	51	37
11-16 (1933-43)	80	54	46	74
17-19 (1945-49)	87	50	28	63
20-24 (1951-59)	81	53	42	53
25-26 (1961-63)	85	53	..	..

Source: Derived from Appendix, Tables A-4 and A-6.

wings of their party. Hence, if a chart like Figure 19 were presented
to show Republican legislative voting, it would place the various graph
lines a few percentage points higher than these depicting Democratic voting.

The index lines designated A in Figure 19 show that, over time,
there has been a fairly consistent and high level of legislative party

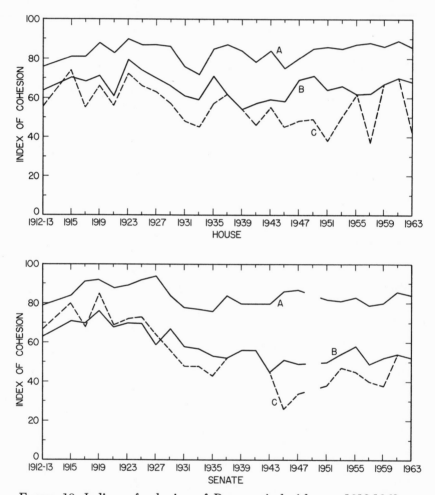

FIGURE 19. Indices of cohesion of Democratic legislators, 1912-1963.
(A. All roll calls inclusive of unanimous votes; B. All roll calls exclusive
of those which were unanimous; and C. Party versus party roll calls when
the minority party held no less than 16 per cent of the total membership.)

cohesion. Perturbations in this measure of cohesion of all Democratic members voting on all recorded roll calls are not great, but they may be read as reflections of variations in the sources or intensity of external influence. Thus, the voting in both house and senate in 1929 and 1931 reflects the impact, described in Chapter V, of the Cutting faction upon the two parties. In the house of 1941-1947, the pattern assumed by line A reveals the presence of persistent, cross-party, factional alignments. Thereafter, in the house, cohesion on the aggregate of roll calls is uniformly high—a matter denoting a consistent pattern of basic legislative agreement. Line A describes a similar situation in the senate.

Lines B, resulting from the exclusion of unanimous roll calls, indicate a significantly lower level of cohesion in the senate than in the house. After 1940, the house was considerably more amenable than the senate to gubernatorial direction, and its speakers have sometimes been able to use their sanctions effectively. The senate could come to a prompt and decisive party vote, but it was seldom disposed to do so and its leaders more often acted as traffic coordinators than as its controllers. Increasingly tied to their communities, highly exposed to a broad range of influences, and operating within a network of fraternal ties, the senators have taken, and accorded to one another, a wide latitude. And, since 1940, they have usually been prone to accept party direction only on their own terms.

In sum, lines A and B may be read for both house and senate as measures of the level of fundamental agreement on the broad range of matters which have come before the legislature. In this sense, they are measures of a capacity of the membership to respond as unified, a-partisan, internally regulated bodies making their own resolution of conflicts coming before them, and determining, as well, what matters become issues.

Scale C, in Figure 19, denotes the level of cohesion of the Democratic members when a majority of the party's members was in opposition to a majority of the Republican members. Except in the senate during the period of party control of 1912-1927, the level of party cohesion is lower on party-versus-party votes than it is on other roll calls. (The intervals when lines C and B coincide are those sessions in which the Republican minority was too small to permit a meaningful calculation of party-versus-party votes.) Hence, the party may be conceived as an external, intrusive, and disruptive force on those occasions when it enforces legislative attention to certain issues. The low degree of cohesion of members in party-aligned votes suggests a strong and continuing legislative resistance to the constraints and disciplines involved in party direction; for, when the parties and governors have created or responded to issues divisive of the public, they have found their legislative followings and oppositions to be similarly divided or divisible.[7]

Yet, this inclination to create its own culture and miniscule internal republic may make the legislature an instrument highly useful in containing and converting to a satisfactory social product the forces at work in the larger society of New Mexico, which, like many another unit at home and abroad, is inherently neither polity nor community.

POSTLUDE AND PRELUDE

Governorship, party, and legislature are not institutions readily subject to radical change; yet, as this account may have made clear, they do change and in directions indicative of the major forces at work from time to time. What, then, are some of the more intriguing possibilities inherent in New Mexico's political system and situation—in its capacity to achieve justice—in the years closing this account?

It might be well to begin by considering the enormous weight of the broader institutions setting the political and economic environment of the state and of which I have had but little to say. Consider, for example, what the state's institutions could have been and what they would have implied for politics and government had New Mexico stayed within the jurisdiction and territory of the government of Mexico (a fearsome stretch of the imagination for those who remember the Alamo and Manifest Destiny, but as an exercise it is improved for that reason). And imagine also what great differences would have ensued had New Mexico become, in 1846 or thereabouts, an independent nation complete with all the appurtenances of sovereignty such as an unlimited right of constitution making. As it is, New Mexico is but a limited political and institutional field, defined and structured by its position within a far greater entity which permits the choice only of that range of directions and of organization amenable to the whole. It is true that the differences between states like New Mexico, Wisconsin, and Alabama are great, but they are as nothing to that which would conceivably be the case if each had been permitted for a hundred years to develop free of the restraints inherent in the Union.

Within that broad national environment, an increasingly sophisticated, increasingly more deliberately planned series of measures—subsumable generically as New Deal, Fair Deal, and the Great Society—have sought or tended to bring new or disadvantaged groups and areas to an increased share of the basic social product, and, some have hoped, to an increased influence on the processes determining the distributive formulas. These developments increasingly derive from what Moynihan has termed "the professionalization of reform" —a phenomenon related to more or less regular increments in public funds available for social purposes, and which has involved, as well, an increasing emphasis on fostering and putting into effective political commission local, ethnic, and similarly distinguishable social and economic groupings. For, as Moynihan makes clear, the groups and individuals developing the ideas and analyzing the data recently going into the computing machines of Washington and the great research institutions no longer seek to foster a homogenized society.[8]

If these emerging elements of the nation's policies are continued, they will serve not to diminish, as have so many policies in the past, but to emphasize the diversity that underlies the political system of New Mexico. In addition, the legislatures of 1967 and some indeterminate period to follow will reflect the fundamental legislative redistricting described in Chapter VIII, for a large proportion of their members can be expected to be faithful reflections of small, relatively homogeneous, one-delegate constituencies. What results will probably not be new in any literal sense, but there is apt to be a greatly increased emphasis on factors which only lately have been broadly perceived as valuable.

The state's new capitol, for example, is a curiously revealing transformation of the symbols of government. Members of the first legislative session in 1912 found, of course, the familiar dome, the ranks of arched windows, and the broad stairway leading to the capitaled columns of a Roman facade. (An ill-favored building, it was converted to the southwestern territorial style after World War II, when facade and dome were removed for a simpler garnish consisting of a coat of white stucco, a brick trim at the roof line, a square bell tower rising high from ground level, and a portal.) The building made ready for the newly reapportioned legislature of 1967 preserves something of the territorial flavor (already a tradition strong enough to demand its hostage from the new), but it is otherwise startlingly like a vast kiva—the round, half-below-ground, ceremonial chamber of the Pueblo Indians. But it is not inappropriate that the members arriving from their highly varied constituencies should confront tokens of the several cultures for which they are to legislate. Los Alamos—a pueblo representative of the tribal culture of science—is but fourteen or fifteen miles from the ancient pueblo or city state of San Ildefonso which lies, in turn, twenty or so miles from Santa Fe—outpost of the lively and graphic arts, seat of the state government, the Roman Catholic Archdiocese, and the Protestant Episcopal Diocese. A few leagues to the west of Santa Fe and Los Alamos is Navajo, Mormon, and tourist country; southward, along the Rio Grande, every major town to the Mexican border boasts university or research and development installations; and eastward, on the plains, are the civic and cultural frontiers of Texas and the South.

Although the new electoral arrangements will admit a new cast of actors to the political scene, and although each turn of the plot may be, I think, more just, it is most unlikely that they will solve any of the ancient paradoxes or remove any of the ancient limits. Government is a process, not a solution, and by it, among other processes, we attempt to achieve from day to day some possible optimum of well-being, but the welfare we seek is itself being constantly redefined. It is a central question of politics, of course, for a good many citizens seem persuaded that government (as causal entity) can be sufficiently well informed and organized so that it will find and execute policies which will achieve an optimum of welfare, and perpetually disappointed because it does not. However, a high level of political participation and information is costly to the citizen, and Anthony Downs, for one, would have it that governments and citizens must always proceed on the basis of insufficient information so that, consequently, the budget must always be too low in a democracy.[9] Key, more optimistic, proposes that there is a large and responsible element of the citizenry which is disposed, not only to vote for what they want, but likely, as well, to invest enough time and energy to find and act upon information instrumental for a public welfare broader than their own.[10] Both, probably, are right (and there is no paradox in that), and we may assume that groups hitherto active in politics will continue to be so, just as we may assume that some citizens and some politicians will continue to seek a broadly equitable and efficient polity within which groups and elements socially and economically disadvantaged can seek those gains their values impel them to seek. Yet, it must be recognized that in a governmental organization such as that of the state of New Mexico, one will find for a long time to come only a limited range of activities—road building, the provision of education, public health services, etc. Others will be added, of course, incrementally and from time to time, for that is what all the noise of politics is about.

There is a strong possibility also that the very intensity and competitiveness of politics in the Hispanic counties and in some urban neighborhoods (and, as it may develop in some Indian communities) will continue to limit the uses to which state and local government can be put. The endless factional maneuverings, the use of office to support and reward factions, the personal and narrowly political obligations which successful candidates for the legislature have so often assumed as the price, apparently, of their election, and the exceedingly close and personal involvement of leaders and potential leaders in their own communities—all these things, and more, operate to limit the capacity of Spanish Americans to use their political power to obtain an increased advantage for their communities. There is no reason to suppose that other disadvantaged groups and communities will behave much differently. (Yet, these activities have gained and will serve to retain at least one great advantage for the Hispanic voter. This group—now mustering only 28 per cent of the population of the state—has recently enjoyed, according to an accurate accountant of such matters, 70 per cent of the positions in the state highway department, 70 per cent of those of the bureau of revenue staff, 72 per cent in the motor vehicle division, 92 per cent of the penitentiary's jobs, 86 per cent in the state mental hospital, and lesser but still large percentages of available positions in nearly every other agency of the state.[11] Many of these workers are now well enough trained and educated to have an even chance in the competitive examinations by which many are admitted, but before the days of a merit system, the bureaucracy was an instrument incidentally useful in training and acculturating at a relatively small cost a large and oftentimes seriously disadvantaged sector of the population. It is a matter which some other states might do well to ponder.)

Yet, when all such limitations have been acknowledged, the conviction remains that a good deal more is possible and this within the
political and economic framework that now exists. For one thing, no
convincing demonstration has been made, although it may be an
assumption of many of us, that the "welfare" of the society is always
at a momentary optimum, and that all that can be done by the political
process is to alter the distribution of social and economic benefits. It
is a loose, rather than a tight and rigidly structured political environment in which New Mexicans live, and the economy, with its tax structure, no doubt permits of more than it has recently produced. Many of
the new legislators will be relatively secure in their new little constituencies, and if, as the statistical probabilities of such matters lead us to
anticipate, a fair number of them are responsible and intelligent men,
they will be in a position to exert a strong leverage upon the legislature.
And, assuming a continuance of the legislature's proclivity to create its
own standards and environment as well as to provide the arena in
which prospective governors and congressmen may demonstrate their
capacity, the legislature should continue to provide a situation in which
a mere handful of astute and adroit individuals could utilize its processes to produce some startling achievements. A few men with a
knowledge of the complex mechanics of legislation, and the ability
and willingness to operate at the administrative and legislative levels
in the manner developed by the better interest-group lobbyists, would
exert an enormous influence. Such skills are always badly needed
wherever policy is determined, and their availability, always for a
suitable—not too high—bargaining price, plus the leverage exerted
at critical moments by minority group voters, could sometimes be decisive. If such a development should occur it might do so as a result of
accident rather than conscious action, but there is nothing in the
politics of the state which should necessarily preclude it. An Hispanic
Lyndon Johnson or another Charles Springer from any group could
move the political mountains; and, if nothing else were at hand, he
could do it with the materials of group politics already available. To
create the optimal system even momentarily is probably a problem that
can never be solved. To create an improved situation for a group is
quite another matter, although it would probably require assumption
of the heavy burden of mutual responsibility.

And, unless the new legislature and the political system of which it
is part, undergoes some profound, and unforeseeable alteration, it is

quite likely that those young men of Albuquerque, Santa Fe, and the southern and eastern counties who aspire to the governorship will continue not only to try their spurs in the legislature, but to give hostage to it. If they are to be serious contenders, and if they are from the urban or eastern counties, they must demonstrate the capacity to lead, and follow, men of antecedents and aspirations much different than their own. And, to gain credence as serious contenders for legislative leadership or higher office, they will be quite likely to be even more constrained than in the recent past to see and reach policy objectives not sought and perhaps not wanted by their own constituencies.

Notes

CHAPTER ONE

1. V. O. Key, Jr., *American State Politics: An Introduction* (New York: Alfred Knopf, Inc., 1956), pp. 28-33.

2. This behavior corresponds to that of the 19 states of Key's tabulation for the period of 1920-1930, in which sample New Mexico was a unit. *Ibid.*, p. 45.

3. *Ibid.*, pp. 72-73.

4. V. O. Key, Jr., *A Primer of Statistics for Political Scientists* (New York: Thomas Y. Crowell Company, 1959), p. 85.

5. V. O. Key, Jr., and Corrine Silverman, "Party and Separation of Powers: A Panorama of Practice in the States," *Public Policy*, (eds.) Carl J. Friedrich and J. Kenneth Galbraith (Cambridge, Mass.: Graduate School of Public Administration, Harvard University, 1954), as cited by Austin Ranney and Willmoore Kendall, *Democracy and the American Party System* (New York: Harcourt, Brace and Company, 1956), pp. 414-415.

6. Austin Ranney and Willmoore Kendall, "The American Party Systems," *American Political Science Review*, XLVIII (June, 1954), 482.

7. Robert T. Golembiewski, "A Taxonomic Approach to State Political Strength," *Western Political Quarterly*, XI (September, 1958), 494-513. The results of various classifications suggest that the particular schemata used for New Mexico might well be chosen to distinguish between different offices, types of elections, and various time periods, or to bring to the surface particular manifestations of political behavior. Thus, in another context, a classification by V. O. Key, Jr. (*American State Politics* . . . , p. 99) relating primaries to general elections is found useful. And see Joseph A. Schlesinger, "A Two-Dimensional Scheme for Classifying the States According to Degree of Inter-Party Competition," *American Political Science Review*, XLIX December, 1955), 1120-1128.

In a classification based on control of the governorship and the two legislative chambers for the period 1947-1962, Jewell distributes 46 states into two broad groups. Twenty-three states fall into three categories of one-party dominance, and an equal number range through four degrees of two-party competition. In Jewell's schema, New Mexico is one of eight "limited two-party states" at the lower end of the scale. Malcolm E. Jewell. *The State Legislature: Politics and Practice* (New York: Random House, 1962), pp. 10-13, by permission of the publisher.

8. "The average intercensal increases through the net migration of native whites were generally high in the Mountain States and in the Northwest. There were two interesting exceptions; neither Utah with its predominantly Mormon population nor New Mexico with its Spanish-Americans has substantial in-migration [1870-1910] from other states." Conrad Taeuber and Irene B. Taeuber, *The Changing Population of the United States*, Census Monograph Series (New York: John Wiley and Sons, 1958), p. 310. That the other laggard state was Utah prompts the conjecture that the socioreligious systems of the two areas served for a time to deter immigration.

9. These data are estimates based on a table of voter registrations by county—a procedure involving the assumption that the voters of the time were reasonably representative of the whole population. The table is: "Division of Vote of the State by Descent," *New Mexico Blue Book, 1915* (Santa Fe: Office of Secretary of State), p. 142.

10. V. O. Key, Jr., *Southern Politics in State and Nation* (New York: Alfred A. Knopf, 1949), p. 86.

11. Figure 9 shows the variations in the relationship of the total vote of the Hispanic counties to the state's total and to that of the six contrasting counties of Little Texas.

Special Report P. E. No. 3C, "Persons of Spanish Surname," *U.S. Census,* 1950, lists the counties as follows (with the percentages Hispanic): Doña Ana, 53; Guadalupe, 75; Mora, 85; Rio Arriba, 80; Sandoval, 53; San Miguel, 77; Santa Fe, 60; Socorro, 59; Taos, 81; and Valencia, 50. The 1960 Census lists Doña Ana with 42 per cent, Sandoval at 32, and Valencia at 36 per cent.

CHAPTER TWO

1. *Albuquerque Journal,* November 7, 1958.

2. Thomas C. Donnelly, *The Government of New Mexico* (2d ed. rev.; Albuquerque: University of New Mexico Press, 1953), pp. 1-5. France V. Scholes, "Civil Government and Society in New Mexico in the Seventeenth Century," *New Mexico Historical Review,* X (April, 1935), 71-111; and Scholes, "Church and State in New Mexico," *ibid.,* XI (January, 1936), 9-76.

3. Harvey Fergusson, *Rio Grande* (New York: Alfred A. Knopf, 1936), p. 81.

4. Herbert O. Brayer, *William Blackmore: The Spanish-Mexican Land Grants of New Mexico and Colorado, 1863-1878* (Denver: Bradford-Robinson, 1949), pp. 10-11; and William J. Parish, "The German Jew and the Commercial Revolution in Territorial New Mexico, 1850-1900," *New Mexico Quarterly,* XXIX (Autumn, 1959), 324. Parish's article is reprinted and documented in *New Mexico Historical Review,* XXXV (January and March, 1960), 1-23 and 129-141.

5. Two extensive and recent bibliographies are available: Frederick C. Irion, "Bibliography on New Mexico Politics," *Western Political Quarterly,* XI (December, 1958), pp. 77-109, Supplement; and Irion, "Selected and Annotated Bibliography on Politics in New Mexico," (4th ed., Santa Fe: New Mexico Legislative Council Service, 1959, mimeographed), pp. 4-117.

6. Key, *Southern Politics . . . ,* pp. 271-275.

7. Edward C. Banfield, *Big City Politics* (New York: Random House, 1965), pp. 66-79; and Robert C. Stone, *et al.,* "An Overview of Economic and Inter-ethnic Patterns in a Border Community," *Arizona Review of Business and Public Administration,* XII (January, 1963), 4-29.

8. William Pryor Irwin, "The Rocky Mountain Ballot: A Study of Political Behavior in the State of Colorado," (unpublished Ph.D. dissertation, University of California, Berkeley, 1955), pp. 188-231.

9. "Los Atarqueños: A Study of Patterns and Configurations in a New Mexico Village," (unpublished Ph.D. dissertation, Radcliffe College, 1941). Extensive excerpts and summaries of this account comprise a central portion of Florence R. Kluckhohn and Fred L. Strodtbeck, *et al., Variations in Value Orientations* (Evanston: Row, Peterson and Co., 1961).

10. Sigurd Johansen, *Rural Social Organization in a Spanish-American Culture*

Area (Albuquerque: University of New Mexico Press, 1948), a study based on a doctoral dissertation of the same title, University of Wisconsin, 1940; Paul A. F. Walter, Jr., "A Study of Isolation and Social Change in Three Spanish-Speaking Villages of New Mexico" (unpublished Ph.D. dissertation, Stanford, 1938) ; Olen Leonard and C. P. Loomis, "Culture of a Contemporary Rural Community: El Cerrito, New Mexico," in Charles P. Loomis, *Studies of Rural Social Organization in the United States, Latin America and Germany* (East Lansing, Mich.: State College Book Store, 1945), pp. 265-338; Olen E. Leonard, "The Role of the Land Grant in the Social Process of a Spanish-American Village in New Mexico" (unpublished Ph.D. dissertation, Louisiana State University, 1943) ; Donovan Senter, "Acculturation Among New Mexican Villagers in Comparison to Adjustment Patterns of Other Spanish-Speaking Americans," *Rural Sociology,* X (March, 1945), 31.

11. Several of the reports are to be found in the various titles of the Values Studies Project of Harvard University. And see E. Z. Vogt and J. M. Roberts, "A Study of Values," *Scientific American,* July, 1956. A related study is M. S. Edmundson, *Los Manitos: A Study of Institutional Values* (New Orleans: Tulane University Press, Middle American Research Institute, 1958).

12. Cf., Kluckholn and Strodtbeck, *op. cit.*; Johansen, *op. cit.*; George I. Sanchez, *Forgotten People: A Study of New Mexico* (Albuquerque: University of New Mexico Press, 1940) ; and Florence Hawley and Donovan Senter, "Group-Designed Behavior Patterns in Two Acculturating Groups," *Southwestern Journal of Anthropology,* I (Spring, 1946), 133-151.

13. Lyle Saunders, *Cultural Difference and Medical Care: The Case of The Spanish-Speaking People of the Southwest* (New York: The Russell Sage Foundation, 1954), p. 48.

14. *Ibid.,* p. 49.

15. *Ibid.,* p. 49. But, such leadership "was nothing to aspire to; neither was it anything to shun." p. 50.

16. *Cultural Patterns and Technical Change,* (ed.) Margaret Mead, Tensions and Technology Series (Paris: UNESCO, 1953). Citations are to the Mentor ed., 1955. The quotation is from p. 157.

17. *Ibid.,* pp. 157-158. Mead states the generally held position, for a recurring theme of frequently cited studies of Spanish American political sociology, is that of the "typical *patrón*-dominated New Mexican village," Kluckhohn and Strodtbeck, *et al.,* *op. cit.,* p. 182. See also Johansen, *op. cit.,* pp. 112-113; and Walter, *op cit.,* pp. 12, 40, and 70.

18. Leonard and Loomis found no current evidence in San Miguel county of *patrón* domination, and they note a frequent occurrence of a factionalism which they deplore: "The village of El Cerrito is peculiar in this area in that it has no acute local political problems. The fact that the village has no factions enables the people to work in unison. . . . In the typical situation two distinct factions work at cross purposes in every situation." *Op. cit.,* p. 323. The authors fail to identify the "factions" as party organizations or alignments.

19. Ralph Emerson Twitchell, *The Leading Facts of New Mexico History,* Vol. II (Cedar Rapids: The Torch Press, 1912), p. 500; Miguel A. Otero, Historical Society of New Mexico, *Papers,* No. 31.

20. Kluckhohn, *op. cit.,* p. 60, generalizes about an absolute control exercised by bosses over entire groups of voters; Walter, *op. cit.,* p. 40, refers to *patrones* whose will was the equivalent of law; Leonard, *op. cit.,* p. 96, reads El Cerrito's election returns as yielding a 100 per cent Republican vote before 1932, a 100 per cent Democratic vote in 1932, and a Democratic vote in each following election.

21. Knowledgeable political activists of New Mexico might be able to surmise which of the following precincts and villages were controlled by family, leader, or faction.

Those counties making Republican shifts of 10 or more points: Mora—Guadalupita, Armenta, Turquillo, Naranjos, and Nolan; Rio Arriba—Los Pinos; San Miguel —Los Alamos, Agua Zarca, and Encinosa; Santa Fe—Stanley, Otto, and Ortiz; Taos —none.

Making Democratic gains of 30 or more points: Mora—none; Rio Arriba—Chimayo, San Jose de Chama, El Rito, Vallecitos, El Vado, and Haynes; San Miguel—La Cuesta, San Geronimo, San Juan, San Pedro, El Cerrito (described by Leonard, *op. cit.*), Los Torres, Ojitos Frios, and Hot Springs; Santa Fe—Galisteo, Chimayo, Rio del Medio, and Cow Springs; Taos—Valdez.

22. The five counties voted in 166 precincts (including urban) in 1920, and in 223 in 1936. Most of the new polling places were in areas of urbanized population. In 1920, 37 per cent of the precincts cast less than 100 votes; 24 per cent cast over 200. In 1936, 34 per cent cast less than 100 votes, but those casting over 200 dropped to 14 per cent.

23. Haniel Long, *Pinon Country* (New York: Appleton, Century, Duell, Sloan and Pearce, 1941), p. 88, by permission of the publisher.

24. *The New Mexican* (Santa Fe), March 8, 1912.

25. Melville J. Herskovits, *Man and His Works* (New York: Alfred A. Knopf, Inc., 1948), pp. 543-545.

26. Fred W. Riggs, "The Prevalence of 'Clects'," *The American Behavioral Scientist* V, (June, 1962), p. 16.

27. Gerald Brenan, *The Spanish Labyrinth: An Account of the Social and Political Background of the Civil War* (2d edition; Cambridge: Cambridge University Press, 1950), p. 336.

28. *Ibid.*, pp. 336-339.

29. George I. Sanchez, *op. cit.*, p. 5.

30. *Ibid.*, pp. 5-6.

31. O. D. Barrett, *The Mora Grant of New Mexico* (Washington, D. C.: R. O. Polkinhorn and Son, 1884), pp. 1, 13-14.

32. Relevant acequia statutes are found in *Compiled Laws of New Mexico*, 1897, Title I, chap. 1. Similar statutes governing land grants are *ibid.*, Title XXII, chap. 2.

33. From a declaration by Edwin V. Byrne, Archbishop of Santa Fe, January 28, 1947, published in the *Register* (Santa Fe), February 7, 1947. The occasion was the acceptance by a group of Penitente chapels of the authority of the Church.

34. Harvey Fergusson, *op. cit.*, p. 78.

35. Mead, *op. cit.*, p. 159.

36. Fray Angélico Chavez, "The Penitentes of New Mexico," *New Mexico Historical Review*, XXIX (April, 1954), p. 122.

37. Charles F. Lummis, *The Land of Poco Tiempo* (New York: Charles Scribner & Sons, 1893), pp. 79-108. See also the materials, chiefly from Lummis, in *El Palacio*, XIII (January 31, 1920). pp. 3-11.

38. *El Palacio, op. cit.*, p. 5.

39. Ralph Emerson Twitchell, *The Leading Facts of New Mexico's History*, V (Cedar Rapids: The Torch Press, 1917), pp. 487-488.

40. John C. Russell, "State Regionalism in New Mexico" (unpublished Ph.D. dissertation, Stanford University, 1938), p. 42.

41. *Ibid.*, p. 43.

42. Harvey Fergusson, *Grant of Kingdom* (New York: William Morrow and Co.,

1950), pp. 288-290, by permission of the publisher. The period covered in the book ends "in the late seventies, just before the completion of the Santa Fe railroad brought the epoch of primary pioneering to an end." p. v.

43. Aurelio M. Espinosa, "Penitentes, Los Hermanos," *The Catholic Encyclopedia,* XI (Robert Appleton and Co., 1911), p. 635.

44, Cf., *Time,* September 1, 1958, pp. 45-46. This account indicates that total membership then totaled 1,200. In an interview in 1960, Don Miguel estimated that there were 400 members in the Walsenburg area of Colorado, and nearly 200 in Colorado's San Luis valley. If so, this would leave only 600 members in New Mexico— a number considerably too low to account for the number of currently active chapels.

45. Interview.

Various views of the implications of the Spanish-American personality and culture differ significantly. Although politicians interviewed stressed that Penitente groups were independent and best reached through bargaining and negotiation, some literary and many formal accounts frequently stress a dependency relationship resulting in easily controlled local groups.

Support for the politicians' interpretation comes from two unexpected sources in studies of psychological aspects of Penitente behavior.

Mills and Grove conclude from a study of eyewitness and secondary source accounts, "that practices of the Brotherhood were pursued with intensity."

"We summarized current ideas of the cultural configurations; shame controls, emphasis upon present time, passivity, the dramatic configuration, and family patterns. An explanation for the Penitentes does not emerge because these concepts of Spanish-American culture are over-simplified." George Mills and Richard Grove, *Lucifer and the Crucifer: The Enigma of the Penitentes* (Colorado Springs Fine Arts Center, Taylor Museum, reprinted from the *1955 Brand Book* of the Denver Westerners), p. 38.

Another observer, a psychiatrist, has observed that by 1850, "Penitentes had so internalized authority (in contrast to the degree of reliance on externalized authority of 19th century Spain) that they were able to develop a political power system in opposition to the Anglos that precluded their complete reabsorption into the Catholic church on anything like the pre-Penitente scale and level." Rudolph Kieve, M. D., "The Penitente Sub-Culture," a paper delivered Sept. 21, 1961, before the Fourth Western Divisional Meeting, American Psychiatric Association, Salt Lake City, Utah.

46. Leonard, *op. cit.,* p. 96. For a pleasant view of Rociada, a Penitente precinct with a strong but not overwhelming Republican vote, see Oliver LaFarge, *Behind the Mountains* (Boston: Houghton Mifflin Co., 1956), an account by a man who married a daughter of the former *patrón* of the San Miguel County village.

47. Several chapels were called the "Cherry moradas" for sharing with Cherryvale a strong Democratic attachment. Other chapels were fostered by adherents of the Cutting Progressive faction and ultimately came to favor the Democratic cause. In consequence, many villages had two moradas.

48. Factional movements involving fusions and splits have long characterized northern-county politics. The spectacular 1924 split was abetted in San Miguel County by Republican U.S. Senator-to-be Bronson Cutting, with the aid of Democratic state chairman and governor-to-be Arthur Seligman.

Appendix, Table A-1, setting out generalized data for the seven elections of 1922-1934 in the five north-central Hispanic counties, shows the narrow range of party majorities in which Cutting's factional influence was decisive. When the precinct is used as the electoral unit, a much more widely varying vote is apparent. Although variances were not as great as they have been reputed to be, they could be significantly affected by intense party or factional activity. The accumulation of a few votes here and there could tip the party scales from election to election in several of the northern counties.

49. The names of some are among the most familiar of New Mexico's history: Thomas B. Catron, Charles Spiess, Albert Bacon Fall, Holm O. Bursum, I, Malaquias Martinez, W. D. Murray, T. D. Burns, Charles Springer, Victor Ortega, and Solomon Luna. For a description of their ethos and political style see chapters 5 and 6.

50. Reuben W. Heflin, "The New Mexico Constitutional Convention," *New Mexico Historical Review*, XXI (January, 1946), 61-62.

51. Art. 7, sec. 2.

52. Art. 7, sec. 3. The italics are added to emphasize the prohibition referred to in connection with a provision of the Enabling Act which specifically barred such a provision.

53. For a parallel appraisal see Carolyn Zeleny, "Relations Between the Spanish-Americans and Anglo-Americans in New Mexico: A Study of Conflict Accommodation in a Dual-Ethnic Situation" (New Haven: unpublished Ph.D. dissertation, Yale University, 1944), pp. 233-236. Zeleny's is one of the few accounts which treats of the institutionalization of political conflict in New Mexico. Cf. the approach sought by Seymour M. Lipset, "Political Sociology," in Robert K. Merton, *et. al.* (eds.), *Sociology Today: Problems and Prospects* (New York: Basic Books, Inc., 1959), pp. 81-114.

54. One writer declares on the basis of an interview that: "The secretary of the convention, George W. Armijo, noted that if anyone could be credited with the inclusion of the famous protective clauses, it would be Solomon Luna and Holm Bursum, Republican bosses who 'ran the show' but that there was no particular opposition." Ernest Barksdale Fincher, "Spanish-Americans as a Political Factor in New Mexico, 1912-1950" (unpublished Ph.D. dissertation, New York University, 1950; Pub. 2506, University Microfilms, Ann Arbor, Michigan), p. 168.

55. Sec. 6, Organic Act Establishing the Territory of New Mexico, 9 *Statutes at Large* 446; 1 *New Mexico Statutes Annotated, 1953 Compilation* 388-403.

56. Par. 5, sec. 2, Enabling Act for New Mexico, 36 *Statutes at Large* 557; 1 *New Mexico Statutes Annotated, 1953 Compilation* 404-425. The case of *Coyle* v. *Smith*, 221 U.S. 559 (1911), was yet to be settled by the Supreme Court, and Congress had long been proceeding upon the assumption that it possessed authority to impose such restrictions upon the powers of new states it admitted.

57. *Proceedings of the Constitutional Convention of the Proposed State of New Mexico* (Albuquerque: Press of the Morning Journal, 1910), p. 288.

58. 37 Stat. J. R. 8, and see 1 *New Mexico Statutes Annotated, 1953 Compilation* 407.

59. The precincts were identified and grouped for the author by local leaders of the two parties.

60. In New Mexico, the speakership can provide a significant leverage, for the members of the house frequently make up a statewide organizational team.

CHAPTER THREE

1. Settlement patterns elsewhere are of relevance to New Mexico. Cf., John H. Fenton, *Politics in the Border States* (New Orleans: The Hauser Press, 1957), pp. 2-7; Key, *American State Politics* . . ., 218-227. Key's data for Oklahoma hint that Union County, for example, should sometimes return a Republican vote.

2. The livestock industry of the counties of the extreme southeast corner (Lea, Eddy, and Chaves) has long been organized and financed as though it were a western extension of the industry in west Texas. There are, however, a few differences in tenure arrangements stemming from the extensive areas of state lands in New Mexico. Since 1930 the oil industry has attracted much of its labor and management forces from west Texas. Seasonal and investment variations in the oil industry, particularly, contribute to a considerable back-and-forth movement of population between the two areas.

3. Alexander Heard, *A Two-Party South?* (Chapel Hill: University of North Carolina Press, 1952), p. 13.

4. See Key, *Southern Politics* . . . , chap. xii, "Texas: A Politics of Economics," and chaps. xxiii and xxiv on the size and composition of the southern electorate.

5. Key has observed that economic issues had a "deep meaning" for Texans back in 1890-1915. "Political controversy since 1944 has [also] been pitched on the broad level of progressive versus conservative government. . . . During the Populist era and briefly thereafter the conflict was essentially of the same kind as Texans were campaigning about in 1944, 1946, and 1948." *Ibid.*, pp. 261-262.

6. For a summation of radical, third-party activity in the South and West see V. O. Key, Jr., *Politics, Parties and Pressure Groups* (4th ed.; New York: Thomas Y. Crowell Co., 1958), chap. x.

7. Conversely, as is also suggested in the following chapter, the one-party tradition may serve as a powerful weapon to those who can dominate the electoral mechanism and render it an instrument for the preservation of the status quo.

8. Key, *American State Politics* . . . , *passim.*

9. These conjectures receive some support in the theories set out by Lipset, *loc. cit.*, pp. 81-114. "In a one-party system, whether in civil society or in a trade union, abhorrence of the politics of the administration often results in rejection of the whole system, since it is difficult in such a system to distinguish between the permanent rulers and the system of organization itself," (p. 105). Also: "A stable democratic system requires sources of cleavage so that there will be struggle over ruling positions, challenges to parties in power, and shifts of parties in office. . . ." (p. 113.)

10. Key, *Politics* . . . , pp. 288-289.

11. *Ibid.*, p. 289.

12. To sort out the major electoral and sociological components of the voting during the radical era in the counties of New Mexico's eastern plains would be difficult. Ancient party attachments may have produced the heavy votes for conservative Democratic candidates for the U.S. Senate. The movements of the left may have been the primary factor exciting an indigenous opposition in the strong and overt Ku Klux Klan activities in those counties during the 1920's. The many Democratic leaders coming into prominence during the period were tough and agile politicians, but they were conservatives. For several periods in the 1920's and 1940's, the state party was dominated by its members from the eastern counties. My impression is that the appearance of radicalism served to stimulate, and make more effective, those groups striving to protect the status quo.

13. Leon D. Epstein, *Politics in Wisconsin* (Madison: University of Wisconsin Press, 1958), pp. 37, 41, 44-45.

14. Inferences that there was a latent liberal opinion in Little Texas akin to the old Progressive spirit, and that it was denied expression by the conservative forces dominating the one-party system, are supported by the drastic change in voter participation accompanying the candidacies of Franklin D. Roosevelt. The area's increase in voter turnout had been 10 per cent in the course of the decade of the 1920's (about

half the percentage increase in population) ; but over the set of three elections of 1932-1936 (using the abnormally high 1930 vote as a base) there was a 90% gain in voter turnout—more than double that of the state.

15. Philip E. Converse, *et al.*, "Stability and Change in 1960: A Reinstating Election," *American Political Science Review*, LV (June, 1961), 269-280.

16. *Ibid.*, p. 280.

17. Key, *Southern Politics* . . . , p. 278. Alexander Heard examines Presidential Republicans and their voting characteristics at some length, *op. cit.*, chaps. iv and ix.

18. Key, *Southern Politics* . . . , pp. 408-409.

19. Coupling the Republican and minor-party votes of 1911-1928 in Table 14 serves to smooth out some puzzling electoral vagaries. None of the three minor parties was consistently in the field. The socialist vote was most consistent from election to election, and most of the socialist vote came from one county—Curry. Minor-party voting had all but disappeared before the advent of the New Deal.

20. Heard, *op. cit.*, table 20, p. 141.

21. *Ibid.*, table 19, and pp. 138-143.

22. See O. Douglas Weeks, *Texas in the 1960 Presidential Election* (Austin: Institute of Public Affairs, University of Texas, 1961), chap. v. The item includes comparative data from other Southern states. Traditional, rural, and urban voting are compared for Texas elections of 1956 and 1960. Weeks concludes: "Texas and much of the South . . . is drifting toward class and interest group politics and away from sectionalism." p. 80.

23. Generally, Heard found, a Republican increase was registered in the southern states in the elections of 1940-1948, but in the nation Republicans merely held their own. *Op. cit.*, p. 73.

24. Key, *Politics* . . ., pp. 295-296.

25. Registration figures have since become a most uncertain indicator of election results. Application of the same correlation procedure to the Kennedy vote in 1960 results in a coefficient of −.166. The intervening Eisenhower elections of 1952 and 1956 would show a positive but very limited correlation indicative of a heavy stress on Democratic loyalties in Little Texas as well as several other areas. Johnson's 1964 candidacy was rewarded in Little Texas with a vote considerably below his national percentage. The 55.1% returned for him in Little Texas was almost on the region's 1912-1964 trend line (see Figure 12) and 25 percentage points lower than Democratic registration.

26. Cf., Samuel Lubell, *The Future of American Politics* (2nd ed.; Garden City, N. Y.: Doubleday and Company, Inc., 1956), pp. 14-17. As Key describes manifestations of such matters in Texas: ". . . sharp divisions along class lines do not consistently occur in the balloting . . . the one-party system does not assure that the electorate becomes keenly conscious of those differences." *Southern Politics* . . . , p. 261.

27. The big hat and twangy speech are still assets in the politics of Little Texas. As Key has phrased an aspect of the matter: "Possibly the more the voters saw of Mr. Dewey the better Harry Truman looked." *Politics* . . . , p. 530.

28. Cf., Richard Hofstadter, *The Age of Reform: From Bryan to F.D.R.* (New York: Vintage Books, 1960), pp. 5-21 in particular, but the entire thesis, *passim*.

29. David S. Greenberg, "The Myth of the Scientific Elite," *The Public Interest*, I (Fall, 1965), 62.

30. Avery Leiserson, "Scientists and the Policy Process," *American Political Review*, LIX (June, 1965), 416; John Fischer, "Why Our Scientists are About to be Dragged, Moaning, into Politics," *Harper's Magazine*, 233 (September, 1966), 19.

31. James Q. Wilson and Edward C. Banfield, "Public-Regardingness as a Value Premise in Voting Behavior," *American Political Science Review*, LVIII (December, 1964), 876-887.

32. L. G. Cook and G. W. Hazzard, "Mature Research Institutions and the Older Scientist," *Science*, 150 (November 5, 1965), 716.

33. Alvin M. Weinberg, "But is the Teacher also a Citizen," *Science*, 149 (August 6, 1965), 601-606.

34. Don E. Kash, "The Necessary Elements for Research and Development," *Arizona State University Public Affairs Bulletin* (Tempe: Bureau of Government Research), III, No. 4 (1964), p. 4.

35. The *New Mexican* (Santa Fe), March 28, 1965.

36. Robert C. Nichols, "The Financial Status of National Merit Finalists," *Science*, 149 (September 3, 1965), 1071-1073.

37. Clinton Rossiter, *Parties and Politics in America* (Ithaca, N.Y.: Cornell University Press, 1960), pp. 103-104 (copyright, 1960, by Cornell University, and used with permission of Cornell University Press). See also Paul F. Lazarsfeld and Wagner Thielens, Jr., *The Academic Mind* (Glencoe, Ill.: The Free Press, 1958), pp. 14, 28, 131, 401-402. Seymour Lipset, *Political Man: The Social Bases of Politics* (Garden City, N. Y.: Doubleday and Co., Inc., Anchor ed. 1963), reviews similar findings in chap. x, and contrary evidence at pp. 341-343.

38. Cf. Philip E. Converse, Aage R. Clausen, and Warren E. Miller, "Electoral Myth and Reality: The 1964 Election," *American Political Science Review*, LIX (June 1965), 321-336.

39. In a study comparing reactions and forecasts of a set of social scientists with those of a set of physical scientists and engineers in an exercise in strategic forecasting, the authors observe parenthetically: "In general, there seemed to be a tendency throughout the whole set of questionnaire responses for the physical-science-oriented respondents to express themselves with more caution about physical science topics and with less caution about political topics, with the reverse being true of the behavioral scientists." T. W. Milburn and J. F. Milburn, "Predictions of Threats and Beliefs About How to Meet Them," *American Behavorial Scientist*, IX (March, 1966), 5.

40. Robert C. Wood, "Scientists and Politics: The Rise of an Apolitical Elite," in Robert Gilpin and Christopher Wright (eds.), *Scientists and National Policy-Making* (New York: Columbia University Press, 1964), p. 60.

41. Gabriel A. Almond and Sidney Verba, *The Civic Culture: Political Attitudes and Democracy in Five Nations* (Princeton, N. J.: Princeton University Press, 1963), chap. xii.

42. *Ibid.*, pp. 398-399.

43. Alvin M. Weinberg, "Government, Education, and Civilian Technology," in A. W. Warner, Dean Morse, and A. S. Eichner (eds.), *The Impact of Science on Technology* (New York: Columbia University Press, 1965), pp. 80-81.

44. From my notes on remarks by W. G. Pollard, Director, Oak Ridge Institute of Nuclear Studies, to National Science Foundation summer institute, "Impact of Science on Society" (Oak Ridge, 1965).

45. John Swartout, *The Oak Ridger* (Oak Ridge), October 7, 1964.

46. *The New Mexican*, (Santa Fe), September 8, 1964.

47. From my notes on Wigner's remarks to National Science Foundation summer institute, "Impact of Science on Society" (Oak Ridge, 1965).

48. Daniel Lerner, "The Transformation of Institutions," in W. B. Hamilton (ed.), *The Transfer of Institutions* (Durham, N. C., Duke University Press, 1964), pp. 14-20.

49. E. R. Leach "Culture and Social Cohesion: An Anthropologist's View," Vol. 94, No. 1, *Daedalus* (Winter, 1965), 25.

50. *Trujillo vs. Garley*, D.Ct., New Mexico, unreported.

51. Oliver LaFarge, "Termination of Federal Supervision: Disintegration and the American Indians," in George E. Simpson and J. Milton Yinger (eds.), *American Indians and American Life, Annals,* American Academy of Political and Social Science, CCCXI (May, 1957), 42-43; Fred Eggan, *Social Organization of the Western Pueblos* (Chicago: University of Chicago Press, 1950), *passim*; Charles H. Lange, *Cochiti: A New Mexico Pueblo, Past and Present* (Austin: University of Texas Press, 1959), pp. 191-226.

52. Guy J. Pauker, "Political Structure," in Evon Z. Vogt and John M. Roberts (eds.), *Peoples of Rimrock: A Comparative Study of Value Systems* (unpublished MS, Values Study Project, Harvard University), chap. xv, pp. 1, 28-31; Robert Bunker, *Other Men's Skies* (Bloomington: Indiana University Press, 1965), pp. 220-225.

53. Eggan, *op. cit.,* pp. 301-324.

54. *Ibid.,* p. 251.

55. Pauker, *op. cit.,* pp. 14-18 and 57-58.

56. Analyses of Navajo political development upon which I have relied heavily here and in related contexts are: Mary Shepardson, *Navajo Ways in Government: A Study in Political Process,* Memoir 96, American Anthropological Association (June 1963); and Jane M. Christian, "The Navajo: A People in Transition," *Southwestern Studies,* Vol. II, Nos. 3 and 4 (Fall, 1964, and Winter, 1965). A similarly useful review of Jicarilla politics is H. Clyde Wilson, *Jicarilla Apache Political and Economic Structures,* University of California Publications in American Archeology and Ethnology, Vol. 48, No. 4, (1964).

57. Shepardson, *op. cit.,* p. 82.

58. *Ibid.,* pp. 83-97.

59. Oliver LaFarge, in *Annals . . ., op. cit.,* p. 43.

60. Helen L. Peterson, "American Indian Political Participation," in *Annals . . . , op. cit.,* p. 124.

61. See C. L. Sonnichsen, *The Mescalero Apaches* (Norman: University of Oklahoma Press, 1958), chaps. xiv and xv, and Clyde Kluckhohn and Dorothea Leighton, *The Navaho* (Cambridge: Harvard University Press, 1948), pp. 100-120.

62. Cf., Lubell, *op. cit., passim.*

63. The matters involved are similar to those anticipated by Key: "Urbanization may have introduced a new element of volatility into electoral behavior rather than a stable and continuing class cleavage." *Politics . . . ,* pp. 274-275. An aspect of the matter as measured by the extent of shifts in a party majority is examined in the following chapter.

CHAPTER FOUR

1. Key, *Politics . . . ,* p. 632. Wilmoore Kendall, in "The Two Majorities," *Midwest Journal of Political Science,* IV (November, 1960), 317-345, proposes that the "congressional majority" is based on a different electorate and arises from issues seen at firsthand in the states and congressional districts.

2. Paul T. David, "The Changing Party Pattern," *The Antioch Review,* XVI (Fall, 1956), 337-338. As E. E. Schattschneider put an aspect of the matter: "The area and

scale of party competition has been expanded greatly by the extension of the two-party system and by the establishment of the conditions for a much more rapid alternation of the parties in power." "The United States: The Functional Approach to Party Government," in Sigmund Neumann (ed.), *Modern Political Parties* (Chicago: University of Chicago Press, 1956), p. 214 (copyright, 1956, by University of Chicago Press).

3. V. O. Key, Jr., "Secular Realignment and the Party System," *Journal of Politics*, XXI, (May, 1959), 198. And see his "A Theory of Critical Elections," *ibid.*, XVII (February, 1955), 3-18. Also, Duncan MacRae, Jr., and James A. Meldrun, "Critical Elections in Illinois: 1888-1958," *American Political Science Review*, LIV (September, 1960), 669-683.

4. The measures used in Figures 10 and 11, and Tables 23 and 24 are explained in Chapter 1 in connection with Figure 2.

5. See Leon D. Epstein, *op. cit.*, pp. 53-54.

6. Cf., Key, *American State Politics* . . . , chap. iii, and pp. 242-254.

7. Cf., *ibid.*, pp. 15-16.

8. Warren E. Miller, "One-Party Politics and the Voter," *American Political Science Review*, L (September, 1956), 707-725.

9. Charles Press, "Voting Statistics and Presidential Coattails," *American Political Science Review*, LII (December, 1958), 1050.

10. The classifications used here have some rough correspondence to those suggested by Peter H. Rossi in "Power and Community Structure," *Midwest Journal of Political Science*, IV (November, 1960), 390-401. Some of the problems involved in the analysis of local power systems are reviewed in Lawrence J. R. Herson, "In the Footsteps of Community Power," *American Political Science Review*, LV (December, 1961), 817-830.

11. Cf. Rossi, *op. cit.*, pp. 397-399.

12. Morris Janowitz, editorial summaries in "Converging Perspectives in Community Political Analysis," *Community Political Systems*, (Glencoe, Ill.: The Free Press, 1961), pp. 13-16.

13. Cf., Key, *American State Politics* . . . , p. 227; and Epstein, *op. cit.*, pp. 66-70.

14. Cf., Key, *Southern Politics* . . . , pp. 507-508.

15. Thereafter, for nearly two decades, Albuquerque's political organization and behavior were much like those of city "Alpha" in Oliver P. Williams and Charles R. Adrian, "The Insulation of Local Politics under the Non-Partisan Ballot," *American Political Science Review*, LIII (December, 1959), 1052-1063.

16. J. Leiper Freeman, "Local Party Systems: Theoretical Considerations and a Case Analysis," *The American Journal of Sociology*. LXIV (November, 1958), 183. Copyright, 1958, by the University of Chicago.

17. Cf., Janowitz, *loc. cit.*, p. 16.

18. Key, "A Theory of Critical Elections," *op cit.*, p. 12.

19. John H. Fenton, *op. cit.*, pp. 213-215.

20. Cf., Key, *Public Opinion* . . . , pp. 108-109.

21. MacRae and Meldrum, *op. cit.*, p. 678.

22. Cf., Miller, "One-Party Politics and the Voter," *op. cit.*, 707-725; and Angus Campbell and Warren E. Miller, "The Motivational Basis of Straight and Split Ticket Voting," *American Political Science Review*, LI (June, 1957), 293-312.

23. Miller, "One-Party Politics and the Voter," *op. cit.*, 716.

24. *Ibid.*, p. 722.

CHAPTER FIVE

1. *George Curry, 1861-1947, An Autobiography*, (ed.) H. B. Hening (Albuquerque University of New Mexico Press, 1958), p. 212.

2. Ralph Emerson Twitchell, *The Leading Facts of New Mexico History* (Cedar Rapids, Iowa: The Torch Press, 1911-17), II, p. 524, f.n. 441.

3. David H. Stratton, "New Mexico Machiavellian? The Story of Albert Bacon Fall," *Montana: The Magazine of Western History* (Autumn, 1957), p. 12.

4. Letter from Thomas Benton Catron, quoted in Donnelly, op. cit., p. 43.

5. Key notes that in the nation "about the same proportion of the potential electorate voted in 1932 and 1928, but the division of the vote between the two parties shifted markedly." *Politics, . . .*, p. 638. In New Mexico the percentage of the potential electorate voting in 1928 was 58. In 1932 it was 67 — the highest point ever reached, although the figure was approached within a few points in 1936 and 1940.

6. The Republican percentage of the vote was a few points lower than normal, for the Democratic candidate was O. A. Larrazolo, a dynamic and effective politician.

7. Robert A. Dahl and Charles E. Lindblom, *Politics, Economics, and Welfare* (New York: Harper and Brothers, 1953), chaps. x and xi.

8. Robert Michels, *Political Parties* (Glencoe: The Free Press, 1949), p. 222. Cf. Dahl and Lindblom, *op. cit.*, pp. 279-280.

9. James G. McNary, *This is My Life* (Albuquerque: University of New Mexico Press, 1956), p. 42.

10. Interview.

11. Stratton, *op. cit.*, p. 8, and W. H. Hutchinson, *A Bar Cross Man: The Life and Personal Writings of Eugene Manlove Rhodes* (Norman: University of Oklahoma Press, 1956), p. 86.

12. New Mexico Archives, Governor, *Correspondence*, July 8, 1919.

13. *Bursum Collection*, University of New Mexico Library, April 16, 1919. (Italics added.)

14. *New Mexico Tax Bulletin*, III (March, 1924), 4.

15. McNary, *op. cit.*, pp. 205-206.

A list of those subscribers provided this writer by McNary will no doubt be of of interest to a good many New Mexicans:

James G. McNary, Burton Mossman, Charles Springer, Col. Breece, Ed Sargent, and Frank Bond, $1,000 each per year.

Nathan Salmon, Governor Hagerman, Richard Dillon, Herbert Denny, H. B. Holt, $500 each.

Percy Wilson, Judge Holloman, Lon Pullen, Oliver Lee, Powell Stackhouse, Joe Tondre, A. B. Renehan, Governor Hill, Manuel Otero, William Dooley, Tom Gable, Judge Roberts, Mike Gonzales, W. C. Reid, Ed Mitchell, Ed Safford, Narciso Francis, Arch Hurley, and Eugenio Perez, $250 each.

Charles Closson and Jose Ortiz y Pino, $200 each.

Nathan Jaffa, Hugo Seaberg, D. J. Leahy, Bob Halley, Judge Mechem, Governor Merritt C. Mechem, L. S. Wilson, Clinton, H. O. Bursum, Dr. J. J. de Praslin, B. Marcus, Fred Eicholas, J. D. Sena, John Burguete, and the Fernandez Co. by Floyd Lee, $100 each.

Max Fernandez, $60; Francisco Urrea and Jose D. Martinez, $30 each.

16. *Ibid.*, p. 206, and interview.

17. Quoted by Alfred C. Cordova and Charles B. Judah in *Octaviano Larrazolo: A Political Portrait* (Albuquerque: Division of Research, Department of Government,

University of New Mexico, 1952), p. 10. Reprinted from the *New Mexican* (Santa Fe), August 31, 1911.

18. *The New Mexican* (Santa Fe), September 28, 1918.

19. Vorley Michael Rexroad, "The Two Administrations of Governor Richard C. Dillon" (unpublished Master's thesis, University of New Mexico, 1947), p. 91.

20. Paul A. F. Walter, "Necrology: Arthur Seligman," *New Mexico Historical Review*, VIII (October, 1933), 314.

21. Interview.

22. *Otero Collection*, "Cutting Letters," University of New Mexico Library, March 20, 1930.

23. New Mexico Archives, Governor Seligman Scrapbooks: *Clippings*, Vol. II (*Albuquerque Journal*, November 24, 1931).

24. *The New Mexican* (Santa Fe), October 17, 1924.

25. Curry, *op. cit.*, p. 260.

26. Cf., Key, *American State Politics* . . . , pp. 254-264.

27. Interview.

28. Ranney and Kendall, *Democracy* . . . , p. 126. (Their italics.)

29. Avery Leiserson, *Parties and Politics: An Institutional and Behavioral Approach* (New York: Alfred A. Knopf, Inc., 1958), p. 306.

30. Robert M. and Philip LaFollette received $50,000 and $25,000 respectively in 1935 from the Cutting estate.

31. Key, *American State Politics* . . . , p. 95.

32. Patricia Cadigan Armstrong, *A Portrait of Bronson Cutting Through His Papers, 1910-1927* (Albuquerque: Division of Government Research, Department of Government, University of New Mexico, 1959), p. 11.

33. Letter from William Bayard Cutting, December 15, 1911, quoted by Armstrong, *ibid.*, p. 7.

34. Robert Thompson and Charles B. Judah, *Arthur T. Hannett: Governor of New Mexico* (Albuquerque: Division of Research, Department of Government, University of New Mexico, 1950), pp. 5-6.

35. *Ibid.*, p. 17.

36. Charles B. Judah, *Governor Richard C. Dillon: A Study in New Mexico Politics* (Albuquerque: Division of Research, Department of Government, University of New Mexico, 1948), pp. 37-38.

37. Interview.

38. From transcript of probate filings provided the author by Hugh Woodward.

39. *Ibid.*

40. *The New Mexican* (Santa Fe), October 10 and 11, 1934.

41. *Ibid.*, February 27, 1929.

42. *Otero Collection*, Cutting Letters, University of New Mexico Library. Letter of May 29, 1934.

43. New Mexico Archives, Governor Seligman Scrapbooks: *Clippings*, Vol. X (The Las Vegas *Optic*, March 31, 1933).

44. *The New Mexican* (Santa Fe), June 24, 1935.

45. June 21, 1935.

46. Armstrong, *op. cit.*, p. 32.

47. *Ibid.*, p. 35.

48. *Ibid.*, p. 35.

49. Interview. And see his parallel account in Thompson and Judah, *op. cit.*, p. 19.

50. Letter to Mrs. Olive (Harry) Carey, 1932, in Hutchinson, *op. cit.*, pp. 324-327. Copyright, 1956, by the University of Oklahoma Press.

51. If, during the early 20's, the Cutting adherents were a legislative faction responding to a recognized leadership, the correspondence of Cutting's temporary alliances and interests with Hinkle's, Hannett's, and Dillon's administrations may have tended to obscure it. Scale analysis or some such technique might reveal that Cutting men could be identified by a greater measure of administration support than typical members, but that result does not seem likely.

52. The measure used is the Rice index of cohesion. See Stuart A. Rice, *Quantitative Methods in Politics* (New York: Alfred A. Knopf, 1928), pp. 208-209. Illustrations of the method are also given in Julius Turner, *Party and Constituency: Pressures on Congress* (Baltimore: The Johns Hopkins Press, 1951), p. 26; and in Leiserson, *op. cit.*, pp. 342-344.

53. Special Message of February 28, 1929, *House Journal*, Ninth Legislature.

54. *New Mexico Tax Bulletin*, VIII (March-April, 1929), pp. 35-37.

55. Interview.

56. *The New Mexican* (Santa Fe), February 22, 1933.

57. *The New Mexican* (Santa Fe), March 13, 1933. The "Two Per Cent" is in reference to a system of assessments on state employees. It provided sufficient funds to lessen the Democratic party's dependence upon Cutting. The reference to the "confused proceedings" probably alludes to then current gossip that several prominent lawyers spent several hectic days after the session revising (illegally) and checking (legally) the statutes enacted.

58. New Mexico Archives, Governor Seligman Scrapbooks: *Clippings*, Vol. XI (*Albuquerque Journal*, April 6, 1933); and *The New Mexican*, (Santa Fe), April 7, 1933.

59. Sir George Younger in a speech after the Conservative Party crisis of 1922. Quoted in R. T. McKenzie, *British Political Parties* (New York: St. Martin's Press, Inc., 1955), p. 107.

60. *Otero Collection*, University of New Mexico Library, May 5, 1934.

61. *Idem.*

62. *The New Mexican* (Santa Fe), July 9, 1934.

63. *Ibid.*, July 10 and 11, 1934.

64. *Ibid.*, July 7, 1934.

65. *Idem.*

66. *Ibid.*, July 12, 1934.

67. *Otero Collection*, University of New Mexico Library, July 13, 1934.

68. *The New Mexican* (Santa Fe), July 17, 1934.

69. *Ibid.*, July 19, 1934.

70. *Ibid.*, July 23, 1934.

71. *Ibid.*, September 11, 1934.

72. *Ibid.*, July 23, 1934.

73. *Ibid.*, July 23, 1934.

74. Interview.

CHAPTER SIX

1. Key, *American State Politics* . . ., p. 5. See also pp. 275, ff.

2. Paul A. F. Walter, "Necrology," *loc. cit.*, XIX (October, 1944), 349.

3. Key, *Southern Politics* . . . , p. 265.

4. As Key describes the North Carolina system: "An aggressive aristocracy of manufacturing and banking . . . has not been remiss in protecting and advancing what it visualizes as its interests. Consequently a sympathetic respect for the problems of corporate capital and of large employers permeates the state's politics and government. For half a century an economic oligarchy has held sway." The dominant group, says Key, has exhibited a "sense of responsibility in community matters. It has not been blind to broad community needs. . . . The kind of economic-political system favored by the oligarchy was described by a former governor as the 'capitalistic system liberally and fairly interpreted.' And that pretty well sums up the view of the prevailing forces in North Carolina." *Ibid.*, p. 211.

5. Holm O. Bursum in a letter to the editor of the *Rock Island Tribune* (Quay County), reprinted in *The New Mexican* (Santa Fe), July 30, 1910. And see the party resolution reprinted in *The New Mexican* of July 12, 1910.

6. Frank Springer's collection of fossils is still housed in the Smithsonian Institution, which published his *Crinoidea Flexibilia*, 2 volumes, 1920; and *American Silurian Crinoids*, 1926. New Mexico has sparingly used such manifestations of tribute to its citizens, but a Scarpitti bust of Springer is to be found in the auditorium of the Museum of New Mexico (which he helped found). "It was his habit to spend the greater part of the night with his scientific studies. . . . Often as the daylight approached I would hear the sound of his flute and know that he had come to the end of a perfect day." "Memorial Orations," *El Palacio*, XXIII (October, 1927), 382. The two Springers, Frank and Charles, came about as close to manifesting the Renaissance ideal of intellectual accomplishment as have any in the state. They were also formidably endowed politicians.

7. Cordova and Judah, *op. cit.*, pp. 15-21.

8. *The New Mexican* (Santa Fe), September 7, 1920, quoted in John Paul Seman, "The Administration of Governor Merritt Cramer Mechem," (Unpublished Master's Thesis, University of New Mexico, 1953), p. 15.

9. *The New Mexican* (Santa Fe), March 13, 1921.

10. *Ibid.*, August 14, 1924.

11. *Roswell Dispatch*, August 20, 1926, quoted by Judah in *Governor Richard C. Dillon* . . ., p. 16.

12. *The New Mexican* (Santa Fe), January 18, 1923.

13. Key, *American State Politics* . . ., chap. ix.

14. Paul T. David and Ralph Eisenberg, *Devaluation of the Urban and Suburban Vote*, II (Charlottesville: Bureau of Public Administration, University of Virginia, 1962), Part 1, p. 107.

15. Key *American State Politics* . . ., p. 278.

16. An electoral district of three counties could well contain some 10,000 square miles and only 20,000 inhabitants.

17. Charles S. Hyneman, "Tenure and Turnover of Legislative Personnel," *Annals of the American Academy of Political and Social Science*, CXCV (January, 1938), Table I, and pp. 22-25.

18. Key, *American State Politics* . . ., pp. 181-196.

19. The strategy is somewhat similar to that employed in Illinois legislative elections where the electoral system permits a voter to concentrate his several legislative votes on the designee of his party. See George S. Blair, "Cumulative Voting: Patterns of Party Allegiance and Political Choice in Illinois State Legislative Contests," *American Political Science Review*, LII (March, 1958), 123-130.

20. *The New Mexican* (Santa Fe), January 9, 1915.

21. *Ibid.*

22. *Ibid.*, January 12, 1915.

23. Jewell, *op. cit.*, pp. 86-87, finds similar practices existing in several states: "It is often a powerful committee and a major tool of majority control." P. 86.

24. *The New Mexican* (Santa Fe), March 5, 1925.

25. *Ibid.*, March 4, 1925.

26. David B. Truman, *The Governmental Process* (New York: Alfred A. Knopf, Inc., 1951), pp. 143 and 330.

27. Dayton D. McKean, *Pressures on the Legislature of New Jersey* (New York: Columbia University Press, 1938), pp. 47-49, as cited by Truman, *op. cit.*, p. 331. It may be significant in this regard that the power of party has not been much diminished in New Jersey by the direct primary. See Key, *American State Politics . . .*, p. 92. For a similar situation in New York, a convention state, see Warren Moscow, *Politics in the Empire State* (New York: Alfred A. Knopf, Inc., 1948), p. 170.

28. Leiserson, *op. cit., pp.* 335-336. Truman also makes the point that in a "single party organization that regularly succeeds in electing an executive and a majority in the legislature . . . the channels will be predominantly within the party leadership, and the pattern will be relatively stable and orderly." Truman, *op. cit.*, p. 325.

29. W. Duane Lockard, "Legislative Politics in Connecticut," *American Political Science Review,* XLVIII (March, 1954), 167.

30. *Ibid.*, pp. 171-172.

31. Gabriel Almond, "Comparative Political Systems," *Journal of Politics,* XVIII (August, 1956), 392-399. The Old Guard were more than passive brokers, however, for they sought to develop the New Mexico political system as an instrument efficient in the satisfaction of the demands they brought to it. That other demands were also satisfied was but part of the price they paid for maintaining the system. Cf. David Easton, *A Framework for Political Analysis* (Englewood Cliffs, N.J.: Prentice-Hall, 1965), *passim.*

32. Schattschneider, *loc. cit.*, p. 199.

33. Cf., Dahl and Lindblom, *op. cit.*, p. 360. Those writers use the term "programmatic" in suggesting that "party government" goes to the "heart of the problem" of necessary prerequisites to "rational" social action in the United States. As they put it: "the political process as it now operates penalizes politicians who develop local programs and rewards those who operate by personal favors. . . . Unified parties would not automatically become programmatic; but they would make programmatic parties possible."

34. Walter, "Necrology: Arthur Seligman," *loc cit.*, p. 311. The legislature was so much the instrument of the men named that it was normally impossible to achieve significant legislation without their assent.

35. *New Mexico Tax Bulletin,* XII (May-June, 1933), 77-78.

36. New Mexico Archives, Governor, *Correspondence,* January 12, 1920. In explaining the state's mounted police, Governor Larrazolo stated that the force of about 25 members had "been in existence for many years. . . . The main purpose of the police is to protect the interests of the livestock industry." *Ibid.*, February 17, 1920.

37. *The New Mexican* (Santa Fe), March 9, 1915.

38. Nearly a prototype, it was the second established in the United States. For years its staff and directorate were an unofficial governmental institution.

39. *New Mexico Tax Bulletin,* I (January, 1922), 5.

40. *Ibid.*, XII (November-December, 1933), 125.
41. Warren Aldrich Roberts, *State Taxation of Metallic Deposits*, Harvard Economic Studies, LXXVII (Cambridge: Harvard University Press, 1944), 279.
42. *New Mexico Tax Bulletin*, IV (April, 1925), 6.
43. Some insight into economic and social mechanisms involved may be obtained from William J. Parish, *The Charles Ilfeld Company: A Study of the Rise and Decline of Mercantile Capitalism in New Mexico* (Cambridge: Harvard University Press, 1961). See particularly Part Three, pp. 109-245.

CHAPTER SEVEN

1. *The New Mexican* (Santa Fe), March 9, 1937, near the close of the session, reported that Dailey was reputed to be the administration's "chief adviser" in legislative matters.
2. Some of the more important Law Chapters of the 1935 session were: 9, creating the state bureau of revenue; 16, authorizing banks to come under the Federal Deposit Insurance Corp.; 27, broadening powers of the state board of finance; 66, creating public school equalization fund; 72, creating oil conservation commission and allowing pooling and prorationing; 128, ratifying Interstate Oil and Gas Compact; 73, excise tax act for emergency school purposes; 86, creating agency to receive and expend federal emergency and relief funds; 107, National Recovery Administration enabling act; 112, amending liquor laws of 1933 and 1934 regulating manufacture and sale; 119, establishing state police force. *Laws of New Mexico, 1935.*
3. *New Mexico Tax Bulletin*, XV (December, 1936), 180.
4. *Ibid.*, XVI (January, 1937), 4-8.
5. *The New Mexican* (Santa Fe), January 28, 1937.
6. *Ibid.*, March 15, 1937.
7. See Tables 50 and 51, and Figure 19. Variations of the states in degree of party voting are analyzed by Jewell, *op. cit.*, chap. iii.
8. Interview.
9. Cf. Leiserson's test: "When committees are appointed on a basis of seniority and committee nominations rather than by the majority party leadership, the latter is reduced to informal methods of consultation and pressure." *Op. cit.*, p. 336.
10. *Senate Journal*, 1943, p. 164. The statute is found as Section 2-1-1 and following, New Mexico Statutes Annotated, 1953 Compilation.
11. *The New Mexican* (Santa Fe), January 15, 1943.
12. Employment of legislators has been found to be an effective means of control in several New England states. See Lockard, *New England State Politics*, pp. 68, 219, and 298.
13. New Mexico Archives, Governor Seligman Scrapbooks: *Clippings*, IX. (*The New Mexican* [Santa Fe], November 3, 1932.)
14. *The New Mexican* (Santa Fe), March 9, 1933.
15. For examples, *ibid.*, January 6, 1944 and February 3, 1943. One individual received $5,900 for a summer's rental, and, "in 1941 and 1942, the years [Ceferino] Quintana served as lieutenant governor, the state paid . . . $23,774.92 for the use of his equipment." *Ibid.*, January 7, 1943.
16. *Ibid.*, March 3, 1943.
17. *Ibid.*, April 17, 1944.

18. *Idem.*

19. See *Officers and Employees of State Departments and Institutions,* Santa Fe: Secretary of State, January 1, 1940).

20. Jewell, *op. cit.,* pp. 67-69.

21. In 1919 Governor Merritt Mechem and the Republican party had endorsed the primary, and although Mechem urged the legislature to pass a bill limited to optional county primaries, the relatively innocuous bill died with only 16 favorable votes. Of those, 11 were cast by Democratic house members from the counties of the eastern and southern parts of the state.

22. Curry, *op. cit.,* p. 70.

23. Interview.

24. Message to the special session, 1934, of the Eleventh Legislature. The governor overstated his case a bit, for the dominant groups of politicians in the northern and most of the central counties had no intention of using the primary unless it were to be forced on them.

25. Paul Beckett and Walter L. McNutt, *The Direct Primary in New Mexico* (Albuquerque: Division of Government Research, University of New Mexico, 1947), pp. 4-8.

CHAPTER EIGHT

1. *Silver City Enterprise,* editorial reprinted in *The New Mexican* (Santa Fe), July 10, 1939. See also *The New Mexican* editorial of July 19, 1939.

2. Roland Young, *The American Congress* (New York: Harper and Brothers, 1958), pp. 9-13.

3. Key, *American State Politics . . .,* pp. 181-182, 192-194; *contra,* see Epstein, *op. cit.,* pp. 135-138, and 144.

4. Legislative reapportionments enacted in 1949 and 1953 reduced the representation of the northern counties in favor of urban and eastern areas. Had this not occurred, the 20% of seats uncontested by Republicans might have been a few points lower.

5. Jewell, *op. cit.,* p. 37, finds no "clear and simple correlation between party competition on the statewide level and the frequency of [local legislative] election contests."

6. The author was the assistant hired.

7. Jack E. Holmes, *Patterns of Voting in New Mexico Gubernatorial Elections, 1911-1958, and Relation to Population and Minor Offices* (Albuquerque: Republican State Headquarters, mimeo, 1959).

8. Key, *American State Politics . . . ,* p. 196.

9. The usage here of the term "politico" is similar to that of John C. Wahlke, Heinz Eulau, William Buchanan, and LeRoy C. Ferguson in *The Legislative System: Explorations in Legislative Behavior* (New York; John Wiley and Sons, Inc., 1962), chap. xii.

10. *The New Mexican* (Santa Fe), February 17, 1920.

11. Gordon E. Baker, *The Reapportionment Revolution: Representation, Political Power, and the Supreme Court* (New York: Random House, 1966), pp. 32-37.

12. Key, *Politics . . . ,* pp. 625-626.

13. Key, *American State Politics . . . ,* pp. 134-138.

14. Key, *American State Politics . . . ,* p. 104.

15. *Ibid.,* Table 9, and pp. 98-100.

16. *Ibid.,* p. 145.

17. *Ibid.*, Tables 18-20, pp. 145-152.

18. Attempts to restore the convention system have occurred frequently. See, for example, Dorothy I. Cline, "New Mexico Retains the Primary," *National Municipal Review*, XXXIX (May, 1950), 233-236. The legislature enacted a pre-primary convention statute which governed the nominations of 1952 and 1954, repealed it, and then adopted a similar law in 1963 which governed the elections of 1964 and 1966 before it was also repealed in 1967. For a review of the causes and consequences of the earlier experiment see Charles B. Judah, *Aspects of the Nominating Systems in New Mexico* (Albuquerque: Division of Research, Department of Government, University of New Mexico, 1957) ; and Jack E. Holmes, *Problems Relating to Various Nominating Procedures in New Mexico* (Santa Fe: New Mexico Legislative Council Service, 1954).

19. Don Dickason, as reported by *The New Mexican* (Santa Fe), January 12, 1943. It was later reported, for example: "A bill advocating an increase in the tax on minerals for school purposes was killed by opposition led by [House] Majority Leader H. Vearle Payne, who stressed in this case he was not speaking for the administration because he did not know the administration's views on the bill." *Ibid.*, March 26, 1943.

20. Interview. In Tennessee, the tag is forthright: "administrative floor leaders." Wahlke, *et al., op. cit.*, pp. 56-57.

21. The phrases, "party vote" and "index of cohesion" are explained in Chapter V. Figures 18 and 19 in the following chapter, and data in the related appendix tables, permit a session-by-session comparison of this aspect of legislative behavior.

22. Bryan Johnson was Democratic state chairman. Clyde Tingley, as described in Chapter VII, was mayor of Albuquerque for some years before and after his terms as governor.

23. Cf., William S. White, *Citadel: The Story of the U.S. Senate* (New York: Harper and Brothers, 1956), *passim*.

24. Charles B. Judah and Dorothy Powell Goldberg, *The Recruitment of Candidates from Bernalillo County to the New Mexico House of Representatives, 1956* (Albuquerque: Division of Research, Department of Government, University of New Mexico, 1959), p. 3.

25. *Ibid.*, p. 4.

26. The party had been much more active in building the primary lists in the previous election, when the county's legislative candidates of that year had been among the active supporters of John F. Simms, Jr., the winning gubernatorial candidate at the pre-primary convention. These and subsequent events in the 1955 legislature indicate that legislators of that year were more "party men" than usual.

27. *Ibid.*, p. 4.

28. Charles B. Judah, *Recruitment of Candidates from the Northern and Eastern Counties to the New Mexico House of Representatives—1956* (Albuquerque: Division of Research, Department of Government, University of New Mexico, 1961), p. 5.

29. *Ibid.*, pp. 9-11.

30. *Ibid.*, p. 18.

31. *Ibid.*, p. 18.

32. *Ibid.*, pp. 19-20. Such characteristics as Judah found generally closely parallel those found in a similar survey in Wisconsin. Epstein, *op. cit.*, pp. 119-120. The principal exception is the findings related to the two-party Hispanic counties.

33. Cf., Jewell, *op. cit.*, pp. 67-70.

34. The system described here is not that of the party model; it has entailed some of those "frustrations of party" described in Chapter III of Key's *American State Politics*; yet it did not bar a wide and sometimes decisive range of party influences.

By the test of Ranney and Kendall's *Democracy and the American Party System*, pp. 519-525, it has generally been open to direction by a majority that knows what it wants.

35. During my struggles to sketch the evolving character of New Mexico's politics, I found it grimly satisfying to read of a related aspect of the matter in a four-state comparative study: "Whatever the causal mechanism linking . . . sociological variables to legislative behavior, it seems necessary to visualize a 'political culture' intervening to give to the legislative and political systems of each state a characteristic structure which is more immediately significant in determining what gets done there than is the sociological composition of the population or the day-to-day specifics of pressure-group activity." [John C. Wahlke, *et al.*, "American State Legislators' Role Orientations Toward Pressure Groups," *The Journal of Politics*, XXII (May, 1960), p. 227.] Unfortunately, to seek to attribute differences to the "political culture" merely recreates the problem in another corner.

36. Jewell, *op. cit.*, points out "that statewide factional alignments are seldom reflected in legislative primaries," p. 63.

37. Jewell summarizes a range of findings on the matter: "Wherever there is intensive campaigning [by candidates for the speakership], the promise of choice committee assignments seems to be the most important bargaining weapon in the hands of candidates. The governor often has a decisive voice in the choice of elected leaders, but this is not consistently true even in states with a strong governor." *Ibid.*, p. 79.

38. This has not always been the case, and the number of caucuses per session has greatly increased since 1951. Cf., *American State Legislatures: Report of the Committee on American Legislatures, American Political Science Association*, (ed.), Belle Zeller (New York: Thomas Y. Crowell Company, 1954), pp. 203-207.

39. *The New Mexican* (Santa Fe), January 30, 1951.

40. Minutes of the Senate Caucus (undated, but subsequent to meetings of January 7 and January 13, 1957). The minutes came into my possession easily enough: I simply asked for them. It was a rare find, for most caucuses have not included a stenographer or member designated to keep minutes.

41. *Ibid.*

42. Bob Brown, *Albuquerque Journal*, May 5, 1966.

43. Richard H. Folmar, *Piecemeal Amendment of the New Mexico Constitution, 1911-1961* (Santa Fe: New Mexico Legislative Council Service, 1961), Tables 1 and 3.

44. Leiserson, *op. cit.*, pp. 335-336.

45. The final report of the 29th American Assembly is contained in *State Legislatures in American Politics*, (ed.), Alexander Heard (Englewood Cliffs, N.J.: Prentice-Hall, Inc., 1966).

CHAPTER NINE

1. Key, *American State Politics* . . ., p. 194.

2. *Ibid.*, fn. 20, p. 195.

3. *Op. cit.*, p. 157.

4. Jewell, *op. cit.*, p. 106.

5. Wahlke, *et al.*, *The Legislative System* . . ., pp. 173-174.

6. Jewell, *op. cit.*, pp. 50-52.

7. The foregoing view or interpretation of these several indices is suggested by the analysis of Wahlke, *et al.*, *The Legislative System* . . ., *passim*. The approaches are on quite different levels; the conclusions are congruent.

8. Daniel Patrick Moynihan, "The Professionalization of Reform," *The Public Interest*, I (Fall, 1965), 6-17.

9. "Why the Government Budget Is Too Small in a Democracy," *World Politics*, XII (July, 1960), 541-563.

10. V. O. Key, *The Responsible Electorate* (Cambridge, Mass.: The Belknap Press of Harvard University Press, 1966), *passim*.

11. Will Harrison, in *The New Mexican* (Santa Fe), September 14, 1964.

Appendix

TABLE A-1. RELATIVE POLITICAL INFLUENCE OF U.S. SENATOR CUTTING AND DELGADO—PERCENTAGE OF VOTE REPUBLICAN IN FIVE HISPANIC PENITENTE COUNTIES

	1920	1922	1924	1926	1928	1930	1932	1934
GUADALUPE								
Congress	55	51	53	57	59	41	46[a]	53
Governor	55	50	56	60	60	43	51	52
Lt. Gov.	55	51	50	57[b]	60	...	47	52
Sheriff	53	49	54	55	58	...	47	53
Average	54	50	53	57	59	42	48	53
U.S. Senator					61			55
MORA								
Congress	50	46	51	53	53	48	35[a]	52
Governor	49	46	53	55	54	49	37	51
Lt. Gov.	50	46	50	50[b]	54	...	35	50
Sheriff	47	43	48	53	51	...	38	50
Average	49	45	51	53	53	49	36	51
U.S. Senator					55			49
RIO ARRIBA								
Congress	64	58	57	63	64	48	37[a]	49
Governor	63	57	59	64	65	50	41	47
Lt. Gov.	...	58	61	64[b]	65	...	40	46
Sheriff	...	56	52	56	63	...	41	46
Average	64	57	57	62	64	49	40	47
U.S. Senator					68			48
SAN MIGUEL								
Congress	57	62	50	49	61	56	56[a]	66
Governor	57	60	52	52	64	58	58	65
Lt. Gov.	58	60	51	46[b]	64	...	56	64
Sheriff	56	62[c]	50[b]	51	55[b]	...	56	66
Average	57	61	51	50	61	57	57	65
U.S. Senator					66			63
TAOS								
Congress	64	59	59	57	58	41	49[a]	59
Governor	63	59	65	59	60	49	50	56
Lt. Gov.	64	59	59	55[c]	60	...	50	56
Sheriff	57	41	49	53	53	...	49	54
Average	62	54	58	56	58	45	50	56
U.S. Senator					64			54

a. The Democratic candidate for Congress in 1932 was Dennis Chavez. Note that his Republican opponent was low. Chavez then ran against Cutting for the U.S. Senate in 1934.

b. In opposition to Lorenzo Delgado running as a Democrat.

c. Lorenzo Delgado running as a Republican.

Source: New Mexico *Blue Books*.

TABLE A-2 VARIABILITY IN THE VOTE OF RURAL PENITENTE PRECINCTS OF
SAN MIGUEL COUNTY

(Republican percentages in four elections involving Republican and Democratic
candidacies of Lorenzo Delgado)

Republican Percentage

Precinct No. Name	1922 (Sheriff) DELGADO (R) Lucero (D)	1924 (Sheriff) Romero (R) DELGADO (D)	1926 (Lt. Gov.) Sargent (R) DELGADO (D)	1928 (Sheriff) DELGADO (R) Sena (D)	Variation Range	Variation Points
1. San Miguel	75	62	51	64	75-51	24
2. La Cuesta	93	95	18	86	95-18	77
4. Tecolote	71	44	39	32	71-32	39
7. San Antonio	83	69	95	87	95-69	26
9. Pecos	60	59	56	61	61-56	5
11. San Geronimo	55	n.a.	48	53	55-48	7
13. Rociada	57	42	35	58	58-35	23
14. Sapello	58	38	42	47	58-38	20
15. Las Manuelitas	89	72	57	61	89-57	32
21. Casa Colorada	61	45	51	90	90-45	45
22. Sabinoso	80	80	47	54	80-47	33
26. Los Alamos	51	32	55	69	69-32	37
30. Canon Manuelitas	54	34	28	63	63-28	35
31. Puerticito	62	65	36	51	65-36	29
34. San Isidro	56	42	43	46	56-42	14
35. Las Gallinas	94	57	53	93	94-53	41
37. El Cerrito	98	98	78	81	98-78	20
38. Los Torres	92	71	92	92	92-71	21
39. Tecolotito	61	47	64	46	64-46	18
40. Bernal	53	44	41	81	81-41	40
44. Ojitos Frios	90	29	45	80	90-29	61
45. Cherryvale	38	21	39	53	53-21	32
46. Emplazado	75	58	43	70	75-43	32
48. Trementina	58	52	63	35	63-35	28
49. Agua Zarca	78	59	74	56	78-56	22
51. San Ignacio	64	51	46	72	72-46	26
52. Las Colonias	46	48	44	50	50-44	6
56. Gonzales	53	47	29	52	53-29	24
58. Santa Ana	85	91	41	83	91-41	50
Total vote	2,944	2,696	2,783	2,643		
Republican majority	1,016	269	−91	647		
Per cent Republican	67.3	55.5	48.4	62.2		
Precincts carried by Democrat	2	13	17	5		

Source: New Mexico *Blue Books*.

TABLE A-3. Party and Roll Call Voting, House of Representatives, 1912-1963

Legislature[b] number and year	Percentage of members Democrat	Roll calls[a]							Party versus party			
		Total roll calls	Unanimous		Non-party minority[c]			Number	%	Cohesion index[d]	
			Number	%	Number	%	Voting "no," %			Dem.	Rep.
1. 1912-13[e]	34.7	683	221	32.4	327	47.9	14.6	135	19.8	56.0	59.3
2. 1915	28.6	392	142	36.2	140	35.7	9.9	110	28.1	73.5	81.7
3. 1917	38.7	324	130	40.1	145	44.8	11.6	49	15.1	55.2	60.7
4. 1919	32.6	326	194	59.5	90	27.6	11.1	42	12.9	65.9	70.4
5. 1921	30.6	377	184	48.8	131	34.7	12.4	62	16.4	56.0	61.5
6. 1923	67.3	369	196	53.1	111	30.2	8.3	62	16.8	71.8	75.3
7. 1925	59.2	307	154	50.2	108	35.2	12.1	45	14.7	65.9	63.2
8. 1927	36.7	366	206	56.3	113	30.9	10.3	47	12.8	62.5	69.3
	41.1	3,144	1,427	45.4	1,165	37.1	11.3	552	17.6	63.3	67.9
9. 1929[f]	24.5	374	211	56.4	135	36.1	11.8	28	7.5	57.2	40.4
10. 1931	57.1	450	176	39.1	199	44.2	14.9	75	16.7	48.3	62.5
	40.8	824	387	47.0	334	40.5	13.4	103	12.5	50.7	56.5
11. 1933	83.7	613	195	31.8	307	50.1	17.6	111	18.1	45.1	58.9
12. 1935	75.5	314	153	48.7	114	36.3	13.6	47	15.0	57.1	48.4
13. 1937	95.9	450	293	65.1	157	34.9	19.3	...	...	...	...
14. 1939	85.7	406	268	66.0	138	34.0	25.1	...	...	...	...
15. 1941	81.6	356	174	48.9	116	32.6	17.9	66	18.5	45.8	63.5
	84.5	2,139	1,083	50.6	832	38.9	18.7	(224)	(17.5)	(47.8)	(58.1)

16. 1943	67.3	291	173	59.5	56	19.2	17.2	62	21.3	55.4	78.9
17. 1945	61.2	321	135	42.1	122	38.0	17.4	64	19.9	44.7	52.8
18. 1947	61.2	377	126	33.4	200	53.1	15.1	51	13.5	48.3	41.5
19. 1949	73.4	324	163	50.3	142	43.8	13.8	19	5.9	49.2	32.3
	65.8	1,313	597	45.5	520	39.6	15.9	196	14.9	49.5	56.1
20. 1951	83.6	431	262	60.8	137	31.8	14.0	32	7.4	37.5	59.4
21. 1953	49.0	430	242	56.3	149	34.6	14.9	39	9.1	50.0	63.8
22. 1955	92.7	553	357	64.6	196	35.4	19.8	…	…	…	…
23. 1957	65.1	552	377	68.3	141	25.5	14.1	34	6.2	37.2	63.0
24. 1959	90.9	586	334	57.0	252	43.0	16.8	…	…	…	…
25. 1961	89.4	610	384	63.0	226	37.0	15.5	…	…	…	…
26. 1963	83.3	537	301	56.1	187	34.8	13.7	49	9.1	43.2	45.0
	79.1	3,699	2,257	61.0	1,288	34.8	15.5	(154)	(7.9)	(42.4)	(56.7)

aCompiled from House Journals.

bInclusive of special sessions.

cBased on number voting "no" (against the deciding majority) except in votes involving a party majority against a party majority.

dRice Index of Cohesion. Party vs. party votes not used if minority party held less than 16% of the seats.

eThe first legislature met in two sessions of 60 and 90 days.

fThe Journal of the regular 1929 session is incomplete, and after the first half of the session does not give the votes of individuals. Democratic score for the 18 regular session index of cohesion votes listed is 50.5; the Republican, 42.5. The plotted House votes for the session in Figure 18 are for the regular session.

TABLE A-4. PARTY AND ROLL CALL VOTING, SENATE, NEW MEXICO LEGISLATURE 1912-1963

Legislature[b] number and year	Percentage of members Democrat	Total roll calls	Roll calls[a]								
			Unanimous		Non-party minority[c]			Party versus party			
			Number	%	Number	%	Voting "no" %	Number	%	Cohesion index[d] Dem.	Rep.
1. 1912-13[e]	29.1	492	213	43.3	161	32.7	12.5	118	24.0	66.7	75.8
2. 1915	29.1	245	112	45.7	73	29.8	16.0	60	24.5	80.2	79.8
3. 1917	41.7	291	206	70.8	45	15.5	12.6	40	13.7	68.2	82.7
4. 1919	41.7	304	198	65.1	51	16.8	13.8	55	18.1	84.7	83.3
5. 1921	37.5	371	236	63.6	76	20.5	15.4	59	15.9	68.6	68.3
6. 1923	37.5	299	192	64.2	70	23.4	13.3	37	12.4	71.9	80.5
7. 1925	37.5	253	183	72.3	34	13.4	12.8	36	14.2	73.3	64.2
8. 1927	41.6	264	224	84.8	31	11.7	13.1	9	3.4	64.0	78.6
	37.0	2,519	1,564	62.1	541	21.5	13.7	414	16.4	72.4	76.5
9. 1929	25.0	366	187	51.1	144	39.3	16.2	35	9.6	56.3	28.3
10. 1931	33.3	330	158	47.9	117	35.4	18.4	55	16.7	48.1	43.1
	29.2	696	345	49.6	261	37.5	17.3	90	12.9	51.3	37.4
11. 1933	83.3	520	243	46.7	206	39.6	19.0	71	13.7	47.8	82.2
12. 1935	75.0	271	130	48.0	94	34.7	19.8	47	17.3	42.6	62.1
13. 1937	95.8	454	303	66.7	151	33.3	24.8	…	…	…	…
14. 1939	95.8	370	204	55.1	166	44.9	22.6	…	…	…	…
15. 1941	87.5	316	171	54.1	145	45.9	22.2	…	…	…	…
16. 1943	87.5	265	166	62.6	99	37.4	27.8	…	…	…	…
	87.5	2,196	1,217	55.4	861	39.2	22.7	(118)	(14.9)	(45.8)	(74.2)

17. 1945	75.0	273	197	72.2	59	21.6	19.9	17	6.2	25.8	69.8
18. 1947	75.0	344	257	74.7	79	23.0	22.5	8	2.3	33.8	48.3
19. 1949f	79.1	299	200	66.9	99	33.1	19.1	n.a.	n.a.	n.a.	n.a.
	76.4	916	654	71.4	237	25.9	20.5	(25)	(4.1)	28.4	62.9
20. 1951	75.0	400	255	63.7	115	28.8	20.2	30	7.5	38.3	62.6
21. 1953	70.9	442	260	58.8	129	29.2	21.3	53	12.0	47.1	45.8
22. 1955	71.8	608	366	60.2	180	29.6	18.3	62	10.2	45.4	60.8
23. 1957	75.0	620	349	56.3	198	31.9	22.7	73	11.8	39.5	55.4
24. 1959	75.0	670	395	59.0	226	33.7	22.2	49	7.3	37.6	38.4
	73.5	2,740	1,625	59.3	848	30.9	20.9	267	9.7	41.9	52.5
25. 1961	87.5	644	442	68.6	202	31.4	24.0	...	...	...	...
26. 1963	87.5	600	404	67.3	196	32.7	22.7	...	...	...	...
	87.5	1,244	846	68.0	398	32.0	23.4	...	...	...	...

aCompiled from Senate Journals.

bInclusive of special sessions.

cBased on number voting "no" (against the deciding majority) except in votes involving a party majority against a party majority.

dRice Index of Cohesion. Party vs. party votes not used if minority party held less than 16% of the seats.

eThe first legislature met in two sessions of 60 and 90 days.

fThe Senate Journal for the 1949 session records only total "yes" and "no" votes.

TABLE A-5. DEMOCRATIC INDICES OF COHESION, HOUSE OF REPRESENTATIVES, 1912-1963

Legislature number and year	All roll calls		All voting less unanimous roll call votes		Party vs. party roll call votes[a]	
	Number	*Index*	*Number*	*Index*	*Number*	*Index*
1. 1912-13	683	75.7	462	64.1	135	56.0
2. 1915	392	81.1	250	70.3	110	73.5
3. 1917	324	80.9	194	68.0	49	55.2
4. 1919	326	88.4	132	71.3	42	65.9
5. 1921	377	82.6	193	61.4	62	56.0
6. 1923	369	90.2	173	79.1	62	71.8
7. 1925	307	86.8	153	73.5	45	65.9
8. 1927	366	87.0	160	70.2	47	62.5
	3,144	83.1	1,717	68.6	552	63.3
9. 1929	234[b]	85.6	98	65.6	28	57.2
10. 1931	450	76.0	274	60.5	75	48.3
	684	79.3	372	61.9	103	50.7
11. 1933	613	72.3	418	59.3	111	45.1
12. 1935	314	85.0	160	70.6	47	57.1
13. 1937	450	86.6	157	61.7	...	(61.7)
14. 1939	406	84.3	138	53.7	...	(53.7)
15. 1941	356	78.1	182	57.1	66	45.8
	2,139	80.4	1,055	60.3	224	47.8
16. 1943	291	83.5	118	59.4	62	55.4
17. 1945	321	75.4	186	57.6	64	44.7
18. 1947	377	79.6	251	69.3	51	48.3
19. 1949	324	85.3	161	70.5	19	49.2
	1,313	80.9	716	64.9	196	49.5
20. 1951	431	85.8	169	63.8	32	37.5
21. 1953	430	85.0	188	65.6	39	50.0
22. 1955	553	86.6	196	62.1	...	(62.1)
23. 1957	552	88.1	175	62.4	34	37.2
24. 1959	586	85.6	252	66.6	...	(66.6)
25. 1961	610	88.9	226	70.0	...	(70.0)
26. 1963	537	85.7	236	67.6	49	43.2
	3,699	86.6	1,442	65.7	154	42.4

[a]Party vs. party indices not calculated when the minority held less than 16% of the seats.

[b]Of 374 roll calls of the session, only 234 were so recorded in the Journal that they may be used in these calculations.

TABLE A-6. Democratic Indices of Cohesion, Senate, 1912-1963

Session number and year	All roll calls		All voting less unanimous roll call votes		Party vs. party roll call votes[a]	
	Number	Index	Number	Index	Number	Index
1. 1912-13	492	78.8	279	62.6	118	66.7
2. 1915	245	84.4	133	71.3	60	80.2
3. 1917	291	91.3	85	70.1	40	68.2
4. 1919	304	91.7	106	76.1	55	84.7
5. 1921	371	88.4	135	68.2	59	68.6
6. 1923	299	89.1	107	69.5	37	71.9
7. 1925	253	91.7	70	70.2	36	73.3
8. 1927	264	93.8	40	59.2	9	64.0
	2,519	87.9	955	67.9	414	72.4
9. 1929	366	83.6	179	66.5	35	56.3
10. 1931	330	78.0	173	57.9	55	48.1
	696	80.9	352	62.2	90	51.3
11. 1933	520	77.0	277	56.8	71	47.8
12. 1935	271	75.5	141	52.9	47	42.6
13. 1937	454	84.0	151	51.7	...	(51.7)
14. 1939	370	80.4	166	56.4	...	(56.4)
15. 1941	316	79.9	145	56.2	...	(56.2)
16. 1943	265	79.6	99	45.3	...	(45.3)
	2,196	79.6	979	54.1	118	45.8
17. 1945	273	86.3	76	50.8	17	25.8
18. 1947	344	87.0	87	48.5	8	33.8
19. 1949[b]	(299)	n.a.	(99)	n.a.	n.a.	n.a.
	617	86.7	163	49.5	25	28.4
20. 1951	400	82.0	144	50.1	30	38.3
21. 1953	442	81.1	182	54.1	53	47.1
22. 1955	608	83.3	242	58.1	62	45.4
23. 1957	620	77.8	271	49.3	73	39.5
24. 1959	670	80.2	275	51.7	49	37.6
	2,740	80.8	1,114	52.7	267	41.9
25. 1961	644	85.5	202	53.9	...	(53.9)
26. 1963	600	84.2	196	51.8	...	(51.8)
	1,244	84.9	398	52.8	...	(52.8)

[a]Party vs. party indices not calculated when the minority held less than 16% of the seats.

[b]The *Journal* records only the numbers voting "yes" and "no."

Bibliography

Save for inadvertent or careless omissions, the books and articles which most shaped the objectives and assumptions of this study of New Mexico's politics are duly acknowledged in notes to the text. So also, I hope, are those from which I most freely borrowed information. My intention here is primarily to indicate sources or bibliographies more or less peculiar to the state, so only two items broadly useful for comparative study are included.

Students of New Mexico's politics, economics, sociology, and cultural anthropology are fortunate in having available several exhaustive annotated bibliographies. The two below by Irion are recent enough to provide access to most of the conventional sources as well as to abundant materials relating to Spanish-American culture and politics, and to a smaller group of items relating to Indian social and political life. As Irion notes, the extensive anthropological literature relating to Indians of the Southwest provides relatively few explicit references to politics. Some of this material is cited above in the section of Chapter III relating to Indian participation in the state's politics. Additional bibliographic materials on culturally differentiated groups are available through the Comparative Values Studies program of Harvard University. The several unpublished doctoral theses consulted on topics related to New Mexico's Spanish-American politics are listed separately below. Irion's bibliographies and that of Lyle Saunders contain a broad and useful listing of other such unpublished materials as well as pamphlet length items.

Bibliographies

Herndon, James, Charles Press, and Oliver P. Williams, (eds.). *A Selected Bibliography of Materials in State Government and Politics.* Lexington: Bureau of Government Research, University of Kentucky, 1963.

Irion, Frederick C. "Selected and Annotated Bibliography on Politics in New Mexico," 4th ed., Santa Fe: New Mexico Legislative Council Service, 1959. (Mimeographed.)

Jonas, Frank H. (ed.). *Bibliography on Western Politics: Selected, Annotated, with Introductory Essays.* Supplement, *Western Political Quarterly*, XI (December, 1958). Includes Frederick C. Irion, "Bibliography on New Mexico Politics," p. 77-109.

New Mexico Quarterly. "A Guide to the Literature of the Southwest," XII (May, 1942) to XXIV (Autumn, 1954).

Saunders, Lyle. *A Guide to Materials Bearing on Cultural Relations in New Mexico.* Albuquerque: University of New Mexico Press, 1944.

DISSERTATIONS: SPANISH-AMERICAN POLITICS

Fincher, Ernest Barksdale. "Spanish Americans as a Political Factor in New Mexico, 1912-1950." New York University, 1950.

Irwin, William Pryor. "The Rocky Mountain Ballot: A Study of Political Behavior in the State of Colorado." University of California (Berkeley), 1956.

Kluckhohn, Florence. "Los Atarqueños: A Study of Patterns and Configurations in a New Mexico Village." Radcliffe College, 1941.

Leonard, Olen E. "The Role of the Land Grant in the Social Process of a Spanish-American Village in New Mexico." Louisiana State University, 1943.

Russell, John C. "State Regionalism in New Mexico." Stanford University, 1938.

Samora, Julian. "Minority Leadership in a Bi-Cultural Community." Washington University, St. Louis, 1953.

Walter, Paul A. F., Jr. "A Study of Isolation and Social Change in Three Spanish-Speaking Villages of New Mexico." Stanford University, 1938.

Zeleny, Carolyn. "Relations Between Spanish Americans and Anglo Americans in New Mexico: A Study of Conflict and Accommodation in a Dual-Ethnic Situation." Yale University, 1944.

ELECTION STATISTICS

Ramsay, Dwight M., Jr. "Election Returns in New Mexico—1912-1950: Tables on Election Returns by Counties for President, U.S. Representative and Governor." Albuquerque: Division of Government Research, University of New Mexico, 1951. (Mimeographed.)

Secretary of State, State of New Mexico. *Blue Books* (and Supplements), biennial, 1913-1940; *Official Returns of Primary and General Elections*, biennial, 1942—. (Much of these data will be available after 1967 in machine-readable form from the Inter University Consortium for Political Research, University of Michigan, Ann Arbor.)

LEGISLATIVE JOURNALS

Journals, of the New Mexico Senate and House of Representatives. Santa Fe: Office of Secretary of State.

LETTERS, PAPERS, AND COLLECTIONS

Letters and Papers of New Mexico Governors and State Agencies. Santa Fe: Museum of New Mexico, *New Mexico Archives,* 1897-1920; 1935-1941. Albuquerque: Special Collections, University of New Mexico Library, *Territorial Archives,* 1848-1912; *State Archives,* 1912-1935.

Papers and Collections of Holm O. Bursum, Richard C. Dillon, Albert Bacon Fall, and Miguel A. Otero. Albuquerque: Special Collections, University of New Mexico Library.

Index